PHILOSOPHICAL EXPLORATIONS

EDWARD POLS

THE RECOGNITION

OF REASON

FOREWORD BY

George Kimball Plochmann

Southern Illinois University Press CARBONDALE

FOREWORD

PHILOSOPHIC INQUIRY, to remain vital, must turn up new subject matters, or must formulate in new ways the problems that old subject matters suggest, using new methods to solve them. To find unfathomed seas is not easy, nor is it easy to invent new and more precise methods to fathom them. Nevertheless, the present Series is founded upon the conviction that from time to time books are written that have something new to say. The first in the list of *Philosophical Explorations* is, I think, a work of this sort.

Dr. Edward Pols deals with important parts of the time-honored subject matters of metaphysics and theory of knowledge, but he is clearly impatient with the ways, traditional or recent, of dealing with the topics customarily suggested by them. *The Recognition of Reason* implies a criticism of the ways in which reason has been conceived by thinkers from Kant onward: some men have unduly exalted reason even when they have detached its object while others have arrogantly criticized it, at the same time allowing its solid base to remain untouched. The philosophical predicament (which is not fundamentally different from that of common sense, although more interesting to pursue at length) arises from the fact that few have taken the trouble to reformulate what reason really is in terms of its powers *and* its forms and objects. Mr. Pols takes the "self-reflexive character" of reason to be at the heart of this issue, but holds that it is now so taken for granted that it falls short of what it might be, and therefore fails to yield the philosophical fruits it might yield. Reason must now be scrutinized as a power concretely engaged, reflecting upon itself, in intimate conjunction with its object. In other words, perhaps a little more loosely, the old Aristotelian notion that the activity of God is thinking on thinking is spelled out in this book in terms more appropriate to human experience, feeling, and ratiocination. Reason which is concretely engaged and ontically extended so that in itself it becomes an act of being as much as an act of mind, is called *radically originative reflection* (a term which marks a resting place and a point of departure, both, for this dialectic). It both is and is *about* a union of awareness and understanding; or, if you like, of the empirical and the rational. Mr. Pols is in this, as in all other parts of his exploration, concerned with what lies in the very junction between two classically balanced opposites. He expends considerable effort showing how the mind becomes integral with the thing known. But the thing known—and here is perhaps the most important and striking point of the book—is neither a bare particular nor a disemboweled universal, but an object which is a fusion of the one and the many, of the singular form and the plural "thises." It is not hard to see from this that perception is creative; it is a constructive selection of many relevant aspects of the object from among many more. Let us get rid of the superstition and paradox of a perceptive act which is wholly passive, the author is saying, and we shall be well started on the way to an epistemology giving due regard both to concreteness and abstraction.

It should be plain from this that Pols is not in sympathy with the methods and most of the conclusions of the analytical schools of Britain. Their work is sequential, as a rule, but they have concentrated upon individual problems, problems which sometimes have been selected almost at random. Nor is our author content to write a phenomenological description of experience as such; he would rather take account of what lies partly beyond immediate experience—the nature of being. His individual points bear many resemblances to those of Aristotle, but the line of argument is developed in a very different fashion. Where Aristotle has literally hundreds of distinctions, Pols looks to concrete fusions of categories; where Aristotle has multiple approaches ("Let us now make a fresh start"), Pols has a single train of concrete reflection, one that would have made Descartes himself jubilant; where Aristotle scatters his epistemology, distributing it in the disciplines of logic, psychology, and metaphysics, Pols collects *his* doctrines all together, in a massive single sorites that constitutes this book. (My logical image does some little violence, if you take it literally, to the author's concrete approach, suggesting as it does a deductive method he does not employ, but at any rate it emphasizes the unity of his argument.)

For myself, I am not *quite* convinced by Mr. Pols, though this may be for temperamental reasons. The method which persistently aims at the midpoint, though it is excellent at hitting this bullseye, does not give an account of the rest of the circles on the target. What Pols is interested in is that moment in thinking when subject, object, and their appropriate symbols are gathered "like the scattered leaves of the universe into one volume," and distinction of thought, being, and language is done away with. I agree with the description that he gives of this, but I should also like to know what takes place when this intellectual fusion—to the unconvinced it might seem a kind of articulated rapture—does not come forth: there are the hours when we are lazy, unconstructive, when our minds give over and we are passive to sensation; or when we are imperceptive, and even our senses flounder. And there are also the minutes when like the Stranger from Elea or like Hegel we are splitting categories less substantial than hairs. Perhaps this is an unconstructive use of reason, but it is one to be taken into epistemological account.

The book's unity, as I have said, has the impact of a sorites of remarkable length and force, and scarcely any new theses are put forward without some indication of their connection with old ones. Nevertheless, certain metaphysical statements show themselves more prominently than the rest. Being itself is not static, but is a common formative power, and from this Pols builds an account of the way being, which is the presupposition of all entities, charges these with cause and (in certain cases) with purpose. To be an entity at all, he says, is to dominate an extensive span within which other entities are subordinated by being constrained to contribute to the character of this dominating entity. One might think of the dominating monads or occasions of Leibniz and Whitehead, respectively; but in fact this is more like a system of nature in which, far from deliberately fractionating the real, one seeks to descry certain stabilities existing as such in virtue of a set relation between their modes of being. Being, matter, and individual causes are all powers, varying in their generality. The lower levels (or modes) of being are causal with respect to the higher, just as the higher are supervenient with respect to the lower—as for instance organism supervenes upon the disparate and wandering molecules, but cannot be ontically independent of their already-instituted structure. Personality supervenes in like manner upon organism, reason upon the lower levels of personality. We come full circle: reason grows in a generalized mode of action, in which our own formative power, or being, issues in theoretic knowledge. But this very knowledge, because it is creative, adds to being and to all the levels of being upon which reason has at last supervened.

Mr. Pols has a formidable rhetoric: he marshalls ideas with ferocious strength into a pattern most effective for their dissemination to other minds. One must look to a writer of the type of F. H. Bradley for a ready parallel to the rigor with which a track of discourse is followed up, and for the intensity with which it is communicated. Here is plainly a book to be read with pleasure and studied with attention.

George Kimball Plochmann

Southern Illinois University
April 24, 1963

PREFACE

I HAVE TRIED in this book to justify the ancient view of philosophy as a synoptic mode of knowing that informs all our reasonable activities, and that so engages and transforms our passional natures as to warrant our calling it a wisdom. Although I intend "synoptic" in what I hope is a new and modest enough sense, conveyed in the book itself in terms less familiar and therefore less suitable for a preface, the undertaking is still a brash one. Yet I have compounded the offense by representing the justification as an expansion of reason's nature in an act of self-recognition, and by holding this justifying act to be a necessary condition for the right exercise of the synoptic mode of knowing. The justification therefore purports to make of philosophy what it ought to be and has not yet managed to become.

My excuse for this outrageous claim is that I have here only represented dramatically, and as already completed, an ontological expansion of reason that is in fact still in train in our time—in train, I mean, in reason, for which general power any philosopher must make bold to speak and act. If the expansion were in fact what I hope it will some day be, my expression of it would have been clearer than I know it to be.

Readers familiar with phenomenology will note that this book has in common with that movement the theme of the reflexive, or self-reflective, character of reason. Since my own philosophical roots are of a different sort, I should observe that I have handled that theme with a difference. I might approximate it here by saying that although there are modes of reflection that may appropriately be thought of in terms of *experience*, the reflective act in which both the nature of reason's possession of the real and the nature of reflection itself become transparent to us exceeds that category. The same point may be made by saying that the basic *philosophical* act of reflection does not yield us a phenomenological description of consciousness. The sense in which the categories of experience and of phenomenological description are exceeded I have tried to capture in the lengthy discussion of *radically originative reflection* that forms Chapter 4. I am happy nevertheless to make common cause with all those who see in the reflective exercise a hope, not so much for the *restoration* of philosophy, as for the *finding* of it in our time. I would hold, in any case, that the *general* power in whose expansion we all participate is such that influence gives us only part of the story.

I wrote most of the first draft of the book during the academic year 1958–59, when I was on sabbatic leave from my duties at Bowdoin College. A grant from Bowdoin's Faculty Development Fund enabled me to live abroad that year and to devote my time chiefly to writing. I am grateful for this indispensable help, and for the spirit of confidence in which it was extended to me. I am also grateful for several grants from the Faculty Research Fund.

From September 1958 until April 1959 I enjoyed the hospitality of the Warburg Institute of the University of London. I am grateful to Professor G. Bing, then Director of the Institute, for providing me with a room to work in, and for many other kindnesses. One of these led me indeed to the villa in the Alban Hills that was for some time one of my happiest working places, so that my book owes very much to the Warburg influence. I thank also my friend Professor Charles

Mitchell, now of Bryn Mawr College, but at that time still at the Warburg, who first introduced me there. Yet I do not suppose that the ties between the Warburg and Bowdoin would have been so close if it were not for the presence on the Bowdoin Faculty of a member of the Warburg circle, my friend and close colleague, the late Professor Walter M. Solmitz, whose death as this book was going to press leaves so many associates and students with a profound sense of loss.

To the General Editor of this series, Professor George Kimball Plochmann, I owe especial thanks; first, for his sympathetic reception of the book; second, for the valuable suggestions he made when I agreed to shorten a somewhat longer version to bring the book within the limits laid down for the series; and finally, for the searching reading he gave the typescript before it went to press. In the course of this reading he made many suggestions, most of which I have adopted, always, I think, with a gain in clarity.

The professional wisdom and the kindness of Mr. Vernon Sternberg, Director of the Southern Illinois University Press, have made themselves felt from the very beginning. I am very grateful to him, to Mr. James E. McSherry of the Press, and to other members of the staff.

Last, I wish to acknowledge the part played in the development of the book by my old friend Professor Richard G. Tansey of San Jose State College. It is perhaps inappropriate to speak of a *debt* in an association of such long standing and so full of a readiness to listen on both sides. It is, however, typical of our alliance that I worked out my first statement of some of the chief themes of the book in the course of a summer's correspondence with him.

Edward Pols

Bowdoin College
February 1, 1963

CONTENTS

THE RECOGNITION OF REASON

PHILOSOPHERS IN SEARCH OF PHILOSOPHY

I.   The contemporary debate about the proper role of philosophy centers on the question whether philosophy is a first-order way of knowing that aspires to wisdom. The radical character of the point at issue has so far prevented a successful revolution in philosophy: there is still an openness to the philosophic situation that calls out for new beginnings of a most radical sort.

These are revolutionary times in philosophy. The crisis is a deep one, for the truly revolutionary movements are not concerned merely with advancing new doctrines within the framework of a generally accepted discipline, but with revising our conception of the discipline itself. It is not too much to say that among professional academic philosophers there is no dispute carried on more implacably than the one about the very nature of philosophy; it is in fact the form in which that Protean thing, the spiritual crisis of our times, reveals itself in these circles. The dispute has ramifications throughout the contemporary world, and whether symptom or cause, or like most things, having something of each, its importance can not be set too high, seeing that it is a dispute about the whole structure of reasonable life. It is one main purpose of this book to show that our time demands of philosophy new beginnings of a most radical sort, and that, in understanding the nature of this demand, and the possibility of our fulfilling it, we begin also to understand what we have indeed long been in some confusion about, namely, the role of philosophy itself. In so far as the book is directed, despite some of the technicalities of its later reaches, to the educated layman, who is probably in any case a specialist off duty and well accustomed to technicalities, it attempts to give precise form to our spiritual crisis in a sphere in which it is perhaps more open than elsewhere to such formulation; in so far as it is directed to the philosophical specialist—a conception, incidentally, that I shall later question—its intent is irenic, as befits a situation in which, despite all the acrimony of debate, so many men are honestly concerned to find a surer footing for reason. And because, as I trust to show, we can not even understand the peculiar nature of our problem without in some sort making a new beginning, this book is an attempt to make such a beginning and to press on with its consequences some little way.

It is no part of my plan to offer, even in a summary fashion, a survey of the contemporary philosophical scene, but in order to make as vivid as possible the revolutionary atmosphere in which philosophy is now carried on we shall look briefly at two revolutionary extremes.

Consider first the analytic revolution, of which we hear so much in the English-speaking world that we might well suppose that it has been completely successful, and that its gains have been consolidated in what is now truly an age of analysis. "Philosophy" was once a term embracing all knowledge as organized under a presiding mode called metaphysics, which, at its highest pitch, was known as wisdom. Except in one brief phase early in the century, the chief mark of the analytic movement has been its hostility to metaphysics. Until quite recently, and as the converse of this attitude to metaphysics, the movement has also been disposed to regard science as the very prototype of knowledge, against which the pretensions of all other disciplines, including philosophy, must be measured. This is of course a common enough theme in our era, by no means limited to analytic philosophers. As the realm of organized knowledge has gradually been parcelled out to the special sciences, the philosopher, including of course the analytic philosopher, has been left with the burden of demonstrating that he still has a useful task to perform. One of the chief themes in the analytic movement is therefore the search for a philosophic specialty. There has been general agreement that this was to be found in the analysis of the concepts, categories, symbolic forms, or "languages" in which the findings of common sense and science were embodied, and philosophy was therefore thought of as a "second-order" activity as over against these "first-order" activities. It was sometimes loosely thought of as a second-order *knowledge*, but the revelation of certain paradoxes, chiefly by Wittgenstein in the *Tractatus Logico-Philosophicus* (1922) made the conception of even a second-order philosophical knowledge dubious.

For much of its history the analytic movement took as its major concern the development of a "perfect" language, in which the vagueness, obscurities, and logical puzzles of ordinary language and scientific language would be eliminated. This perfect language was thought of as nothing more than the ideal towards which science had in fact been groping all this while. That concern has now been given up as illusory by the dominant wing of the movement, which has now in effect taken its own past errors, together with the errors of traditional metaphysically oriented philosophy, as an important part of its subject matter. Largely through the later work of Wittgenstein, whose posthumously published *Philosophical Investigations* (1953) is the chief document of the "ordinary language" phase of the movement, the view has gained currency that our everyday grasp of things, embodied in the logic of our everyday or ordinary language, needs no correction by either philosophy or science. It is in fact the proper job of the philosopher to *show* or display by multifarious examples, discovered or invented, the logic of our ordinary language, which is a completely satisfying logic when we *really* understand it. The persistent temptation to misunderstand it is made possible by analogies between forms of expression in different regions of language. We find ourselves divagating into the "unusual," "peculiar," or "strange" language of metaphysics, the direction taken by our divagations being explained by unconscious pressures, so that many ordinary language philosophers think that it is their job to deal with metaphysical beliefs much as a psychoanalyst deals with neuroses. The possibility thus arises that philosophy (new sense) is the specialty whose chief function is the abolishment of what has until this century been taken to be the principal function of philosophy. Nor can this second-order activity be considered a mode of theoretic *knowledge*, seeing that we are *shown* the logic of our language by learning to *use* it, until, comfortable at last in its infinitely delicate ramifications, we acquiesce in its magisterial persuasiveness.[1]

But we have not yet come at the point that made me choose this as one example of a revolutionary extreme. Notice that we are no longer dealing only with the question "What is philosophy?" but also with the questions "Why is there philosophy?" and "Should there be philosophy?" "What *is* this peculiar compulsion," it has now become possible to ask, "what is this compulsion that drives me not just to try (however warily) to get some special knowledge of things, that does not even permit me to stop with assessing the nature of knowledge, but causes me to try to surprise itself at work?" Such questions are everywhere with us today, especially in the English-speaking world, tempting us away from all questions of a substantive sort, and at the same time nurturing the seeds of despair. Reflexive about the very reflexivity of philosophy, we experience a sudden revulsion that leads us to dismiss the whole affair. *Our* new beginning, some writers have become capable of telling themselves, lies on the other side of sophistication in a new innocence in which the very word "philosophy" takes on an unhealthy ring. There are already some writers, philosophers in the sense that they hold posts in academic philosophy, who answer to the name very reluctantly. It is not unusual to have philosophers of this sort tell you, with a kind of higher Philistinism, designed to make the rest of us feel like the most everyday Philistines, that it is time to drop all this nonsense about a special study called philosophy. I am talking, to be sure, of a view more commonly ventured in conversation than in print, although the theoretical basis for such a final step has been set down in print often enough. I recall in particular a conversation in Oxford with one of the most prominent members of the ordinary language movement, in which he maintained that a philosopher should never concern himself with theoretic matters, and that he might have profitable enough occupation if he confined himself entirely to an examination of the particularities of usage, accumulating in his diligence a vast body of observational material, much as Tycho Brahe did for astronomy (the illustration is his). And would it not be infinitely better, he went on, if we simply dropped that pretentious old title "philosopher," and adopted some more modest one for our future proceedings? There is a subject that we investigate and teach, but surely we do not pretend that it is our job to find and inculcate wisdom.

At the other extreme, within continental movements nourished by existentialism and phenomenology, equally revolutionary forces have been at work. In these movements philosophy is represented sometimes as a peculiar way of knowing—or perhaps experiencing—in which philosophers may hope to find at last something like that presiding perspective at which the old metaphysics aimed, yet free of all pretentious and ungrounded claims; sometimes as something beyond knowledge, and therefore free, by virtue of quite different aims, from the irremediable defects of the theoretic, something so enveloped in an atmosphere of moral and ontological crisis as best to be conceived of as a way of acting, although a way of acting without which a higher Reason beyond the objective reason can not come into its own.

At one revolutionary extreme then, philosophy is concerned with the abolition of philosophy of the traditional sort; at the other with a thorough-going revision of the traditional view of philosophy—a revision that at its most ambitious reveals what must surely be the ultimate philosophic *hubris* in seeming to aim, not just at a revision of our *knowledge* of God and man, but quite simply, at a *revision* of God and man. There is no use pretending, as so many analytic writers appear to do, that continental philosophy of this sort, and its counterparts on the more various American scene, need not be entertained as serious impediments to the analytic revolution; plainly they must be so entertained, and to think otherwise is nothing but the most complacent provincialism. But on the other hand it is quite clear that phenomenology has not managed to establish philosophy on a new and unquestioned theoretic footing; and as for existentialism, whatever its virtues in bringing home to us the concreteness of our natures, it has not rendered other modes of philosophy obsolete, seeing that it imperils the cultivation of the clarity and articulation that we value in the life of reason. We may well say, then, that these are revolutionary times in philosophy, but we are very rash if we claim that anyone has yet brought off a successful revolution. We are willing to entertain the most radical reformulations of the nature of philosophy, but we have not really been persuaded that we now see clearly what it ought to be—have not been persuaded, that is, that any of the revolutionary movements gives us at last unquestionable grounds upon which we may delimit the sphere of the reasonable. And yet this is just what we want and want the more exigently because of the revolutionary situation in which we find ourselves.

It is all too easy not to notice how deep these revolutionary movements go, for philosophy has always seemed, to a certain kind of philosopher at least, to demand a self-examination on the part of reason. Descartes, Locke, Kant, and Bergson come readily to mind as philosophers who were concerned to make radically new beginnings by reassessing reason itself. They set out, that is, not as a scientist might, to transform their understanding of some more or less familiar subject matter by hitting upon some new "first principles," but to come to a better understanding of reason itself—its situation, its capacities, its limits—and then, and only by this means, to come to an understanding of whatever it is that a philosopher ought to have as his subject matter. For all these thinkers, philosophy calls itself implicitly in question, since we can not know what it is while we remain uncertain about precisely what the appropriate subject matter of reason is. It is therefore the discipline that is concerned first of all with the discovery of its own nature; or, less paradoxically, it is reason in search of itself and therefore in search of its own subject matter. The modern controversy over the possibility of metaphysical knowledge has made this side of philosophy familiar enough. Yet the search for the nature of philosophy has been conducted in an atmosphere of underlying agreement that has persisted even in the face of all the radical reassessments that the attack on metaphysics has made necessary: it has, that is, always been assumed that philosophy is in some sense a way of knowing, and one that at its best deserves to be called wisdom. It is just this agreement that we miss in the present revolutionary situation, and it is its absence that makes the crisis so radical.

The crisis is truly radical not just because there is disagreement about a point upon which there had been agreement, but because of the nature of the point itself. For, once we are in doubt about philosophy's capacity as a special way of knowing that aspires to wisdom, how shall we ever settle the status of philosophy to our satisfaction? How convince anyone that philosophy *is*, after all, something like what it was traditionally supposed to be, without invoking the capacity whose status is in doubt? How defend the view that philosophy *is not* a special way of knowing without invoking, however indirectly and circumspectly, some knowledge of reason and its situation, some wisdom that warns us against trying to do what cannot be done? The atmosphere grows suddenly Kafka-like: credentials are exacted, but no credentials will pass muster, for we are not sure there is authority competent to issue them; credentials are exacted, and the very presentation of credentials is an admission of imposture. And the more bewildering the situation, the more insistent our need to break out of it; the more paradoxical it becomes the more we suspect that the key to it all is simplicity itself, if only we could see it.

That new beginnings are possible we are assured by all the revolutionary movements of our time, if only because they tell us that we can join them only by breaking off an old and pernicious habit under the influence of a new insight. But we are placed in an ambiguous situation: called upon from all sides to make a new beginning, we are not sure how, or indeed whether, we can do it. We cannot even be sure, when we consider any of the new beginnings we see all around us, that it is not the final abdication of reason rather than its renewed life. As for tradition, there is nothing in it that is wholly sound, nothing that we cannot call in question. We are only sure that a profound effort is exacted of us: we do not know reason at all, and thus, despite all the virtuosities that in some sense belong to it, seeing that in science alone so much has been accomplished, there is a nagging unease at the heart of all our knowledge, and one which it is our duty to remove. But at least the situation is an open one, and thus more auspicious for philosophy than one might have expected of a time in which philosophic controversy has been so remorseless as to bring the whole subject into disrepute. This book is an attempt to profit from this open situation.

I write this at the end of an investigation that has confirmed me in my belief that philosophy is both a first-order discipline and a way of knowing. But my beginning was in a situation in which I held this traditional belief in considerable obscurity, my respect for tradition merely compounding the difficulty and increasing the demand for a new beginning, since it was the *intent* of the tradition, and not any final achievement, that held me. All that is new in present day philosophy seemed to me to demand a new beginning that should bring about a redefinition of the subject; all that made me venerate a still living tradition, and that made me feel called upon to answer these new claims, cried out no less for a new beginning, and told me that we had so far not quite got things right. It was the Kafka-like paradoxes mentioned just now that held me first, and made me think that the first task of philosophy was to face directly the problem of its own implicit reflexivity. Philosophy must, I felt, become reason recognizing itself and justifying its right to such recognition, and must see how inseparable this task is from all "substantive" ones. And it dare not underestimate the potential creativity and transforming power of its first reflective act, lest that underestimation should make that act fall short of what it might be.

2

NEW BEGINNINGS AND OUR SITUATION:

PARADOXES OF REASON AND EXPERIENCE

I.   To attempt a radically new beginning is not to try to begin entirely de novo: we begin rather from a cognitive situation that in some respects satisfies us and in others puzzles us, and we try to transform it from within.

We are naturally wary of any proposal to attempt a radically new beginning. For one thing, it seems to raise once more the tiresome delusion of an indefeasible starting point for philosophy—a state of pure certainty like that Descartes thought to be necessary for knowledge. And even if we should not go so far as to regard this as a delusion, we might still fear, having the contemporary preoccupation with the philosophy of philosophy constantly before us, an endless and neurotic preparation that becomes an end in itself: a puritanical niceness that keeps us from the honest piecemeal jobs that the world affords in abundance. There is also the fear that all this scrupulosity is in fact a screen for subjective forces that have already decided for us the position we shall at length take up: it is all too likely that the real beginning has been made long ago and in a different place, and that we are in fact only escaping from a world divided between the approach of science and that of common sense by allowing temperament and childhood training to project quite another world for us—the world as the heart would have it.

As to the second problem, it might well be that the source of the energy that we draw on to make any new beginning is not one we may rightfully tap, and that to do so must lead us eventually to postulate a pattern in ourselves and in things more propitious to our wants than real. But this is a risk we all take, for there is no pattern that some temperament will not find propitious. The question is nevertheless a complicated one, requiring a judgment about the whole relation of the theoretic to the practical life, and I therefore reserve it for the next chapter, where it is also related to a consideration of the motives of philosophical reflection and indeed of the motives behind the choice of philosophy as a profession.

As to the first problem, it is a convenient one for establishing the exact character of our new beginning, since it is an important feature of what I propose that it is in no sense a Cartesian effort to rid ourselves of all presuppositions in order to establish an unquestionable basis for advance. I imagine ourselves rather as summoning up our energies *within* an obscure situation in order to transform it. We do not however doubt, deny, or otherwise suspend our grasp of it in order to move to another one, but accept it, in all its mingling of light and obscurity, all its *internal* tension of certainty, doubt, and opinion, as the necessary platform for advance no less than as a hindrance to advance; nor do we suppose for a moment that, in whatever further enlightenment we are able to bring about, all the obscurity now inherent in our situation will be dispersed, or indeed that that situation will, in most respects relevant to the general purposes of action, be transcended. For although it is the situation of reason that is at issue, a situation which reason is able to transcend at will so soon as it is in a position to lighten the obscurities in it, it is also the human situation seen from a certain perspective; and this we never really leave by taking thought.

But just what this situation *is*, it is impossible to say with simplicity. Only if it did not puzzle us, only if it yielded up to inquiry or to alert attention what it unambiguously and ineluctably *is*, should we be able to characterize it adequately. What it is *not* is just that clear, or at least univocal, "world," "reality," or even "experience" that this or that philosophy, religion, science, or art has urged upon us. It is rather our world as we know it when in any one mood or mode of attention, however respectable, basic, or habitual, we are aware of that mood's contingency, aware that it could, and in due course will, be displaced by another, which for the moment at least will import its own standards. It is the world of common sense; not, however, the abstract version of that world that as philosophers we might postulate for the sake of some epistemological theory, but that world as all of us know it and believe in it when we do not function as epistemologists: a world in which massive certainties exist side by side with perilous doubts and mortal fears. It includes, but is by no means identical with, the "external world," which has furnished philosophy with so much of its pabulum of problems from the time of Descartes and indeed earlier, but which here is non-problematic, at least in some of our more commonplace moods. It therefore includes, what is much the same, the world as it is for what phenomenologists call the natural standpoint—in Husserl's phrase, a fact-world thought of as "out there," and which therefore occupies our attention in much of our scientific and our commonplace concerns. Yet it is just as important that it includes as well many features that will on occasion discredit a fact-world, and leave us, while quite unable to shake off the claims of the latter, still quite unwilling to take it as the only natural and viable framework. It is a very complex situation, and this is what made it appropriate to speak, in the first instance, of a "situation" rather than of a "world."

A major complication is that it is qualified throughout its frame by the enigma of consciousness. From one familiar perspective the world of common sense is *within* consciousness, which then furnishes the situation for it. We do not need to

call upon the long train of epistemological investigation leading to idealism to convince us of this: your unreflective man
knows it from moments of casual and relaxed introspection, or
from other moments of moral or emotional tension, as when,
for instance, some issue is momentarily suspended between
two persons, and the whole world of the natural standpoint is
for the moment suspended within a consciousness they seem
to share. Such attitudes are intermittent, but even when they
give way to more "normal" moods, our own consciousness remains an environment of commanding importance, whose
interior space, together with the flux and reflux of it, we have
no need to reach by any setting aside of the external world.
The importance of this other environment is coeval with that
of the external world in this sense, that our true situation is
something wide enough to contain both, together with all that
perplexes us about the relation between them. There are to
be sure major perplexities here, but they merely qualify our
certainties about these matters and do not annul them. Thus
we know that our bodies, which in some respects are part of
the external world for consciousness, mediate our consciousness of it; we know, in Whitehead's words, that we see *with*
our eyes, and hear *with* our ears; we know also, in fact, that
our very consciousness of ourselves as individuals is dependent
upon the body's mediation. As for that self-consciousness, we
are aware of a subtle difference between our apprehension of
it and our apprehension of the ordinary world, but we are
aware also that the two go together. We are conscious *with*
our bodies and *of* the world; also of our bodies *in* the world;
and, turning then to consciousness itself, we find it made up
in great part of the world, our bodies, and our bodies' mediation. This leaves out some important features of consciousness, but it is at least true that, under one aspect at least,
consciousness is constituted by these things it is directly aware
of, and by the things it is aware of also as mediating its awareness. Consciousness is, in the technical phrase, internally related to the things we are aware of; much, though not all, of
its character therefore is given by that which is "other" than

consciousness. Yet despite all the perplexity about how it is related to its world and to the body, it does remain an aspect of our environment that is itself of unique importance. It is a sea moving beneath us, whose power and general shape we feel as it rises and falls; we know it is given shape by the shores and winds and the sea-bottom, but it remains itself a power, a receptive and active force, and an environment. While we are aware of being in a world, of being resisted and supported in our whole being, including that of consciousness, by that world, we are also aware of moving *within* consciousness, being resisted and supported by it in our cognitive and other efforts. And qualifying this environment, coloring everything we are aware of, but not always in the foreground, and not always with the full shapeliness of complete utterance, lies language, and with it some part of the great range of symbolisms that reason has built upon this substructure.

Our situation is therefore qualified by everything that attentive introspection can yield us—itself a various world full of light and obscurity. Whether consciousness is an indivisible stream, or granular in character; whether we can find in it features that are in principle not to be clarified by the explanatory procedures that science and common sense bring to the external world; whether becoming and flow are the essential features of it, or instead something that demands the word "eternal"; whether it is only individual and private, so that we are enclosed in it and have to employ dodges to reach even an external world, not to speak of other minds or consciousnesses, or is on the other hand common, permitting and even demanding communication with others, so that awareness of being in a society is as primordial as any of our experiences; whether it is only, what it so obviously in some sense is, multiple, or, as so many traditions and some current speculation tell us, in essence one—a common environment to which we all in some sense belong; all these are real enough questions that contribute variety, uncertainty, and ambiguity to a situation that is nevertheless certainly the one we find ourselves in.

It is also the situation of our feelings and valuations.

This of course the presence of consciousness makes possible, but it is not primarily consciousness considered as something unique and irreducible that we are concerned with when we notice this. Things, persons, events, possible actions, possible attitudes even, all these form an environment that is not neutral for us, but is charged with all the intricacy of our feeling for them, and charged also with some feelings that announce themselves as more than feelings—I mean duty, love, piety, the response to beauty, the impulse to make art, and all the other tendencies that have been philosophically problematic over the centuries. From one point of view this is the common world about us, viewed as concretely as may be; from another it is consciousness, viewed as concretely as may be in its concrete interplay with the world. Even the impulse to philosophize, as I shall maintain in the next chapter, belongs here, for it appears to us as one tendency among others; appears indeed so bound up with our whole affective life, that from one perspective at least we think of it as one feeling rooted in a complex of others. And as one dominant aspect of consciousness is its enigmatic association with the body, we may say of philosophy, as of this whole affective life, that it is rooted in our flesh.

From this it may seem that I am talking only about the situation of the philosopher: so many of these factors I see in the situation are just those that, taken as problems, provide him with much of his professional employment. But although it is true that we are speaking about the situation of the philosopher, and true also that in their acute and technical form many of these problems are philosophic ones in the strict sense, they are by no means unknown to the non-systematic reflection of Everyman, who is quite aware that he lives in many dimensions, whose proper order and relation he cannot establish. Even that most sophisticated philosophic issue, the search for the ultimate occupant of the situation—a Self or Ego that is *within* the body, indeed *within* consciousness, no less than these are within the general situation—is not something we are moved to only after a course in philosophy. It is probably true that we need formal philosophy to suggest to us that there are technical reasons why we cannot observe or otherwise surprise this ultimate occupant who yet so directly and vividly insists that he is after all *there*, but we are familiar enough with that paradoxically vivid insistence. For it is after all a situation in which we *will* reflect—reflect, I mean, in the sense of trying to make ourselves aware even of the whole structure of awareness—long before and long after we learn of the technical formulation of the conditions under which we do so. Although we should (it would seem) recognize that we are defeated by the paradoxes of reflection, paradoxes that I may sum up for the moment by saying that we must presumably stand outside ourselves and our situation in order to do what reflection requires us to do, we do not acknowledge defeat but persist in reflection *in* our situation, which thus takes on an additional problematic complication.

But it is after all a situation in great part made by philosophy. If there are in it complications that it does not need technical philosophy to provide, it is plain that technical philosophy has increased them. What were mere perplexities become cruxes that make us unwilling to accept some salient feature of our situation, and this can happen to us even when the only philosophy we have is second-hand, by way of absorption of some dominant epistemological or metaphysical bias of the day. In this sense the situation of Everyman, or at least Everyman *qua* reasonably concerned about his situation and thus able to conceive of it *as* a situation, becomes, at last, the situation of the philosopher. Let us acknowledge it then, for we are after all not thinking of a pre-philosophic situation, but of the situation within which anyone who philosophizes must find himself; much of what newer currents in philosophy have urged upon us is true: this is a situation that bears the marks of past philosophic efforts. Philosophy is a set of Pyrrhic victories: we try repeatedly to leave our situation in this sense, that we strive to establish a point of view that should bring order into it by ranging the tasks it confronts us with in terms of feasibility and importance; yet each advance seems only to

*II.   It is agreed on all sides that reason has been in funda-
mental error about its capacities and its proper tasks,
but that it is capable of repairing its deficiencies. The
interest in the problem of experience in our times
makes it tempting to look for a solution in some "new
empiricism"; it soon appears, however, that we cannot approach experience in any fresh way without
appealing also to the creative autonomy of reason.
We require a really radical new effort to know the
extent and proper disposition of reason's powers; and
this must respect the intent, if not the findings, of
both rationalistic and empirical appeals.*

There is hardly a fresh philosophic development of the last
fifty years that does not tell us either that past philosophers
have been fundamentally mistaken about their job, or that
there has been a decline into confusion after an earlier clarity.[2]
Philosophers of this century are very far from agreeing about
how reason's stance is deficient and how the deficiency is to
be remedied, but there is general agreement that something
can be done about it: reason is capable of righting itself: it
can find its way out of this maze, and go on—or backward—
to its proper employment.

We are at first tempted to a premature formulation of
our task in terms laden with all the traditional difficulties of
the problem of experience, for most of the stated or implied
remedies suggest that the best stance of reason is to be had in
a proper appreciation of what, among all the varieties of
"experience" that are urged upon us, really deserves that name.
Sometimes it is the common world that goes with the unreflective moods we all know; sometimes it is something having
a narrower and sharper focus to it than this, as in logical
positivism; sometimes it is something supposedly more "real,"
"concrete," or "absolute" than competing modes of experience. The banner of experience is an equivocal one, and those

enrich our perception of the situation while rendering it mor
enigmatic, so that we are precipitated by each new effort mor
deeply into the situation that confuses us. From one perspective we see progress: that is the enrichment, which any dis-
passionate observer of the history of philosophy must recognize; from another perspective we see a hopelessly persistent
situation in which profound disagreements multiply and the
influence of philosophy diminishes: that is the multiplication
of perspectives enigmatic in their competition. One sees readily
enough why some writers think we cannot afford any more
such victories.

Our situation, then, is the situation of reason in all of
us: absorbed in its tasks in a world in which myriad perspectives are open to it; discontent with a variety that will not
remain a mere variety; tempted to take its own true measure
and ultimately that of its situation by observation of some of
its own more successful works, as today science tempts us to
model all reasonable pursuits upon it; attracted still by a variety
of interests and tasks that persist in keeping the situation a
many-sided one, as still today the arts, religion, and metaphysics refuse to be dismissed as belonging only to our affective
lives; distrustful, finally, of a philosophic task that seems
endlessly self-defeating. And it is this complex situation in
which we seem nevertheless to be called upon for a new
philosophic effort of a radical sort.

who march under it are looking for a groundwork that is hard to find. They are, however, aware of this, and it is surely true that the problem of experience presents itself in this century exigently and in a new guise, so that from now on no rationalism or idealism, however austere and remote from what we usually think of as empirical concerns, will be able to neglect it. It is not for nothing that so many new approaches present themselves as radical empiricisms, or new empiricisms, or true empiricisms; not for nothing that the word "concrete," which brings in its train so many aspects of empiricism—sense, feeling, growth, indefeasible presence—has so honorific a tone in recent philosophy; not for nothing too that so many otherwise discordant philosophies recall us to the recognition of at least one putative mode of experience—that of the common world about us.

Yet formulation of the issue in terms of the problem of experience *would* be premature. We have something essential to learn from the experience-oriented philosophies of the last half century, but we must correct an overemphasis that has surely vitiated their attempts at new beginnings. The correction, which is itself all too easy to overstate, lies in seeing the sense in which all our philosophic advances, including any adjustment of the relation between reason and experience, any more ample grasp of experience, any assessment of the relative importance of whatever modes of experience there may be, must wait upon the creative autonomy of reason. There can be no question of settling our problems by turning to an experience that lies unambiguously, publicly, and as it were nakedly, before us, and calling upon it to arbitrate the issue for us merely by being what it is, because it is precisely our inability to *decide* what it is that troubles us. I do not mean that we are not able to consult it for certain purposes: obviously we can do so in many different ways, but then the purpose dictates what we shall take experience to be. There are probably occasions on which it is appropriate to appeal to the sort of sense-content that is the positivistic ideal; there are surely a vast variety of occasions upon which appeal to the everyday certainties of common sense is legitimate—these indeed probably form the bulk of our empirical appeals; and we are familiar enough with alternative approaches to experience by existential philosophers, moralists, artists, and mystics to know that we may at least entertain the possibility of a whole spectrum of empirical appeals. What is of course always then at issue is the legitimacy, in the sense of the *reasonableness*, of the purpose that dictates our view of experience. There is obviously a sense of "experience" that lies behind all these appeals, presumably furnishing a common orientation that enables us to speak of them all as empirical appeals, or at least putative empirical appeals. But if, bent on making a philosophic advance of the kind we are now considering, we ask just *what is* this experience upon which all our empirical appeals are directed, and if we conceive of ourselves as expecting an answer from experience itself, we shall surely be disappointed. There is no answer that an uninterpreted experience could make to us: it does not lie there guileless, open to a disinterested inspection however passively receptive, however intent on allowing it to speak to us. To ask what experience *really* is, is presumably to ask after some primordial empirical warrant upon which our whole cognitive structure might then be based; more realistically, perhaps, it is to ask after a whole set of empirical warrants suitable to various interests and occasions, these latter being ranged in order of importance— in effect a range of modes of experience related in some systematic way. To ask such a question of experience is to expect it to establish unshakably and as it were on its own authority what we usually establish by the very attitudes we adopt, attitudes in which the "empirical" and "rational" components mingle confusedly. There may be ways out of this confusion, but surely we cannot help matters by trying to submit—however patiently and ingeniously—to what is incapable of imposing itself upon us unaided.

And yet—the correction *is* an overstatement: there is something in the demand for newer and deeper empiricisms, and something we brush off all too peremptorily when we make the point I have just made—a point that has after all been made often enough, though with a different emphasis, by distinguishing the "given" from "experience." An empiricist might now step in to redress the balance by observing that what I have called the creative autonomy of reason cannot seize upon the whole framework of experience and know it for what it is, cannot establish a whole range of empirical warrants suited to our various reasonable interests, without somehow consulting the very patent character of experience. Grant the autonomous power of reason in this sphere, and it would still seem that reason can only exercise it in so far as it is capable of enjoying some of that satisfaction (whatever it may be) that we enjoy when we rest our case (whatever it may be) on experience. And so it goes: we oscillate between the claims of experience and those of reason and never tend towards that unknown but desired pole that should bring us at last to rest.

The lesson of this is that we cannot neglect either the "rational" or the "empirical" side in any attempt to secure a better stance for reason. Let us suppose for the moment that we are justified in attempting to secure this better stance by a fresh effort at *knowing* what is before us—that there are indeed some grounds for a renewed first-order effort not just at solving some particular philosophical problem but also at reestablishing the whole status of reason and therefore of philosophy. If we then attack the issue by setting reason to work in an effort to *know* its own situation as concretely as may be, we must be wary to preserve, even as we set about a new beginning, the sound intents both of rationalists and of empiricists, whose apparent conflict a more controlled and more passionate release of reason's energy might remove. It is not what rationalists and empiricists *formulate* that we want, for it is just these formulations that we oscillate between: we must succeed in expressing instead what each *intends* to honor in his formulations.

Therefore our effort must be truely radical: we are attempting not to neglect two things we cannot possibly know adequately in advance; we grope after archetypes of rational satisfaction and experiential grounding, and grope after them as being at root connected. There is no contradiction here, for how should we direct ourselves and expend our powers towards any end if it were not in *some* sense already with us? There is a creativity and autonomy to the mind as it expands into the familiar enlightenment that accompanies the unfolding, or at least the fresh ordering, of the articulated realm of concepts; and though we may not grasp the full significance of the accompanying satisfaction, we know it as an expansion in which understanding is completed, and know also that part of the satisfaction lies in its being the successful exercise of creativity and autonomy. Besides this satisfaction there is another that consists in the enjoyment of and repose in the independent and supporting character of what we are aware of, and we are familiar enough with this even if we cannot say definitively what exactly so supports our awareness or how we should go about finding this secure support. And we are not without some sense that the two kinds of satisfaction should march together, even though we can say as yet little more about an ideal joint satisfaction than this negative observation, that the first satisfaction is menaced with emptiness and the second with inarticulateness when we conceive of them in isolation one from the other.

III. *But in finding our way out of our situation we must do more than satisfy simultaneously the ideal demands of "reason" and "experience" in a new beginning, for it is exactly the ideal "relation" between "reason" and "experience" that is the primary subject matter of our new beginning. A paradox: we feel the need to satisfy the demands of both "reason" and "experience" by finding a standpoint that is "beyond" reason and experience yet enlightens us about reason and experience. The paradox inhibits attempts at a really radical solution: it discourages us from attempting to release what insist on presenting themselves as latent resources of reason.*

In the previous section I emphasized our hope of achieving in our new beginning archetypes of rational satisfaction and experiential grounding. But the common perplexity that makes our situation one of manifold modes of experience, manifold criteria of the reasonable, manifold perspectives in which philosophies compete inconclusively, is precisely our uncertainty about what the most fundamental relation between reason and experience is. We grope after an ideal satisfaction and hope to attain it in a reflexive perusal *of* reason and experience, but it is the general stance of reason with respect to experience, and experience itself, thought of as a general ground of authenticity, that we do not understand. To speak of the "fundamental relation" is to introduce a normative note: we wish archetypes of rational and empirical satisfaction and wish to find that satisfaction in an archetypal relation of reason and experience, now taken as our subject matter. Our failure to grasp this at the outset is perfectly compatible with the large certainties that must exist, side by side with uncertainties, *within* any settled, viable, and habitual mode of attention: science with its methodological certainties existing side by side with much methodological obscurity is a case in point. I made this point in the previous section by noticing that we pursue various explicit reasonable ideals and consult experience in various explicit ways, in accordance with the nature of various more or less well characterized tasks. What we fail to understand, then, is the role reason and experience play in establishing the framework within which these well established tasks are carried on. And one reason why we fail to understand it is that we tend to conceive of this role in terms of the relation that exists between explicit reasonable criteria and explicit experiential criteria *within* these settled tasks. Perhaps our first misunderstanding is the use of the word "relation" with regard to the framework. This is the obverse of the normative note mentioned above: our failure to understand reason and experience in their most fundamental or framework roles produces a deficiency in reason's most fundamental stance "relative" to experience. Our effort to begin anew is then, with respect to this issue at least, an effort to transform reason's general stance and thus to release that part of its resources heretofore suppressed by a faulty self-knowledge.

The task is therefore paradoxical: we wish to place ourselves "beyond" the interplay of reason and experience in order to determine the role reason and experience (now in a more fundamental sense) play in establishing the framework for that interplay and hope thus to perfect reason's stance. Yet, as we saw in the last section, while thus placing ourselves "beyond" or "outside," we wish nevertheless to bring about that simultaneous satisfaction and actualization of the still obscure demands of reason and experience that we proposed to ourselves as the first object of our new beginning. We wish to go to the root of reason and experience, to satisfy there the ideal demands of reason and experience, and to bring about reason's best stance by this means.

Is it any wonder, then, that philosophers of many different temperaments should find a reflexive demand both for the real and our means of access to it excessive, and that they should, within their several frameworks, reject it? They might well agree with us that our situation is not entirely satisfactory: that reason, just because of the multiple perspectives open to it, is unable to give any task it embarks upon, whether in science, art, religion, or morals, or in that daily routine that forms a background for all of these, its proper weight and relation to the others; that reason may therefore either set itself impossible tasks or neglect important possible tasks; and that all this is symptomatic both of a deficiency in self-knowledge and of a lack of a secure foundation in the concrete. But they may also be unable to see how reason is to step outside itself, rid itself of all the confusions that go with its present engagement, and see its main task for what it really is, and therefore its special tasks for what they really are. They may be right; the question of reason's best stance may not be a legitimate one, and we may have to put up with the present deep disagreement about the philosopher's vocation, although we must probably then reconcile ourselves to the disappearance of philosophy in an intellectual world divided between reasonable specialties and the manifold life of feeling.

The language in which I call for a radical remedy is, however, the language of our situation, and consequently makes that seem impossible which, once the situation should be transformed, would seem the most natural thing in the world. A more suitable way of putting the issue might well remove the air of paradox, but this can only develop in and with the insight it should articulate. To speak of going to the root of reason and experience must remain little more than a flourish until the development of the topic of radically originative reflection in Chapter 4.

3

NEW BEGINNINGS AND OUR SITUATION:
PARADOXES OF SUBJECTIVITY

I.   The abstractness of our discussion in the first two chapters masks the problem of subjectivity. Does the participation of our subjective dynamism in a new beginning of this sort doom it to subjectivity? Besides the obvious difficulties of this issue there is the opportunity of transforming our whole understanding of subjectivity.

Philosophy is not so abstract and theoretical an affair as the previous two chapters suggest. The motives that lead any of us to defend a philosophical position, or indeed even to begin philosophical inquiry, are complex and deep-rooted. We misrepresent what is at stake here if we express ourselves in ways appropriate to some purely epistemological problem, engaging some supposed purely theoretic side of our nature in a perfectly determinate, clear-cut, and objective situation. It is true that the governing feature of the present discussion has been the obscurity and ambiguity of our situation, and this should have warned us that there are depths here to be explored cautiously; but the exact role played by our subjectivity both in defining our contemporary situation and in pointing a way out of it needs to be made explicit before we can undertake the new beginning for which we stand poised. There are difficulties here, but it may turn out that there are unexpected opportunities as well.

The contribution made to all our activities by our various conscious and unconscious interests, appetites, passions, wants, inclinations, impulses, or tendencies I shall call the contribution of subjective dynamism. I mean to point by this term to everything in one's nature that makes the life of the mind an affective and passional one, whatever else that life may be. Our problem, then, is this: does not our whole definition of the philosophical situation, and the whole enterprise of a new beginning, owe more to subjective dynamism than would appear in the first two chapters? And is this presence of subjective dynamism compatible with what we see at this point as an effort to establish philosophy as a first-order way of *knowing*, with all the commitment to the theoretic and the "objective" that this implies? It is possible that we can summon our subjective dynamism to the service of reason only if certain components in that dynamism—it might be certain interests, certain wants, certain aspirations—are suppressed and certain others allowed their head. Is the interest in truth the only one that we gratify when we see ourselves confronted with the philosophical situation and task that I have described? Or do we then give free play to other interests that we ought to suppress in the philosophical undertaking?

The question is one philosophers of all sorts might well ask themselves, but it is especially exigent here; for, if we are concerned with the problem of subjective dynamism, we are concerned with it in an especially concrete way. We are in the first place not altogether clear about reason itself: we know it as it appears in some of its works and acts, but we do not know its precise limits, and we therefore remain uncertain to what degree the pattern of subjective dynamism must be enlisted to give reason all the scope it needs for self-recognition. It might well be that more of that subjective pattern must be enlisted than we usually think appropriate where we talk of knowing: might well indeed be that dynamisms we are accustomed to think only appropriate to moral and artistic activity—dynamisms we tend to group under such headings as valuing, feeling, expressing—must be enlisted in order to loose reason to its proper work. It is a possibility we must at least consider in a starting point of this sort. And more than this, if our intent is concrete in the sense that we are not concerned for reason as an isolated function only, but think of it as something whose best stance affects the whole pattern of subjective dynamism, then we are also concerned to bring about an appropriate organization of that subjective dynamism. So it is here: we are concerned to employ subjective dynamism in the way best suited to make reason live, and we are concerned that reason should live to so govern us as to bring about an ideal subjective organization.

Opinion on the proper role of subjective dynamism in philosophy is sharply divided today. Many ordinary language philosophers tell us that the wish to bring about a philosophical knowledge deeper than that we express in ordinary knowledge is the result of unconscious drives—directed, it might be, towards a cosmic security we do not in fact possess—which issue finally in the application of certain language turns beyond the range in which they can do good service. They hold the metaphysical nisus to be a subjective tendency that sets reason an illusory task, and the resulting "metaphysics" to be a pseudo-knowledge emerging from an inappropriate organization of subjective dynamism. On the other hand, many existentialists tell us that our most appropriate attitudes must deploy a very concrete pattern of subjectivity indeed: out of the interplay of the forces composing our individualities there arises the sense of loss, of emptiness, of disgust, of nothingness, of meaninglessness, of the shipwreck of reason, from which our appropriate attitude, whether a perfect freedom analogous to religious belief, or a perfect freedom of disillusion in which we shape ourselves by gratuitous acts, ultimately springs. We would, with the former, not have our subjective dynamism enter into the life of reason in a way that would mar it; with the latter, we should prefer to believe that our appropriate reasonable attitude to the world must grow out of a more concrete pattern of subjective dynamism than the former would allow. Notice, though, how deeply subjective dynamism appears to enter into *both* attitudes with respect to the formulation of our whole conception of philosophy. Whatever subjective forces an ordinary language philosopher suppresses when he eschews metaphysics, he engages a whole complex of such forces when he embraces analysis as a way of life. He offers us by this gesture a commitment on such matters as unconscious motivation, the significance of religion, and the proper approach to moral, political, and esthetic issues. The gesture is always implicitly passional, but it often bears besides all the outward marks of passional engagement: there is as much *Angst* in certain pages in which Wittgenstein or Wisdom tell us of their conceptions of the discipline of philosophy as you will find anywhere in Heidegger. There is, then, no doubt that in *some* sense we must think of the search for philosophy as a passional one. Even if we do not agree with Plato that philosophy consists in the turning upward of the whole soul, and may thus in part depend, for better or worse, on temperamental considerations and training, we must still admit that commitments like these touch upon our whole attitude to life. This is why, when we are wrong in philosophy, we may be so totally wrong, and why we do not find in philosophical debates the same coolness a scientist theoretically brings to his. What we do as philosophers must resound through all our moral and intellectual attitudes and touch even our self-respect. To have taken a transient feeling for a metaphysical profundity, or again to have dismissed someone else's valid insight as a matter of transient feeling, is to have made a mistake of some concrete significance. Philosophy cuts very deep. We cannot settle the issue of the proper significance of our subjective dynamism without using its resources; and if we wish to establish some one objective attitude in which our subjective dynamism plays only its proper role, we can not be sure that in doing this we have inevitably employed it in only the ideal way envisaged.

In the terminology of the previous chapter, these are difficulties about the proper relationship between experience and the subjective dynamism upon which all of it is in some sense based. Can we settle the status of the various modes of experience that are put forward as the proper correlatives of reason, or at least of an ideal human adjustment to things, without employing more of subjective dynamism than we suppose ourselves to be doing? This is not just the question whether certain modes of experience are subjective because they employ too much of this dynamism; it is the question whether, even when we judge that only a minimal involvement of our passional nature is desirable, that judgment itself exhibits only the desired minimum.

A new beginning of this sort labors then under many difficulties. It is not without presuppositions; how could it be? We all of us begin advantaged or disadvantaged by our whole intellectual situation. But, more than this, the very roots of our interpretation of it are questionable. Here, at least, we try to bring these questions into the open, and grant at the outset that the enterprise is not just a scientific one, and not just a logical one; that in fact it is not aimed at the solution of certain problems whose frame of reference is clearly understood. We feel that if we could but free ourselves from the encumbrances of tradition and from the too importunate problems of the day—if we could free ourselves, that is, from the corporate practice of philosophy as we know it—we might see things with an innocence and freshness so far denied us. Our situation itself already includes a prescience of a solution, which, most charitably interpreted, appears as one already dimly apprehended; and, less charitably, as the drawings of temperament.

These are all difficult questions, which in one form or another have played a major role in the modern controversies about philosophy. Yet if we face them directly, it may well turn

out that the way we now formulate them is merely symptomatic of the obscurity in which we presently move. And it
may well be that if we face them in this spirit we may find
that this so persistent problem of subjectivity—a problem as
old as Plato's discussion of the role the different functional
levels of the soul play in wisdom, and as new as modern
psychoanalytic theory—so transforms itself as to appear at
last an ally rather than an obstacle to our efforts.

II.   *The aim that dictates this effort at a new beginning
       engages a very concrete pattern of subjective dyna-
       mism. The objective: to find "total significance" in
       the real—though in a way different from that ad-
       vanced in metaphysical systems; to shape our sub-
       jective dynamism under a corresponding ideal of
       reason. It is an effort at self-expression: a cry from
       the heart that is a cry for the heart. Yet the possibility
       of achieving this objective is by no means authenti-
       cated at this stage.*

When subjective dynamism plays a more complete, or more
concrete, role in a philosophical outlook than is usually
thought desirable in a scientific or common-sense undertaking,
it is not always through a mere inadvertence. The concreteness
of the philosophic motivation that led to the present view of
the situation is not present because I could not exclude it; it
is, if not deliberate in the sense of being contrived, at least
affirmatively acknowledged. In terms of knowing, it is a self-
conscious demand for total significance, made in the face of
our contemporary assumption that this is something that
reason must do without, even if some darker and less articulate
"significance" should yet be open to us. "I want everything
to be explained to me or nothing," says Camus in *The Myth
of Sisyphus*, "and the reason is impotent when it hears this
cry from the heart." [3] This impotence of reason I have already

held to be an illusion arising from a faulty self-knowledge, which suppresses powers that we can learn to release; and in releasing them one hopes not just for a more adequate view of the role of philosophy and of the role of reason itself, but for a more ample use of reason's powers in the direction of "total significance." That objective is a much more modest one than critical accounts of metaphysics usually represent it to be. In the first place, one does not look for explanations in any of the senses one might exact within a context that is itself accepted without explanation; such explanations permit in principle a systematic completeness not attainable where the framework itself comes in question. In the second place, the recognition of significance is perfectly compatible with tentativeness of formulation. But with these reservations, it must be insisted here that it really is a cry from the heart that leads us to try to begin in this way, and that it is freely acknowledged to be so.

This cry from the heart leads us not just in the direction of a more adequate knowing based upon a freeing of reason from its self-imposed bonds, where that knowing is purely theoretic in intent; the cry *from* the heart is also a cry *for* the heart: we would shape and order the whole pattern of our subjective dynamism, releasing it to its proper life to just the extent that that proper life is dependent upon the adequate exercise of reason. The most modest way of stating this objective is to say that we are concerned that our attitudes should assume a pattern as little arbitrary and as little symptomatic as possible: we do not, that is, think it appropriate that our attitudes should merely grow out of other components of our subjective dynamism that are too mute to be described as attitudes, and grow in such a way that an account of that growth should be an exhaustive account of those attitudes. Therefore, and to just the extent that attitudes contribute to action, we are also concerned indirectly with the whole realm of action, including making no less than doing. I am not suggesting a view of the philosophic effort as so intimately bound up with the training of all our functions as it is held to be in the *Republic*, but only supposing that there is some appropriate relationship between action, attitude, and knowing.

A cry *from* the heart that is a cry *for* the heart: the concern for an appropriate pattern of our subjective dynamism is not a concern on the part of an abstract reason that observes that pattern from the outside, but is itself the expression of a most exigent affective pattern under the dominance of an ideal of reason. The pattern would "express" itself: it would, that is, become what it might be if the ideal were capable of realization. In this sense the philosophic effort is an effort at self-expression. One uses that term warily, for it brings with it overtones of the multifarious confusions of esthetic doctrine. The meaning I give it is tentative enough, as what we rightly intend by "self" must remain for a long while an open question; but this much at least is clear, that a pattern of subjective dynamism is in process of evolution; that an important factor in the evolution is a complex of feelings, emotions, or drives directed upon an obscure norm, standard, or ideal, called reason; and that the presence of this complex has an important bearing on the course of that evolution. In one sense, of course, any pattern of subjectivity is a self-expression; but I apply the term here because one component in the developing pattern is an ideal of the self. And, remembering that the development is directed towards the shaping and ordering of the whole pattern of our subjectivity with the aim of bringing about its proper fulfillment, one can speak also of a drive towards self-integration. The cry from the heart is a cry for the significance of what lies all about us, and a cry also for an internal order congruent with what that significance should turn out to be. It is therefore also a cry for self-knowledge, issuing from a subjective pattern of interests under the dominance of what we take to be an interest of reason; but it may also be taken as signalizing reason's effort at a self-knowledge which should be both a knowledge of its own appropriate role and of the whole pattern of subjective dynamism.

Whether we have any right to use such conceptions as

self-expression, self-integration, and self-knowledge depends upon the validity of that ideal of reason. The basic image is of a complex personality pressing for as complete a realization of itself as possible, where its very self-identity, together with the sense the word "complete" has, is given by that ideal. I do not mean that we regard the ideal as potentially so related to our subjectivity as to promise ultimately the extinction of all our passions in a contemplative one; or even that we should expect individual patterns of subjectivity that distinguish us one from another to give way to a common pattern imposed by a common ideal. We are not in fact primarily concerned with self-knowledge in that so familiar sense of the uncovering of the very particularity of our individual subjective patterns, but with a self-knowledge in which one hopes to recognize the status and appropriate role of subjective dynamism in general. In the century of psychoanalysis the former sort is so clamant that we forget that the latter is by right prior, and that in the neglect of it we shall probably find ourselves proceeding upon unexamined and perhaps dangerous assumptions about the status of our affective nature. At this point, in any case, being as we are unsure of the status of subjective dynamism, the fate of our whole complex of tendencies making for a new beginning and of the ideal that we wish to see dominate it hangs in the balance: there may be no real satisfaction for what seems like a complex and concrete need—the need of a reason not yet fully conscious of itself. And the situation in which we claim to find ourselves, with all the opportunities it seems to present to us, and all the demands it seems to make upon us may, as it is defined by this complex "need," be a delusion, from which a more modest and more precisely definable ideal would awaken us.

III. *The ideal of reason that moves us is admittedly ob-*
scure, but two correlatives of the ideal help give
definition to our enterprise: (a) an unauthenticated
grasp of the real is an insistent factor in our situation;
(b) an unauthenticated view of the task of philoso-
phy governs our whole enterprise.

An explicit ideal of rationality is most easily formulated if we
give our entire allegiance to some settled framework within
which the interplay of reason and experience (or the theoretical and the empirical) takes place. If we refuse to rest
easily in any framework until we have faced and answered the
question of the role of reason and experience (now in a more
fundamental sense) in establishing that or any framework,
we must expect some obscurity in our ideal of reason. This is
merely a consequence of being responsive to the reflexive character of the problem of reason and experience; a definite ideal
awaits the release of the powers that should define it.

Yet putting the matter in this way does less than justice
to our enterprise, for even at this stage, when subjectivity is
still a problem for us, it is not quite true to say that we are
moved only by an obscure ideal dominating a subjective dynamism of uncertain import. For me, and I suspect for many
others as well, the ideal was associated with an unauthenticated mode of knowing that seemed to be directed upon the
irrecusably real, and that gave some promise of being clarified
by, and in turn of clarifying, the whole significance and tendency of that subjective dynamism.

But let me approach these matters through the more
convenient medium of what accompanies this unauthenticated mode of knowing and this unauthenticated ideal,
namely, an equally unauthenticated view of philosophy. I have
already claimed that there is a fundamental defect in the self-
consciousness of all philosophy, and in the next chapter shall
be concerned to try to make an advance in that self-consciousness. Here I want to point out that if philosophy is a study

whose appropriate "nature" we do not yet clearly know, it is not at any rate to be identified with just one of the several more or less clear interests *of* reason that one might specify, since it is clearly also an interest *in* the whole life of reason, and consequently also an interest in ideals of reason that we have not yet managed to express adequately. Seen from this point of view, our whole account of a subjective dynamism developing under an obscure ideal of reason might stand just as well for an account of the development of the philosophic impulse towards self-consciousness.

But to come at this view of philosophy I must put the matter in a more personal way than the reader expects, indeed than he perhaps feels it appropriate, to hear from a professional philosopher. I persist in this both because I think we can not otherwise be as concrete as the present topic demands that we should be, and because I suspect that in a surprising number of cases we shall find something very like these feelings lying just under the professional aplomb that most of us are able to bring to our duties.

The question whether philosophy is properly a specialty was touched upon in Chapter 1; the question whether it is properly a profession will dominate the present discussion. The same subjective pattern that issued in an obscure ideal for reason and for philosophy was part of a more complex web of motivation that led me to take up a career as a professional philosopher, but it was so controlling a part as to make me uneasy from the start in the role of professional, and to cause me to bring what I hope is a salutary ambiguity to it. In concerning myself seriously with philosophy, I thought of myself as concerned with the nature of man and his place in the scheme of things; in wishing to see philosophy become what it could be, I supposed myself to be intent upon as complete a self-realization as might be; and the whole field of knowledge seemed to me deficient except as it could be related to those matters. One has only to state such aims—enunciated here in so unsophisticated, so informal a way—to understand how unsuitable they are for a professional career. A professional man can hardly avoid taking an interest in such matters *qua* lay person, but *qua* professional he will presumably do better to work in some field whose interests are more modest and exact, and in which he may work without constantly questioning, not his axioms—for in many fields he must expect to call these constantly in question—but the very character of the interests those axioms should subserve. And it is not just that times have changed, that it had once been possible to be a professional philosopher, and that we have now lost the courage, the confidence, indeed the *hubris* to profess so ambitious a subject in the manner of the great professor-philosophers of the past. No, clearly they were in the wrong, those great professors, and even should some such ambitious goal as I had envisaged for philosophy be possible, it is clearly no matter to be *professed*, and no matter for a profession, no more than poetry is, although it is bootless to make very much of this issue in a day when poets have joined philosophers as professional academics. Socrates pointed this out long ago in criticizing not so much the professionalism of the sophists— and "professor" is not so bad a translation for the original sense of that word—in the several fields of learning that they have some claim to having invented, as their wish to professionalize wisdom. Should *that* be teachable, it is not teachable along professional lines, and this is no less true today than in Socrates' time. One hoped, of course, that the philosophy would manage to live amidst professional routine, as a poet presumably hopes that he may yet write poetry amidst all the criticism and the teaching of creative writing. But it is this long-standing orientation of the philosophic effort as I understood it that keeps me from being impressed when now, the logic of professionalism having run its course to produce the ideal of the specialty, we are solemnly told by learned men that they have just discovered that it is not appropriate to profess wisdom and to pursue the traditional ends of philosophy, and that we should leave off doing it. From this they draw the conclusion touched upon in the first chapter: that we should, belonging to a profession having something of the corporate structure possessed by the other professions, find something suitable to profess—some specialty like the others. They have missed the point: we are in fact interlopers among the professions and at best play at it. There is probably no great harm in this, for the world wags in this way, and like poets we need our disguises. But we need not mistake the disguise for the reality: it is in itself a worthy thing, the profession of philosophy in the academic sense—the sense that carries with it learned journals, symposia, professional meetings, and all the rest of the panoply of a profession—and by patience and single-mindedness one may yet hope to get the best of two worlds, as some few have indeed managed to do; yet the thing it disguises is more solitary, more demanding, and more concrete. If we forget this, our philosophy may be as deficient in its kind as that academic poetry that seems to have been written only so that it may then be analyzed in literature classes. All this, of course, seems to have been especially forgotten in the analytic world of English-speaking philosophy, in which the major preoccupation is with the problems raised by earlier philosophic efforts: I have even heard a colleague speak of the *repertory* of philosophic problems.

But who can avoid some misgivings about opposing professionalism in a day when the tide runs so inexorably in that direction? For if one is unwilling to define philosophy in somewhat the same way in which we define any of the tasks of reason, he seems to call the whole fabric of a settled reasonable life in question, and to do so in the name of what might turn out to be a merely personal ideal. We distrust these pretensions in others and in ourselves. There is something of the poet's pride in this impulse, and something too of the poet's demand for self-expression. Say what you will about the way our times call out for fresh beginnings, and what you will about the demand made by the very ambiguity of philosophy's subject matter for such new beginnings, and one might still suspect that those who approach philosophy in this spirit do so mainly because they feel that without some such effort they do not fully express themselves, do not wholly manage to say what it is in them to say, and thus remain both in thought and action somewhat less than they might have been. They would seem to want to pour into philosophy that completeness of effort that I. A. Richards must have had in mind when he spoke of poetry as our "completest mode of utterance," and we wonder whether the poet's wholehearted effort at concreteness is appropriate in what is put forward as a primarily reasonable enterprise.

There is, however, a difference: the concern for completeness is not necessarily directed at producing, in the mode of philosophy, precisely that kind of complete utterance one surely finds in some poetry. It is rather a concern to use philosophy to release all our powers in their proper order and composure: the very composure of reason in the sense that reason would then permeate our various activities to permit them to achieve what they can achieve; and in the sense too that reason itself, while not embarking on tasks it is unfitted to cope with, would still not neglect tasks that it can deal with and that are indeed imposed upon it. However personal the effort, then, that a man supposes himself to be making; however much he is concerned as much for the proper development of his own personality as for any ideal analogous to those we pursue in science; he is also concerned with establishing reason in its dominions, and there can be nothing more impersonal than this. It is indeed his situation that puzzles and tries him, and out of which he would, under the philosophic motivation, see his individuality grow into its proper life; but he also takes it for the situation of humanity in these times, and can only conceive of himself as acting for something that is general in the sense that he himself only shares in it.

This view of philosophy and its relation to the self was, seen from another angle, a view of beings and of Being of which the self offers but one instance. If I could not extirpate alternative views of the self, I could also not help regarding them as resting on a much less concrete mode of attention to things than that which I enjoyed under the dominance of this ideal.

The main lines of this imperfectly articulated but insistent metaphysical view are worth sketching here despite their familiarity, for I shall eventually try to make the point that our chief metaphysical problem lies in the authentication of the more or less familiar. Any authentication one might hope for would bring with it a more adequate understanding of what we try to embody in familiar metaphysical formulae. I shall begin with the problem of causation, and move from there to related issues.

Metaphysicians from Plato and Aristotle through Whitehead and Bergson have tried to do justice to the very *being* of an entity by employing a many-sided causal analysis, of which Aristotle's four-fold scheme (in some important respects a codification of Platonic insights) is the most famous example. Throughout this tradition there has always been present the idea of a shaping and ordering force, which merely expresses itself in the diversity and mobility of things, and which insists on presenting itself to us in terms that hover about the ancient —and doubtless, taken literally, inadequate—idea of teleology. The intent of this preoccupation with a multi-faceted view of causation has been to take seriously, as itself a vital power, any entity however complex, and not to regard it as merely a function in a continuous analysis that will not rest even in reducing it to simpler component entities, but must go on until the very idea of "an entity" or "a being" is replaced by the idea of homogeneous factors productive in their interplay of all so-called entities. But taking an entity seriously has in practice also meant taking seriously the shaping or ordering force mentioned above, for as soon as we speak of an entity we cannot help seeing it as bound together with all other entities by a common ancestry, thought of as possessing a resource that is not exhausted by its expression in the actual world of multiplicity and interaction. There is something in the very idea of "entity" or "being" that resists an outright pluralism and leads us to the idea of a common Being. And so the wish to do justice to causation as we find it before us, by analyzing it in terms of the various aspects or levels it displays, may also be regarded as a wish to do justice to *Being* by seeing the very category of *Causation* as the outcome of an attitude in some degree abstract.

From this point of view a causal analysis in terms of either of the chief views of causation associated with the rise of the physical sciences appeared highly abstract. The first of these theories of causation is a metaphysical one in which the things we know directly in the world about us are held to be derived from the more basic realities of matter and motion. Causal accounts are in effect restricted to two aspects of the fourfold Aristotelian scheme, namely, the material and the efficient (or moving) causes—or rather, to a narrow interpretation of these two aspects in terms of matter in motion, for, in the Aristotelian scheme, "matter" can be given important senses different from the sense it bears in a naive materialism, as can "movement." The second view of causation associated with science is in effect an anti-metaphysical version of the former, and therefore necessarily lacks its explicit materialistic commitment, even though the type of investigation it envisages is perfectly consistent with, and certainly has favored in the popular mind, a materialistic view. We know it in the powerful classical versions of Hume and Kant, from which the more sophisticated versions of the law of causality current in modern philosophy of science are derived. Despite the necessary refinements needed to apply either of these theories to the procedures of modern science, their main lines have not been altered. Perhaps Hume's doctrine, as the principal philosophical ancestor of logical positivism, has been put forward more often. If it has been objectionable to some, as lacking a strictly reasonable foundation for the general principle (or law) of causality, which we seem to invoke when we set about establishing particular causal laws, it has seemed reasonableness itself to others in that it does not demand what we cannot hope to know. There are various circumspect formulations of Hume's principle of causation; all of them suppose only that we can formulate in symbolic or ordinary linguistic terms laws that enable us to predict certain features of one set of happenings from certain features of another set of happenings. The confirmation of the principle lies in our continuing ability to do just this, and we do not therefore regret our inability to assert a universal determinism in the way in which Kant's formulation permits us to do. Also, we may go on *believing*, if it suits us, that things are universally determined in the way, let us say, that Laplace envisaged; one suspects that Hume and at least some contemporary scientists eat their cake and have it in exactly this way.

The abstractness of these anti-metaphysical approaches to causation seemed to me to lie chiefly in their concern with sequences. To treat of causation in terms of the erection of conceptual structures with whose help we can determine certain features of one spatio-temporal region on the basis of certain features of another region seemed in itself unobjectionable, useful, and important; but it also seemed incomplete. For one thing, it neglected the entities that in their togetherness made it possible (so it seemed from my unauthenticated point of view) for us to speak of spatio-temporal regions.[4] Even in the acknowledged obscurity of my own metaphysical orientation, it seemed to me that I *knew* beings and Being, and knew them in a way that required a complex and concrete view of causation. As for the causal relation itself, it seemed to me that I knew it too, despite all epistemological criticism of our ability to know it. However difficult it might be to formulate it within the framework provided for us by the last three centuries or so of epistemological debate, to know beings was to know them in a concrete and complex causal interaction, and was so because it was *beings* that one dealt with, and not just sensuous impressions from which this idea of being was a dubious derivative. Somehow something had gone wrong, leaving me unable to formulate in a completely trustworthy way a knowledge I could not doubt; and, what was worse, every attempt to formulate the groundwork of my knowledge seemed only to bring greater difficulties.

Whatever difficulties lay in the way of clarifying and substantiating this view, I could not, while under its influence, take seriously the various epiphenomenalistic views of the self, in which consciousness, and reasonable activity in general, is seen as the by-product of the working out of physical forces (whatever these may ultimately be) of which an exhaustive account, or at least the only *reasonable* account, is to be hoped for only from science. Epiphenomenalism as a metaphysical view rests its case primarily on a scientific effort that is, despite many successes, still programmatic only: we know it is possible to alter the quality of consciousness and indeed the whole pattern of behavior by chemically, electrically, or mechanically inducing changes in the body; we know also that in certain biological spheres, notably in the study of viruses and in the study of the cell nucleus, there seems reason to believe that the procedures and theories of physics are just as appropriate and useful as they are elsewhere; but we are very far from the general reduction of biology to physics envisaged in this program. Yet even the successful completion of it would leave us with an account essentially abstract, because concerned only with those aspects of causation that are present in the scientific ideal I have been discussing. The status of the self as an entity would have been left out of consideration.

This was in fact a view of beings and of Being from which the idea of hierarchy could not be excluded. Any entity I could think of presented itself as a field of multiplicity and interaction, but one supported by a resource not fully deployed in that or in any other field. This image not only made it inappropriate to reduce any entity or being to whatever components one might find in it, and inappropriate to think of any scientific causal analysis as exhaustive; it made it appear besides that that irreducible activity I have ascribed to any entity expressed itself precisely by controlling and ordering subordinate functions or components. More precisely, an entity appeared to express itself by constituting *as* subordinate just those functions or components into which we are tempted to analyze it. Beings or entities seemed to win their status by so combining their subordinate components or functions as to produce more than the sum of the parts, at least in the sense that a causal account in terms of these parts leaves out precisely what it is that we thus analyze; and they win this status only as they draw on a common Being to do so. And if in this sense one saw *any* being or entity as drawing upon the latencies of Being in this way, one necessarily saw, in a being that lived under an ideal of reason, a quite special and intimate recourse to the latencies of Being. The idea of hierarchy and the idea of freedom I saw everywhere, in at least the limited sense of these terms permitted by this exposition; but the principle of hierarchy and the principle of freedom seemed to come into their own only as one turned to the problems of self, of consciousness, and of reason. All the ambiguity in which the problem of subjectivity has been lapped in our times seemed to me to cohere around this issue, and all the insights of existentialism and psychoanalysis it seemed here possible to reconcile with a rationalism to which they otherwise so often appear hostile. The conception of the self as contingently and freely shaping itself against the threat of static and deceptive metaphysical models of its own perfection, against the threat of divisive and annihilating powers it should rightly transform and master—powers of which anxiety, nausea, and disgust are only some of many possible psychological manifestations; the enigmatic character of a belief without rational grounds, in continuous tension with doubt and despair, and yet supposed by its advocates to be somehow both self-justifying and the completion of the self and indeed of rationality; the problem of integrating a self so distracted and neurotic that it falls short even of an everyday balance—a problem to which our answers are as many as our philosophies; all these matters seemed to me capable of some resolution if only the role of hierarchy and freedom, here so clamant, were authenticated. To be as under the ideal of reason was not simply to draw upon the freshness of Being to exist in one's own right, dominating by one's existence components that otherwise might seem more real; for, besides this birthright (as it seemed) of all entities—a birthright which, in so far as it expresses itself in the massive regularities of types, in which individual echoes individual, we tend to blur by using the word "essence"—besides this, reason, as the crown of an entity, seemed capable of drawing upon the latencies of Being in all its unemployed resource, bringing the infinitude of it into a context that could not otherwise contain it. To be as under the dominance of reason was to be capable of drawing upon this resource to surpass the level in which one finds himself; but it was also to be subject not just to the competition in which all entities whatsoever are susceptible to dissolution, but to a threat from within as well. This is the creativity and the vulnerability of reason, and it has in other contexts been used to establish a sense of freedom both more ample and more perilous than that which one must (at least on the basis of the present unauthenticated view of causation) accord any entity whatsoever in so far as one takes it seriously *as* an entity.

As for the problem of Form, which any mention of generality, or of what is common, at once invokes, it seemed to me that the continued interest in it was entirely appropriate for anyone seeking to account for the orderly, persistent, and interlocking structures of things, as well as for our ability to know these aspects of things. The intent of a persistent Platonism seemed understandable, but I felt that no one had yet succeeded in doing justice to that aspect of things which so strikes Platonists, without at the same time hypostatizing our own conceptual forms. That this sort of question was inseparable from an ample and concrete view of causation I took for granted. Dominating all these ideas was a concern for the reality of concrete individual things—the *ousiai* of Aristotle— and a refusal to think of their structure, their order, the possibility of classifying them, as condoning our depreciating their reality as over against that of Platonic forms. The source of the possibilitiy of generalizing about them, the source of their congruence with the stability of our conceptual forms, I preferred to find rather in their common ancestry in a Being that remains *One* as over against their *Many,* and that supports in this way that power of generalizing and that patience before generalizing that always goes back in any case to an inscrutable contrast of the One and the Many.

Yet I could see that precisely what kept me from formulating any of these issues more clearly and decisively than I had done, and what kept me from answering all the series of empiricist doubts that led eventually to Kant, was my inability to say just how it is that we know anything at all about any of these issues I have been discussing. This in turn was what produced all that was unsatisfactory in the metaphysical tradition: all the overstatements, all the self-defeating contradictions seemed to me to go back to this decisive point. Yet how to remedy it? When I considered this my "theoretical" view of things, it seemed sometimes that I had only to look at things afresh. The concrete, or the real, is always there, it would seem, and however inexplicably, somehow open to our perusal. The confusion lay in the philosophers: they defeated themselves, and often enough by simply behaving as though their only resource was the examination of theories, ideas, and arguments; while the "freshness deep-down things" remained there, gloriously itself, and capable of resolving all our confusions if we could but see it and formulate it. And this, of course, was just the task foreseen for philosophy, under the rubric of the problem of reason and experience, in my previous chapter. And yet how could I do this? For not only did my misconceptions about reason and its workings make me stumble over myself each time I essayed a fresh start of this sort, but I was besides perfectly aware that this so tentative "theoretic" outlook of mine was bound up with that "practical" concern for the completion of the self under an ideal of reason that I have been describing; I might therefore have no title whatever to the outlook described, and likewise no real grounds for conceiving of the philosophic task in the terms just given. We seem, then, to possess a kind of knowledge that we can neither establish indefeasibly nor yet extirpate, and if we cannot fully persuade ourselves or others of what remains so essentially unclear, neither can we discard it on the basis of evidence brought forward from standpoints that appear to be of lesser concreteness.

What is admittedly in some sense "subjective" in origin insists on presenting itself as an "objective" (if ambiguous and unclear) mode of knowing; what is clearly a "practical" concern aims stubbornly at a "theoretic" or "contemplative" insight, in order to further what it takes to be an already theoretic if imperfect insight—and takes itself in all this for the central philosophic concern; what presents itself as an action, both as being a passage in the developing history of an individual and as being directed towards a framework for all the action of that individual, presents itself also as thought; and we cannot resolve any of these ambiguities until we either successfully complete the task in hand or recognize its impossibility.

IV.   *The possibility of the transformation of the problem of subjectivity: subjective dynamisms that are seen in one light as mere components in a mere complex, may appear in another light as potentially the supporting dynamisms of an overriding unity. In this sense the radical effort to recognize reason appears as a radical effort at self-integration.*

Two things make the problem of subjective dynamism less threatening than it at first appears. In the first place, before we can dismiss a new beginning because of its supposedly subjective side, we must have some patently objective outlook to bring against it to define its subjectivity. Yet we do not know of any objective outlook in which we cannot find a complex of impulses that gives it direction; settles upon its subject matter by a decision as to what is relevant, knowable, and worth knowing; and indeed therefore settles more or less clearly what we mean by knowing. Not that such knowing is necessarily any the worse for that: it is simply that the problem of objectivity is not settled by defining it in relation to some one obviously reliable attitude, mode of attention, or interest; what we want rather is to settle upon the appropriate pattern of our interests, and to determine what standards of objectivity are appropriate to each of them.

Second, and more important now, is the possibility of transforming the problem of subjectivity. As it stands, that problem, and therefore all the problematic side of philosophy conceived of as an effort towards as complete an expression of the self under reason as may be, arises from a deep and inveterate understanding of the self as primarily a *complex* of tendencies and forces, which manifest themselves both consciously and unconsciously, and some of which we recognize as interests and motives. The unity of the self, or as we so often say, its integration, consists in some harmonious balance of these, and this in turn can not come about unless we recognize these *as* forces that require harmonization of some sort, and unless, in certain cases, we unmask them when they insist on presenting themselves to our conscious minds as something other than what they are. Often enough this view is in turn based on an epiphenomenalism whose metaphysical crudity is masked by the overlying sophistication that is brought to the study of the interaction of these forces; so with the early physiologism of Freud, whose effects persist even in his later work. The view of causation that then prevails makes no allowance for latencies other than those inherent in forces already actual; the story of the self is the story of the interplay of these forces. From such a point of view we give vent to all the concreteness of the self, under the guidance of an ideal, at our peril, since that ideal can only arise out of the interplay of various factors in the complex of the self with one another and with factors in the world which, both physically and culturally, environs us; and it is only a deception when that ideal presents itself as having more substantial and more metaphysical roots.

If there were, however, a sufficiently authenticated alternative view, the problem of subjectivity might seem less serious: would perhaps no longer stand for an essential and irremediable defect in human nature, but merely for a potential failing against which we can erect defenses that will serve us in some spheres even though they should fail us in others. Dynamisms that had been mere components of a mere complex, and whose tendencies we could not therefore trust, would then appear as potentially the dynamisms of an overriding unity; their import would then be transformed, as we saw them in terms of a doctrine of causation quite different from that which first caused the problem of subjectivity to arise for us. But the transformation would not be merely in our way of regarding these dynamisms: we should not merely be regarding in a proper light what hitherto we had seen in a false light. We should also *in fact* be transforming them, because, seen in a false light, they tend precisely towards that status as mere components in a mere complex that the false light gives them; tend to go their own way and to bring as close to actuality as possible that reductive view of the self and of causation that we have been dealing with: that was the perilousness of freedom that I spoke of a while ago.

And so, in default of an adequate understanding of the real, there seems no reason to forego a new philosophical effort that should make full use of our subjective dynamism with the aim of releasing its latencies under the ideal of reason. On the one hand we should be pursuing an ideal of the self under reason; but on the other hand we might well hope that we had loosed reason to satisfy its most concrete interest. It is perhaps to bring us in sight at last of the idea of philosophy we are looking for—a first-order way of knowing committed neither to empiricism nor rationalism, but concerned to go to the root of both reason and experience, and to do so in the name of wisdom. From such an effort philosophy might emerge as a way of knowing supported in its "objectivity," or let us say, to avoid some of the confusions of that word, supported in its Truth by the presence in it of "subjectivity." What appeared as a subjective substitute for, or illusion about Truth, now appears as possibly the concrete exercise of reason in search of Truth. We have brought ourselves to the point of utilizing all our subjective resources, and therefore whatever faculties we employ in valuing, in an effort at a theoretic grasp of a Truth which shall be independent of any distortion by these factors. At the same time, we raise at least the possibility of a radical self-integration based on a radical self-knowledge; and if this falls short of offering us an *individual* self-knowledge, it promises, at least, something that is indispensable for such self-knowledge, and without which it is indeed a dangerous exercise, namely, a general knowledge of the *status* of the factors of subjectivity; for I must necessarily confront the stubborn particularity of my own subjectivity in a way that is inseparable from the general significance subjective dynamism has for me.

We have already learned, in the previous chapter, of the hazards of regarding such an effort as simply a more concrete way of experiencing.

4

RADICALLY ORIGINATIVE REFLECTION:
TO THE ROOT OF REASON AND EXPERIENCE

I.   *We make our new beginning by way of the act of radically originative reflection. In this act we do not merely exercise a familiar function but transform a familiar function. Risking the charge of hubris, we describe the act as an ontological expansion of reason.*

The kind of new beginning at which this book is aimed has now been established, and the difficulties that lie in the way of it have been explored. In the present chapter it is contended that our hoped-for new beginning is to be found in the act of radically originative reflection. It is inevitable that much of the chapter must be given over to expounding the nature of that act. But this way of proceeding does violence to what is at issue, for I do not intend to be describing a familiar function that we all exercise, but to be transforming a familiar function: by intent, the expression of what is at issue marches with that transformation, and, should the expression fail, the transformation will be to that degree unsuccessful, leaving us nothing but a more or less adequate description of an existing function. I am willing to risk the charge of *hubris* if that is necessary to be understood: I am claiming for the philosopher that same creativity that we acknowledge in the artist who shapes for us new modes of reality in expanding his own nature, and whose power of expression is inseparable from that expansion.

The point becomes more concrete when we contrast the intended transformation with certain features of reason that are at least implicitly acknowledged by all the contending parties mentioned in the preceding chapters. Consider first the *radically reflective* character of reason—a feature I mean to distinguish from the radically originative reflection of the chapter title. It is widely acknowledged that reason has the capacity of returning upon itself, by a technique, a discipline, or according to some, a moral transformation, in order to see its situation for what it is. It does not matter that philosophers disagree as to *how* reason does this, and that they often give us epistemological models that make this reflexivity unintelligible; what matters, because it is a precondition of the whole philosophic effort, is the assumption that this reflexivity is real, and that reason can really pronounce upon the problem of its limits: in this sense all revolutionary movements suppose, even when they show it to be impossible, that we can step outside the reason-experience relationship to take stock of it. The second feature is the *radical purity* of reason. By this I mean its capacity for a self-assessment undistorted by its physiological, affective, and social conditioning—undistorted indeed by any of the multitudinous layers of conditions that naturalistically oriented investigation reveals to us. Any philosopher, or any scientist for that matter, acknowledges this even in the act of singling out the particular distortions in the affective nature of some other philosopher: the *other* man is prevented from acknowledging *my* version of the appropriate life of reason because of his temperament, his neuroses or obsessions, his social conditioning, even his moral obliquities, but *my* discernment of all this is quite undistorted. The third feature is the *concrete engagement* of reason: I mean its employment in its self-assessment of energies afforded by those conditions just mentioned, and its taming of those energies in the new composure produced in the act of self-assessment. This was the feature dealt with tentatively in the last chapter under the heading of subjective dynamism—clearly a feature less explicit, in the movements reviewed, than are the first two features.

It might now be supposed that the kind of transformation I have in mind under the rubric of radically originative reflection is merely the better understanding of these acknowledged but obscurely apprehended features of reason. Is it possible, one might ask, that the conditions for a new beginning lie ready to hand—that we have only to look clearly at capacities we already acknowledge in order to bring about a genuine revolution in philosophy? But it can hardly be so simple. To look clearly *at* such capacities would be to deploy these capacities more adequately: we should have achieved nothing less than an ontological expansion or flowering of reason in which its reflexivity, its purity, and its concreteness should at last have come into their own. The theme of radically originative reflection is the theme of that expansion and if this should be philosophical *hubris,* it is at least a *hubris* that any revolution must risk, and indeed one that is implicit in all the revolutionary movements of the century.

We are therefore not concerned to remain at our habitual level of reflexive attention, since it is just at that level that our task seems so paradoxical. We are excessively timorous in our approach to the problem of self-knowledge and self-integration, so that the power of reflection itself is only half understood, and so only half released. Being so pent up, it is in fact other than what it could be, for in this sphere, at least, to misunderstand something is not merely to produce a distorted image of it, but to distort the thing itself. So with our passional nature: with self-knowledge made hesitant at its reflective root, our passional energies may fail to find unabashed and confident fulfillment in alliance with reason. They are then other than what they could be, either failing entirely or asserting themselves disharmoniously as a multiplicity of discrete drives into which the unity of the person is accordingly resolved.

II.   We take the first step towards the transformation by means of a preliminary expression that is aimed at completeness: we try to formulate radically originative reflection as one act, taking the risk of some initial obscurity in order to emphasize the claim that it is an act in which we come abruptly into the enjoyment of reason's creative autonomy and responsibility.

Why does one speak of an act of reflection that is both *radical* and *originative?* Is there not a contradiction, first of all, in speaking of an act of reflection as originative? The word reflection is used in many senses, but in those that are relevant to our present concern what leaps to the mind is a kind of introspective stock-taking in which we try to attend to what is going on in one act of consciousness by surveying it in another. The second follows upon the first in at least this sense, that it is the first act that we think of ourselves as reflecting upon. The difficulty about such epistemological reflection is that when we reflect upon *it* in its turn, it must seem to suffer from whatever defects it has revealed in the first act, and must therefore seem to compound them. This is especially noticeable when our reflection about knowledge yields us theories about or models for knowing that are peculiarly suited to rendering the act of reflection unintelligible. If we speak of knowledge in terms of *ideas* that represent *things,* in terms of *forms* or *essences* with which the mind becomes *identified,* in terms of *categories, symbolic forms,* or *linguistic* structures that the mind *constructs* or *uses,* then the act of reflection upon which at least part of these theories or models is based must seem unsuited to giving us just this sort of information; or at least it must seem so to just the extent that we are obliged to think of reflection itself in terms of these same theories or models. If our concern is to establish the limits of reason we are doing so with questionable equipment: our reflective act will have all the defects we think we see in the primary act, with the additional defect of being once removed from it. Our right to establish the limits of reason is then quickly called in question, so that we despair of any progress.

But if we only suppose that all these difficulties arise from our having misconceived of reflection, the situation looks rather different. If reflection has failed to catch the nature of reflection itself, then it may be that reflection has simply been inadequately exercised. If it should become at once originative and radical there is a way out of our difficulty; for reason would then *originate* a direct awareness and understanding of itself as a function of an individual and as a level of being, not surveying its completed acts or products by an activity that then mimics the supposed "given" character of what is thus complete, but confidently bringing into the light of its own attention its own creative autonomy and responsibility. Thus to link "creative autonomy" with "responsibility" is to suggest once again that the ideals sought by rationalists and empiricists respectively are fundamentally inseparable.

We speak of such an act as *reflection* because to be so concerned is to be intent on a self-knowledge in which reason attempts to justify its own procedure. We speak of it as *radical* because it is concerned with reason's whole footing in experience—concerned not with some particular act of knowing, with some particular elaboration of a "rational" structure that then awaits testing against "experience," but with the whole framework of knowing, including that root act that gives us the whole framework. But it is the force of the word originative that marks the chief change: we speak of it as *originative* because it produces an awareness and understanding that was not there before. By *production* of awareness and understanding I do not mean that we produce the objects of our knowledge; I mean that under the stimulus of the presence of the object we produce or originate our *awareness* of the object as a direct response that is *sui generis*, and produce our *understanding* as the completion of that awareness. We do not take awareness and understanding for granted: do not, that is, take consciousness itself for granted as a medium into which completed "objects of knowledge" are then received. What is thus produced or originated is revelatory not only of reason's "primary" act, but of its "secondary" or reflective act as well, and in such a way as to confirm us in our proposed radical use of that reflective act. We may therefore speak of radically originative reflection as reflectively exhaustive, meaning by this that what is originated is an awareness and understanding of reason as a responsible originator, whose reflective power is primary and natural, partaking as it does of that same originative power.

We come to exercise radically originative reflection in the act of coming to understand it, so that all the creativity with which we have heretofore assailed any subject matter that interests us is now turned upon reason itself, disclosing its reflexivity as being free from that indirectness with which we normally tax it, and in the same disclosure releasing that creativity to a deeper employment. Reason *becomes* originatively reflective in the act in which it discovers this to be part of its vocation. The "result" of the act of reflection now marches with the "primary" exercise of reason; or we may say that reflection now perfects the primary exercise in perfecting itself.

In one sense, however, nothing is changed, for reflection in becoming radically originative now merely partakes of the same capacity it discerns to have been native all the while to its "primary" employment. We spoke of origination as the production of awareness and understanding—a direct activity to which we do less than justice when we take consciousness for granted as a medium into which the "objects of knowledge" are then simply received. But this origination is native to reason even when a defect in self-knowledge keeps us from seeing it, and our transformation was merely the extension of this originative power to radical reflection itself. A capacity heretofore exercised without complete self-knowledge, a capacity not yet adequately displayed *in* self-knowledge, now lends its impetus to that self-knowledge, with the result that reflection no longer seems a secondary, strained, and squinting enterprise, but the very condition of the self-confident exercise of reason in *any* enterprise. Reflection now runs "before" the primary act, illuminating it, and directing it where it may go: it becomes identical with the creative and responsible autonomy of reason, or more precisely with our full enjoyment of that.

Seen from the point of view of reason as a *general* function, radically originative reflection is "empty" or "formal," for in it we dwell only upon the originative power of reason as it brings whatever lies before it to an awareness that is completed in the articulation of language. We merely enjoy the creative autonomy with which reason elaborates the framework of its attention, elaborates its articulated awareness of what lies before it within that framework, and elaborates also its reflective awareness; and we acknowledge the responsibility with which that autonomy is bent precisely upon acquiescing in what lies before it. There is nothing in any particular example that will help us in making this clearer. But seen from the point of view of any of the particular acts that it suffuses, radically originative reflection is as full of content as any cognitive act may be, for it is now the pre-condition and accompaniment of our confident apprehension of content of all sorts: *any* example will do.

Yet even when "empty" or "formal," radically originative reflection is so only in the sense that our attention is not focused upon the particularity of what is before us. It is never empty in the sense of being out of contact with that foundation of authenticity that we enshrine in the word "experience." Not that the introduction of that word quite expresses the point I wish to make. It is more appropriate to say that radically originative reflection is both the paradigm for all recognition of being and the justification for all such recognition. As paradigm it is the enjoyment of a prototype of all empirical grounding and of all rational satisfaction as well: we may therefore say that it affords a matrix for all rational and empirical criteria that might be appropriate to situations of less concrete intent; as justification it is the enjoyment of reason's autonomy as it responsibly produces this matrix.

The point is a very concrete one, although the language

is unfamiliar enough to obscure this fact. To remedy this, let me recast it in terms of what radically originative reflection means for our apprehension of any entity, however familiar—say the child on the swing in the garden below the window. When we acknowledge the empirical presence of any such entity we take that presence to display itself throughout a spatio-temporal range. Our survey of this includes a wide variety of sensory data, which, to the extent that we are prepared to acknowledge the entity, we attribute to it—as, for instance, when we should say that that glint of pale gold is a quality of the tossed hair. I am not interested in the fact that epistemologists would differ in their interpretation of any manifold of qualities that we should specify, beginning perhaps with an objection to the word "quality" itself. I merely mean that, when we acknowledge the presence of the entity, we acknowledge some spatio-temporal manifold to "belong" to it. We are also prepared to discern within the manifold other subordinate entities, to which we might, if we wished, accord the same attention we now give to the child—as when, for instance, a biologist might interest himself in organs or in cells, a biophysicist in molecular structures in the cell, and so on. Let us say that the empirical presence of the entity displays itself extensively: call this its *extensive manifold*.

But that same empirical presence is more than this, for the whole extensive manifold turns about a still center, which we recognize in the measure that we accord the entity an irreducible status, and around which the empirical presence of the entity takes shape for us. It is in our recognition of this that our acknowledgment of empirical presence becomes a "rational" no less than an "empirical" satisfaction, for our standing at the still center is not a mere experience, but a matter of rational import as well. The still center is not some particular point or pivot, but is *general* in character, so that it will be the same still center that is at issue, no matter what individual entity I should attend to. In radically originative reflection we refuse to separate the character of empirical presence from the character of generality. Having this in mind,

I shall in the rest of this section speak merely of *presence* rather than of empirical presence.

It will be the same still center around which subordinate entities, *within the extensive manifold of the entity we are attending to, and to that extent contributing to its presence,* also turn. As these subordinate entities—organs, tissues, cells, and yet "lower" entities—promise or foreshadow, sometimes by their order, sometimes by their very incompleteness, the "higher" entity to whose presence they contribute, we may say that the still center is never merely still, never a mere point, but has the character of abundance and the promise of abundance. And coupling this with the *general* character of our still center, we find that it is abundant in levels of being that are of like generality: that is, the extensive manifold of any entity, which, taken together with the still center *is* the entity, exhibits not just a multiplicity of subordinate entities, but a multiplicity of subordinate general levels as well. To acknowledge the presence of an entity is to acknowledge the presence of Being.

We do not, however, stand at this center as mere spectators, with the presence of a multitude of ordered entities, and the presence of Being itself, turning round us. We are placed there in the very exercise of reason's creative autonomy, and only in this sense is the recognition of any entity, with its presence rooted in the generality of Being, authentic for us. It is the recognition of the level we call reason, a recognition in which we take it to be originative of awareness and understanding, and originative in the act of reflection itself, that gives us our right to all this. It is the reflectively exhaustive acknowledgment of *this* presence that authenticates our right to acknowledge *any* presence, and it is in this sense that we are placed at the still center "in the very exercise of reason's creative autonomy." Our acknowledgment of this presence is no less an "empirical" and a "rational" satisfaction: we are at the still center in the enjoyment of the level of reason itself as it dwells in its extensive manifold, but there is this difference, that our enjoyment of this level is also the self-conscious exercise of creative autonomy and responsibility. The character of our recognition of beings and Being is a matrix from which we can then detach "empirical" and "rational" criteria of more limited intent; but our right to do so is given by the act in which we are aware that we both originate and enjoy this matrix.

There is no philosophical enterprise more paradoxical than the attempt to define the resources of reason without deploying the full resources of reason to do so. I have tried to avoid this by refusing to take existing works of reason, established reasonable procedures, and established frameworks of experience as fully definitive of reason's resources, considering them instead to be features of an ambiguous situation. The present enterprise, therefore, has its own paradox: we wish to turn upon reason itself resources we do not fully understand, in order to come to understand those same resources, and we willingly deploy ambiguous "subjective" forces to do so.[5] We press forward, then, *through* the confusions of our situation; through, therefore, the haze of our own unclear intentions and ambitions. It is our aim to understand reason at its work, and at the same time to perfect that work: we do not regard these as quite distinct objectives. Suddenly, though only after many false starts, we find that this concrete effort both to understand reason and to release it to its task has suceeded. Reason becomes abruptly less opaque to itself, and in doing so finds that the dynamisms it so mistrusted have in fact become the dynamisms of what before had been just an ideal: reason comes to *be* itself as it comes to *know* itself, comes, that is, to make ambiguous forces the living tissue of its own dynamism. The sudden confidence and amplitude that supervenes is an ontological expansion—a growth in being whose concreteness one does violence to by too discursive an exposition, so that although I shall have to approach radically originative reflection by three principal descriptive routes, I shall also have to draw all together again by returning to the conception of an ontological expansion.

III. *First descriptive approach to radically originative reflection: it is an abrupt advance in reason's self-knowledge, in which it comes to see that it creatively and responsibly brings about its awareness of its world (taken as a framework) and the elements of that world, but only under the stimulus of their presence; that its understanding is the perfection or fruit of that awareness, rather than a quite different function that merely makes use of it; and that the production of language and other modes of symbolism is the concomitant of this perfection of awareness.*

The first approach is by way of one of the *conclusions* of radically originative reflection. This conclusion is that reason exercises a creative autonomy, under the stimulus of its "object," to produce both our awareness and our understanding of the "object," and that this awareness and understanding, in reason's most concrete activity, coincide. The word "object" stands here because venerable usage decrees it as the usual word for whatever it is that reason may be said to know directly; it has, however, only that neutral sense, and should not be allowed to suggest that we are concerned primarily with common-sense objects, or perhaps with the problem of the external world. Although we are not yet in a position to settle these matters, I shall tentatively suppose that sensed qualities, the sensible collections of entities or objects that common sense deals with, the world (understood as the indeterminately bounded scene in which objects appear), and even Being as such, might all of them be considered objects in this sense. The point might then be restated as follows: reason exercises a creative autonomy, under the stimulus of the presence of the real, to produce both our awareness and our understanding of all the multiplicity, unity, and gradations of the real, so that it is responsible both for the framework within which we are aware and understand, together with all the items (of whatever ontological import) within that framework. Moreover, whether we are concerned with the framework itself, or with some item within it, awareness and understanding are not separable except where, for some more special purpose of reason than that with which we are now concerned, we deliberately make a distinction between awareness and understanding *within* the framework, and then attend to items within it with the more abstract attention dictated by that deliberate distinction. In more conventional terms, we ignore a concrete coincidence of the findings of reason and experience in order to attend to the findings of a reason and an experience now distinguished by the more narrow sense we give them. I shall in what follows frequently use such expressions as "cognitive awareness" and "reason experiences the real," in order to point out that what we are dealing with forms a background for, and should be presupposed by, a later and more usual distinction between reason and experience.

When I say that reason "produces" awareness and understanding it is always understood that it is the object that is the incitement to such production. I shall later attempt to do justice to the original intent of both the rationalist and the empiricist traditions, by speaking of the cognitive activity as unfolding from "within" and yet realizing itself and satisfying itself in what is in some sense independent of it. Meanwhile, it may help to observe that, although the setting is quite different from Kant's, there is in the present union of "innateness" and "the external" somewhat the same paradoxical union of opposites that he expressed in the formula "synthetic *a priori.*"

On this view, then, we are not justified in looking for the paradigm of all direct awareness in a level of sensation and feeling thought of as mute, inarticulate, and wholly taken up with, perhaps, a shifting pattern of narrow percepts; and we are equally unjustified in thinking of understanding as an activity wholly explicable in terms of the entertainment, the manipulation, and the construction of concepts. There is in fact for us no awareness so inarticulate, direct, and cognitively noncommittal as to make some special claim of authenticity upon us; and no understanding doomed to be merely externally related to the insistent concreteness of awareness just because of the articulation it displays.

In repudiating such views of the relation between awareness and understanding, I am not supposing that all philosophers make of them such polar opposites. Yet I would distinguish the present view from at least the doctrine of Kant, which may occur to the reader as one in which awareness and understanding are intimately joined. Kant does indeed propose to us an intimate union of awareness and understanding, implicit in the doctrine of a synthetic *a priori* truth, and made explicit in that portion of the first critique that deals with the "schematism." This is, however, a union of understanding and awareness in which, although the categories of the former are built up, as it were, out of the materials of awareness, the latter receives reciprocally a structure it lacks in itself; it is an understanding that accomplishes its purpose by imposing a structure on awareness to yield an experience (an awareness in another sense) that is phenomenal and to that extent factitious. I am proposing, rather, a continuity of awareness and understanding in which understanding issues from awareness as its fruit, being in fact, as we shall see, an awareness of elements that were present but missed in what we usually speak of as awareness. No doubt there is a sense in which the intensity, directness, and immediacy we demand in awareness is found in the world of sensation and feeling in which our understanding is rooted, and this predisposes us to associate an ideal awareness with what, if it were really available to us in an unambiguous way, we might call a sensuous manifold. But it is not so available to us, and it would seem that we can no further associate awareness with sensation than to concede that the ambiguous world of sensation and feeling must color all our awareness and therefore all our understanding.

It is impossible for us to isolate a "pure" awareness, devoid of any understanding, if only because the act of awareness is always an incipient self-awareness, even when it does not emerge into the explicit self-consciousness that goes with the use of language. But besides, understanding is a perfection of awareness in which the latter grows more extensive and rich. Without losing the intensity and immediacy conferred by its roots in sensation, our awareness expands, as we articulate it in symbolic structures, into fresh dimensions of what we were originally aware of. What were otherwise (we assume) an intense but superficial and non-committal awareness becomes an *awareness of what it is that we are aware of*, so that what we attend to becomes more fully present to us as we articulate our awareness. (A connection of this aspect of awareness with the generality of understanding is made in section V.) Just *what it is* that assails me with such vividness now colors that same vividness as I pronounce even so simple a judgment as "the wall is yellow," or for that matter merely exclaim "yellow, there, now." The intensity and immediacy persist, but to notice this, or even to grant that these characteristics must inevitably qualify any mode of apprehension we enjoy, is by no means to concede that they must serve as a standard for all modes of apprehension.

From this point of view one is struck with the double role played by our language and the whole range of analogous symbolic structures: their growth being coincidental with the emergence of articulate understanding, they are at once by-products of the root function of reason and instruments through which it completes itself.

In recent years the attention that has been devoted to man's role as a symbol-maker has, I think, tended to emphasize the instrumental role at the expense of the other, perhaps because of the continued vigor of Kantian premises in such work as Cassirer's and S. K. Langer's. Thus Mrs. Langer has made current, at least in esthetics, the role of symbols as *mediating* understanding, or as *vehicles* for understanding. In such writing the emphasis upon the use of the symbol, and upon the almost oppressive presence of the symbol-world, has reinforced the impression that the activity of mentality terminates in symbols, and that understanding is identical with the entertainment of symbols. Probably the image of the making of the symbol as the *transformation* of the thing symbolized is also a powerful influence, for this is a way of thought in which it is natural to think (in ways obviously indebted to Kant) of the world of common-sense objects as itself a product of the symbol-making function. To apprehend with reason is on this view to transform a raw material, and the transformed original is then as much a barrier to the apprehension of the original as it is a means of apprehending it.

In radically originative reflection we so place ourselves as not to be deceived by the role our various symbolisms play in understanding. It is true that these symbolisms, in all their intricacy, form part of the environment and the "situation" of all of us. It is even true that for certain legitimate purposes of reason we may well consider ourselves as pent within the languages and other symbols we have produced, and as understanding, within that framework, entirely by means of the construction of new symbolic devices or the manipulation of old ones. Presumably much of the theoretic side of science is conducted in this way, the construction or manipulation of symbols being the vehicle of understanding in at least this sense, that understanding is then *directed upon* the world of symbols. But if, concerned with the larger question of reason's responsibility for the framework itself, we recognize that all symbolisms are by-products no less than instruments of reason's creative autonomy, we recover our dominion over them, and become capable of prolonging our creativity in this sphere, where once we had been in danger of becoming lost in our own constructs. The whole world of symbols now has its existence suspended within that concrete awareness and self-awareness in which we discern—however vaguely—the very possibility of symbolism. Anything that we are aware of through the manipulation of symbols in however "analytic" (or even mechanical) a fashion, therefore appears to us against the background of that same concrete awareness.

We may suppress the sense in which symbols are *products* in which we merely stabilize awareness and understanding, but the life of reason we then concern ourselves with is a very abstract one indeed, in which we find ourselves entertaining the notion of a self-subsistent symbol world with a supposed "life" of its own. Presiding over the whole of our symbol world, and indeed constituting it *as* a symbol world, is a tension between the One and the Many that lies at the heart of all rational awareness, and becomes, as we shall see, explicit in radically originative reflection. This organically apprehended tension permeates the creative autonomy of reason, and by means of it we are able to hold the symbol world together, see its significance, use it in specific situations in which special contrasts of the One and Many arise, and permit it to expand as our own intelligence expands. In this way intelligence, which, in the very act of coming to self-consciousness, finds itself at one remove from temporality, is able to master the variety and intricacy of that same temporal world, while remaining nevertheless itself.

The theme of symbolism is merely an outgrowth of the theme with which we began our first approach. In radically originative reflection we recognize reason's creative autonomy in bringing its world, in all its unity and variety, to awareness and understanding; and we recognize its responsibility by noticing that this creative autonomy is, in intention at least, a response to the presence of that world, to which it would be faithful. But it is the same recognition that tells us that this awareness and understanding is stabilized in the production of a world of symbols, just as it is itself so stabilized.

IV. Second descriptive approach: this reflection is called "radical" and "originative" because it is concerned with reason's whole footing in the real, and because the advance is brought about by the reflexive employment of the same creative but responsible autonomy that is the subject matter of the advance. The act in which we see the general significance of rational and empirical satisfaction is therefore itself characterized by the joint enjoyment of these satisfactions.

We now try to place these conclusions of radically originative reflection in their living setting. We first note that, even before any hoped-for transformation, the act of reflection, reflected upon without epistemological prejudices, reveals itself as the most natural thing in the world. It is in fact coextensive with knowledge itself, being nothing more than that which enables us to give any item of knowledge full articulation, as when I should say, "I *know* that the child is on the swing in the garden," or "I *am aware* of a certain glint of pale gold." What we are talking about is no unusual or strained exertion of reason, but is of the very nature of it. Really to be conscious of anything in a way that deserves to be called knowledge is to be self-conscious. Second, we find that the reflective act does not display itself to us as regressive: to reflect is to reflect once and for all, in an act that gives me the object of thought, myself as knower, and even myself as taking stock of reflection, and gives me these components not successively, but as aspects of an undivided function.

But we are aiming at a *radical* reflection in the sense noted earlier: a reflection that goes to the very root of reason and experience; a reflection that is aimed at revealing not just the quality of what we know, but also our very right to what we think we know. It is thus aimed at the very act in which reason comes into awareness and understanding, not at the content of a completed act. The question arises: can reason come into such an awareness and understanding? That act does not lie already *there* in the same sense that the garden now lies below me, open to my perusal. The spirit of our answer is that a reflective *effort* is needed; we attempt *to become aware*, not at all taking it for granted that becoming aware always and inevitably involves a mere change in direction of attention, as when I should shift my eyes from the desk to the garden; we attempt *to become aware* and then to bring this awareness to the full articulation of understanding. The radically originative reflection we now describe is put forward as the successful issue of such an effort: *this* reflective act responsibly originates an awareness and understanding of reason, and reveals it as reason the responsible originator.

The generality of radically originative reflection was noticed in section *II*, and will be taken up again in more detail in the next section; at this point, however, we must invoke it briefly to complete our account of the possibility of such a reflection. If the act is general in the sense described, reason is no less rooted in Being than any object it might attain. This common root leaves it, in an important sense, already "inside" any object it wishes to attain, so that the very act of cognition requires that reason should set aside this community with the object, placing itself "outside" it in order to return to it in the act of cognitive attainment. It is important that we are here dealing with a primal requirement of any cognitive act: reason, always in a measure "inside" its object, must even in its "primary" (non-reflective) employment, place itself "outside" the object in order to possess it finally in knowledge.

In the same sense, and only in this sense, reason now places itself "outside" its own act in order to return to it in radically originative reflection. "Outside" its own act, reason does not now have that act before itself, available to some habitual mode of perusal, but must originate an awareness and understanding in which it cognitively attains the act. The words "inside" and "outside" appropriately wear quotation marks throughout this discussion, for we are using them in an unusual sense that partakes of some of the obscurity of that contrast of One and Many that we shall shortly meet in our discussion of generality.

Beyond the congruence of this version of reason's activity with the possibility of a reflective return upon itself, no "evidence" can be given that the act is what is claims to be. But then no external "evidence" would be relevant to what purports to be a standpoint from which evidence of all sorts can be judged. To see reason as the responsible originator is to see reason as productive, in the presence of its "object," of both the "empirical" and "rational" components in any acknowledgment of the presence of an entity—an acknowledgment which, as we saw earlier, involved the acknowledgment of Being as well. It was with this in mind that I spoke earlier of reason as productive in radically originative reflection of a matrix for all rational and empirical satisfactions. Our matrix is nothing more than the enjoyment of a joint empirical and rational satisfaction, together with the knowledge that reason produces this in the presence of its "object." The congruence between the reflective and the "primary" act assures us that radically originative reflection is possible, while radically originative reflection itself yields us a joint "empirical" and "rational" satisfaction of its own. Reason becomes master of all rational and empirical criteria in an act that itself yields rational and empirical satisfaction.

It is important to reiterate that we are not dealing with the conclusions of an argument: the reflective act that gives us these "conclusions" does so by employing just the creative autonomy and responsibility that we have been dealing with, and it is this that enables us to possess and exercise that autonomy with a new assurance. Radically originative reflection is neither an act preliminary to the exercise of reason, nor an assessment of reason after the event, but the act in which reason justifies its powers as it exercises them. The presence of reason to itself incites the reflexive exercise of its creative autonomy to produce a self-awareness that culminates in a self-understanding; we thus possess to its depths that same autonomy, which before, just because it was a problem to itself, we enjoyed only partially.

The matter is elusive and delicate enough to invite ingenuity in alternative statements of it. If we stress that side of radically originative reflection that attends to the way reason comes to know, we find that it produces an access of confidence arising from the complete adequacy of a reason, so understood, to its tasks: the expansion or completion of reason's very being takes place in the enjoyment of whatever it is that is before it, and with whatever depth and fullness reason should intend; that enjoyment is *sui generis*, and is no less adequate because we cannot clarify it readily by means of models; and it is both an enjoyment of reason's own powers and of what those powers are directed upon. We are overcome suddenly by the very concreteness of cognitive awareness, and find it not astonishing in its own terms, and quite astonishing when regarded in more abstract terms. Yet the full effect of radically originative reflection is lost on us if we stress only this side of the act. Seen somewhat differently, the content of the reflective act confirms us in reflection itself, displaying to us the penetration and adequacy of reflection, and thus authenticating the view of reason's activity that I have just described. A reason that in reflecting exercises, completes, or expands its nature in bringing about its awareness and understanding, and does so with whatever depth, fullness, and direction it should intend, is a reason equipped to see its powers as they are, even as it exercises them. We reflectively confirm reason's "primary" activity as that "primary" activity is seen to be fitted to a reflective exercise; or, more simply, though more paradoxically, radically originative reflection confirms us in our right to radically originative reflection.

Reflection has in fact always accompanied the primary function of reason, but its exact role has been obscure, and it has tended as often to impede reason's progress as to further it. Here the primary and the reflective components march together, for the responsible autonomy we exercise in coming to know our world we only possess securely to the degree that it is concerned also with itself. We transform reflection by discovering our autonomy, and we transform autonomy by the proper exercise of reflection. Under the stimulus of its own imperfectly comprehended "nature," reason initiates a more ample and just cognitive awareness of that "nature." It deploys its own resources precisely to *produce* a more adequate self-knowledge. We do not make a "reasonable" theory and apply it to our "experience" of reason; instead we make a creative advance in reason's self-knowledge in which we attain just such a coincidence of awareness and understanding as we have just been concerned with. *What* we thus attain is reason's responsible autonomy before its task; but we find besides that this responsible autonomy includes a capacity for reflective justification that marches with the exercise of it. In this sense radically originative reflection is an act pellucid to itself, and in such a way as to terminate abruptly any supposed regress of reflective acts. As we shall see, the way in which we understand this coincidence of awareness and understanding in fact precludes the kind of epistemological model upon which the idea of such a regress would have to be based. Transposed into the terminology of freedom, this last point can be put in this way: it is the *exercise* of reason's autonomy that justifies that autonomy; we do not try to establish a groundwork of certainty, anterior to reason's exercise of its birthright, as a precondition of that exercise.

The second approach may be connected with the first somewhat as follows. The motive of the act of radical reflection is the liberation of reason's powers, which at first we feel to be partially frustrated through inadequate self-knowledge. Its impetus, understood only after the act is accomplished, is the creative autonomy of reason in coming to grips with what lies before it: the liberation, that is, is accomplished by reason itself, summoning its pent-up resources, and breaking out of the limitations itself had imposed by the partial success of its past efforts. But the full issue of the act is the liberation of reason in a wider sense, for the partial "content" or "object" of the act of radically originative reflection is precisely the creative

autonomy of reason in producing its awareness and understanding of "objects" of whatever sort; and it can therefore
proceed in confidence to a more adequate grasp of them. We
exercise autonomy to understand and realize it; and we go to
the root of reason and experience in doing so, since we bring
about our awareness and understanding of this autonomy
through the autonomous deployment of reason itself in what
lies before it.

V. *Third descriptive approach: the abrupt advance
achieved in radically originative reflection is an ontological expansion of reason, exhibiting a generality
which, with regard to both reason itself and its world,
reveals a tension between the One and the Many.*

Our third approach is by way of the generality with which the
act is permeated, a consideration of which returns us again to
the theme of ontological expansion. This generality must be
distinguished from a familiar sense that depends upon just
that distinction between awareness and understanding whose
abstractness I have been insisting upon. In this familiar sense
awareness is thought of as being confined to the unique particularity of the "object," which it is then usual to speak of,
following Aristotle, as a "this"; while understanding is held to
be concerned not with what is unique in the object, but with
what that object shares with like objects—its "whatness" (or
essence, or form). A contrast is then presumed to exist between
the general term—it does not matter for the moment what
traditional name we give it—thought of as *one*, and the *many*
individuals to which it applies or might apply. We are not
concerned with that sense of generality, but with one compatible with the coincidence of awareness and understanding afforded by radically originative reflection, a sense which then
forms the background and the sanction for the other, even as
the coincidence of awareness and understanding affords a back-

ground against which distinctions between awareness and understanding may fruitfully be made.

The source of this more fundamental sense of generality is to be found in the very atmosphere with which, in this reflection, we enjoy reason's creative and responsible autonomy before its "world." The act of radically originative reflection, like any act of reason, takes place in some here-and-now, being part of the particular history of any individual that engages in it. Yet in the successful realization of this reflection we find that we no longer live entirely in that here-and-now, but inhabit also a world upon which it has no unique claim, and to which it affords only one of an indefinite number of entries. The very autonomy we came to possess we take, even as we possess it, for no private autonomy, and the atmosphere in which we exercise it we recognize as equally hospitable to others. We possess, in thus possessing reason, something that from the beginning has been imperfectly understood as something common.

In this sense radically originative reflection exhibits a contrast of the *One* and the *Many* so concrete and fundamental that we can not properly expound it in terms of any contrast less fundamental. It is, taken in itself, a very rich contrast, which we can illuminate in several ways. It is first of all a *general assurance* that then supports all future generalizing: we immediately transcend the psychological assurance characterizing any here-and-now in which we should exercise radically originative reflection, in that we see this assurance as an instance of a unique *kind*, repeatable in a multitude of such instances. It is not *my* assurance, but an assurance I find myself *sharing* or *participating* in. Similarly, the unity we all find in consciousness on the phenomenological or even common-sense level, it being nothing more than the unity that permeates all awareness—a unity in which countless elements are bound together, and which has historically tempted us now towards the image of the timeless unity of the Leibnizian subject, now towards the image of the seamless and equable flow of duration or creativity—that unity we now recognize as the same unity that our assurance or certainty shares in. It is clearly not the unity of *my* consciousness, but the unity of *consciousness,* of which my own consciousness is now merely one instance. In either case the possession of generality is the possession of a concrete unity set in contrast with a multiplicity that may be variously understood: the multiplicity of the many here-and-nows in which I am aware; the multiplicity of the many phases and factors *within* any here-and-now in which I am aware; the multiplicity of the many consciousnesses of which I take my own to be one.

It is the unity of *that which is creatively and autonomously responsible* for its awareness and understanding of its world, and, in reaching it, I am aware also of having transcended that aspect of my consciousness that is purely private and my own. As for the quality of the unity we then possess, it is not a blind Parmenidean one. The atmosphere we enter has something *common* in it: communication is not only possible, it is also exacted of us. Here that insistent aspect of all consciousness, *self-communication,* becomes intelligible as but one instance of the social or communicative aspect of consciousness in general. Consequently, the unity of the active and creative consciousness, a unity we exemplify in radically originative reflection, is seen to expand into a multiplicity of a special order—the multiplicity of a "common" unity in which the seeming contradictions of monism and pluralism are set aside. This topic is taken up again, in more detail, in Chapter 6.

This concrete contrast of one and many, which ultimately sanctions and renders intelligible all more limited contrasts implicit in generalizing, is also a contrast with regard to the "objects" of reason. Reason, even as it reflectively confirms itself in the possession of a general creative responsibility, is unable to consider whatever becomes present to it as a purely unique "this," but must regard it as only *this* instance, *this* expression, *this* limitation, or *this* modification of a unity that is exemplified and exemplifiable in a multiplicity of otherwise unique instances.

There is no awareness that consists in the bare immediacy of the here and now. The immediacy is real enough, but we are quite unable to isolate a "pure" awareness which should possess *only* such immediacy. With regard to any "object" of reason we find the multiplicity of all our here-and-nows set in contrast with a no less vivid unity. Whether we deal with some quality (as, for example, a color), some pervasive aspect of things (as space), some mode of experience (as the world of common sense), or some supposed natural entity (as a man, a tree), our assent to the presumed presence of any of them involves both the awareness of an extensive range or manifold, and, besides this factor of multiplicity—a multiplicity inherent in our very ability to distinguish elements within any such a range—a factor of unity, in which that same multiplicity appears as the multiplicity *of* whatever it is that we may be attending to.

This contrast of one and many is part of any experience in which we assent, either explicitly or implicitly, to the right of the content of that experience to some rank of its own, but it is not in itself sufficient to be called generality. It becomes generality only when we notice that the tension between many and one *within* any item of experience is the same tension as that between the manifold character of experience in general and the unity of the framework of experience. The latter is a tension between beings and aspects of being on the one hand and Being on the other, and, although it emerges clearly only in that full articulation of understanding that is the perfection and flowering of awareness, it manifests itself obscurely in all awareness, and is indeed impossible to suppress even when we try to put ourselves into as primitive a state as we can.

In radically originative reflection we recognize that we can not be consciously aware of any individual thing, or any unified aspect of things, without being aware of that utter generality for which only the word Being is appropriate. The unity of any individual thing, for instance, is a unity in contrast with the multiplicity of its various aspects or components, as we saw in contrasting the unity of a person with the complex forces that make up his subjective dynamism; but it is a unity that at once appears factitious to us if we are unable to recognize it as an expression of the unity of that Being in which we find utter generality. (This is not in itself an argument for either the unity of the subject or the unity of Being, but merely a claim that they stand or fall together; the argument consists in our whole enlargement of the topic of radically originative reflection.) It is this failure of recognition that leads to the familiar claim that the unity of the individual entities of the world is something that we *construct,* out of elements that were otherwise purely immediate and discrete data.

It is, then, in direct cognitive presence, in which awareness and understanding are continuous, that we find a concrete tension between the unity of Being and its multiplicity. Within the environment of this tension between the One and the Many, and with its authorization, we carry on all other acts of generalizing, all applications of universals to particulars, all employment of the general features of logical relationships. There is, of course, nothing in all this that we may invoke to enable us to find any particular generalization we happen to be looking for, or to validate any particular deductive relationship we are investigating.

But it is the whole point of radically originative reflection that reason's self-knowledge is coincidental with the right exercise of its powers in what lies before it. The generality we find in the diverse "objects" of reason—a generality we have just associated with Being as such—we only accept as authentic by virtue of this reflection. The generality I discussed earlier as a property of the self-knowledge obtained in radically originative reflection is therefore coincidental with the one I have just been dealing with. Yet it would be a mistake to suppose that we merely impute to the world as reason knows it what reason finds in self-knowledge. The two modes of generality are in fact one: we develop our awareness of what lies before us into an understanding that involves the presence of Being, but we then see that the unity of Being is the same unity we find in reflection: indeed, they support each other in much the same way that we saw the unity of any being and the unity of Being to be in mutual support; so that, where we deny the presence of unity in one, we deny the presence of unity in the other also. As we recognize the unity inherent in the Reason to which each of our reasons awakens—a unity distinguished by its "common" atmosphere of society and communication—we find it to be coincidental with the unity of things in general.

When awareness completes itself in understanding, it does so, then, because it has become an awareness of the generality inherent in the unity of Being, a unity present in each thing, present in each aspect of things, present, indeed, as the indispensable "object" in our apprehension of all objects whatsoever. The possession of this generality then gives us each thing we attend to with a depth that we can not now dismiss as unauthentic, as certain narrow interpretations of experience require us to do. I mean the dimension of the possible or potential we now necessarily find in each entity by virtue of its roots in Being. This is a dimension no less real than the actuality that imposes itself upon us when we suppose that a complete account of what is present to us when we observe some item of experience, such as the bowl of small chrysanthemums, some ruddy, some yellow, on the corner of the writing-table, can be given in terms of a summation of the sense contents inhabiting a certain area and a certain temporal span. This realm of potentiality is present to us in exactly the measure in which the unity in each thing, and in things in general, makes Being present to us, and, although we shall defer consideration of this until later, this holds no less for our apprehension of reason in ourselves than it holds for entities like chrysanthemums.

The association of the unrealized potential of Being with the realized actuality of an entity permits us to account for one aspect of language that has been a persistent puzzle. Why should the unfolding of language seem to be also the unfolding of a whole world of entities that have been called essences, possibilities, Platonic forms, categories, symbolic forms, and so on? On the present view, the whole range of symbolisms, held within the concrete tension of the One and the Many that is now our concern, not only enables us to attend to the diversity of the actual world, but besides refracts for us the common unity of Being, and enables us to attend to its inner diversity as a realm of potentiality. We could not indeed do one without the other. When we enunciate some general concept or concepts, and thus invoke the whole panoply of language, our awareness has in fact become an awareness of the common unity of things as diversified and capable of further diversification, no less than an awareness of some particular item set in the diversified "manyness" of the actual world.

To formulate the issue thus is to avoid both a nominalistic or conventionalistic approach on the one hand, and a Platonic approach on the other: we do not consider that the insistent idea of the refraction of the unity of Being into a realm of essences is a wholly inapposite distortion arising from our use of a structured or formal realm of symbolism to understand a complicated and continually changing world; nor do we feel obliged to consider that the unity of Being is literally the unity of a statically ordered realm of subsistent essences. The deployment of understanding in language merely directs attention to the fact that all potentiality has common roots, and that therefore a close affinity between entities in the actual means a close alliance of their potentialities in the unity of Being. The manner of that alliance we do not now try to settle. Such questions as whether we may rightly speak of man as having an essence, and in what sense we are then using "essence," are obviously pertinent, but all I am trying to establish now is that when we name things with common names, or indeed when we use generally expressed mathematical laws to bind together a variety of physical happenings, we are concerned no less with the articulation of the possible than with the articulation of the actual.

If radically originative reflection confirms us in the exercise of an autonomy that gives us Being in just the measure that it gives us reason and its world, it is, from another point of view, an exercise of being in its own right. Knowing, in the sense of the production of an awareness that issues in understanding, is itself a mode of being, which we now merely turn to a reflexive exercise that is no less an exercise of being. It is this distinctive ontological status of knowing that makes it so familiar and natural a thing to us, when once we recognize it, and removes the enigmatic character that it acquires when we try to understand it in terms of a transaction between things—the knower and its "objects"—whose being is then merely taken for granted, and thus removed from consideration, as when we suppose some object to be represented in, mirrored in, or impressed upon the mind. The same primal simplicity of knowing is capable of dissuading us from a misguided sense of loss at our inability to know the thing "in itself," where by that phrase we attribute to the thing some truly inviolate and deeper state of being than that which manifests itself, I will not say just to our own imperfect powers, but to any reasonable power whatsoever. The demand to know the real "in itself," where that means nothing less than to know it without knowing it—or perhaps more simply to *be* it, and by this identification to attain it more profoundly than any act of knowing can ever do—that demand, thought of as somehow both exacted of us and yet impossible to comply with, is the final obscurantism bequeathed by the idealist tradition to much of contemporary existentialism; it is, in the end, what puts existence above essence, and makes articulate self-knowledge seem like an alienation from some truer and deeper self. Radically originative reflection, in giving us the *being* of knowing in all its freshness and simplicity, makes it clear that it is no disability to lack what it would be stultifying to have. At the same time, it permits us to assess another and genuine limitation at its real worth, by allowing us to distinguish it from the problem of the thing-in-itself. That limitation lies in the inevitable coloring of all knowing by our roots in sensation and by our use of language and other symbolisms—a genuine mark of finitude that need not impede the penetration of reason when once we succeed in recognizing the roles of sensation and symbolisms.

Radically originative reflection, in confirming us in this view of knowing, is not merely an exercise of being, but a growth in being as well: an ontological expansion in which we gain a new assurance of reason's being, derived from the reflective knowledge that it is indeed the *being* of reason that we exercise. This theme appeared above, in our second approach, in terms of an authenticated possession of reason's creative and responsible autonomy; here we see that to enter into that autonomy is to enter into a higher exercise of being.

The theme of ontological expansion may be further developed by noticing that in accepting the presence of a generality as characterizing our world, reason, and the reflective act itself, we were not persuaded by the mere experiential weight of that generality, however much the difficulties of expressing a new point of view might have made it seem so. It was not the mere presence of generality, accepted as one might accept some habitual mode of experience, that was decisive, but our assured possession of a creative autonomy that enabled us to trust the presence of the general, *including the presence of generality in our exercise of radical reflection.* The secure exercise of the autonomy in which we bring about our awareness and understanding is in fact the possession of a power that is, seen from one side, a general power. That it was the expansion of just such a power that brought all this about is what permits us to speak here of an ontological expansion.

If we contrast this expansion and its generality with the diversity of the world and with the multiple here-and-nows in which, saturated with sensation, we attend to that diversity, we may say that radically originative reflection affords us a point of view in which both the diversity and the unity of things make legitimate claims upon us. We are tempted neither towards an absolute monism nor towards an absolute pluralism, since we now take ourselves to be dealing with an ontological expansion in which the being of reason, responding to itself and to what is other than itself, finds itself within *one* Being, which is nevertheless diversified both in the knower and in its world.

Although the principal themes of radically originative reflection have now been stated, the full expression of the position requires more detailed development; the rest of this chapter is devoted to this task.

VI. *The habit of our common knowledge of the world has such a hold upon us that we fail to see that in winning to it we exercise and complete the being of reason in an awareness and understanding that is an enjoyment of the being of its "objects." In radically originative reflection we overcome the misleading ways of regarding the relation between reason and its "objects" that are engendered by habit, and see this relation as sui generis: reason realizes itself in what is before it by bringing it to the fruition of knowing—not by being impressed by it, identifying itself with it, recreating it, or representing it.*

As I look down at the garden square, the passionless clear light of October seems to contain things like a medium, so that the trees—plane, elm, hawthorn, birch, and the single chestnut in the corner—seem to be nurtured not so much in air as in light. There are children playing; a woman knits on a bench, her coat beside her; and the church on the other side of the square has just struck noon. The account is commonplace enough, if mildly impressionistic. I could elaborate upon it, setting what I see in the framework of my own experience, and in the framework of the city itself, and I could say something of myself, and how my knowledge of what is before me is coextensive with a knowledge of myself the beholder, and with a network of general knowledge I already possess, but it is enough to say that my account is certainly not complete, either in foreground detail, or in its background. Besides being incomplete, it is also unsatisfactory in some respects. There are some important demands of reason that were satisfied, but the demands that we try to satisfy in science and philosophy remain unsatisfied: we wish to know our world in ways more detailed, systematic, and profound. And it is this need that gives rise to theory of knowledge, in which we try to be very precise about what we really know, in order to perfect the kinds of knowledge demanded, or in order to perfect some of them and show the others to be illegitimate. This then causes us to question our right to say that we certainly know the things I have enumerated, and leads us to discard them in favor of the putative certainties of some empiricistic or rationalistic starting point, upon which, we hope, we shall be able to erect our structure more securely. Reacting against such claims, which so often end in stultification, we may return to insist that we were right in the beginning after all, and that theory of knowledge can find no better foundation than these first certainties; perhaps we even end in saying that the need for theory of knowledge was a delusion anyway, at least in so far as it was a response to a presumed need for a peculiarly *philosophical* knowledge.

Yet the debate about such matters remains focused upon *what* we know, and it is precisely this that prevents us from being able to say just what it is that we know, and this in turn is what makes us sometimes distrust much of what in some moods at least, we really feel that we *do* know. With this goes the image of a consciousness (or an awareness, a mind) as something passive *on* which things are registered, *in* which things appear, or *to* which things are present. It is not that there is no truth in such an image, but that we allow it too exclusive and too literal a sway. We assume that a knowing subject (a term here used without any particular metaphysical commitment) has before it, or receives in it, certain items *given-as-known, given-as-perceived* (or *given-to-awareness*), or an assemblage of such items; and if our philosophy is of a certain bent we may want to say that Reality or Being itself is *given-as-known*, together with its laws. Sometimes no distinction is preserved between "knowing" and "perceiving"; sometimes a preference for the authenticity of one or the other is advanced, and the epistemology develops accordingly; sometimes we ask ourselves which of the things that we "know" are really trustworthy and worth building upon, and on what grounds. Often we are concerned to ask how we are to use items given in knowledge or perception to proceed to other items not thus given; or how things already assumed to be known are organized into more comprehensive and more simple patterns. It is true that all I have said about the *given* character of things known is sometimes altered by a later analysis—like that of Kant's—which reveals a contribution of reason to what we know, with the result that the *really* given is understood in a different way; still it is argument *from* what is given to the knower before analysis (in Kant's case the universal and necessary features of our knowledge of objects) that permits this turn of argument.

In thus focusing upon *what* we know (or perceive) epistemology fails to do justice to the spontaneity and originative power of reason, not indeed to make its world, but to bring the world to that fruition which is awareness and understanding—in a word, to the fruition of being known. This failing is shared by many movements that react—often in the name of some form of common sense—against epistemology. In radically originative reflection our effort is not directed upon what we know, though we never lose sight of this; neither is it directed upon the character of consciousness itself, considered as a medium within which things as known seem to abide; but instead upon the act that produces awareness and understanding as an achievement coincidental with the whole being of what we call reason. We do not take it for granted that we know what knowing is, but turn the effort to know back upon itself to see itself as a way of being. To know the bowl of asters now on the desk before me, I have, it is true, only to turn my attention to them; but if I attend instead to my knowing self in its act of knowing the bowl of asters, I recognize, in an access of wonder, that I have won, by an exercise of an habitual and now unnoticed power, to that very awareness and understanding that seemed so commonplace. The character-of-being-known of that which I now savor is not simply given to a knower that receives it: it is rather coextensive with the act in which I, as knowing agent, exercise my being. Yet the bowl of asters is not because of this any less luminously itself, and I do not the less steep myself in its uniqueness. There is in fact an intensification of uniqueness that marches paradoxically with the universality that characterizes radically originative reflection. That universality, as I claimed, exhibited itself as a tension between the One and the Many, in which the attainment of the being of the particular knower and of his various particular objects was also an attainment of Being. The uniqueness of just these asters gains an authenticity it would not have had in a mere immediacy not caught up in this tension, which indeed now confirms them as just these unique *beings*, and for this reason neither entirely evanescent, nor entirely a passage of data. We take them the more seriously as we have won to an awareness of them that authenticates them for what they are, as it authenticates its own capacity to attain them. What radically originative reflection tells us of knowing, namely, that it realizes itself *in* what is before us, by bringing it to the fruition of awareness and understanding, fills us with gratification both with the act of knowing itself and with what we attain to in it. The adequacy of the act to what it is directed upon is borne in upon us at the very moment we are struck with the creative responsibility of reason that gives rise to it; while this latter insight carries with it the overwhelming realization that knowing demands to be considered in its own terms, and that we are capable of doing this. Just so, we say, are these small asters burning in the October light, and just so, and needing no model to give us intimations of it the while it leads us astray, is the act in which we attain it. We have in reflection brought reason at its work to the fruition of awareness and understanding, even to the reflexive nature of it, and have therefore no need of images that might falsify it.

There is more modesty in this than at first appears. It is true that epistemological models based on representing, mirroring, and the like, together with all epistemological starting points that begin in any way with the role of the idea, are summarily dismissed; but they are not dismissed in favor of a claim that in cognitively attaining the object I have somehow identified my intellect (or some aspect of it) with the object (or some aspect of it). I have only claimed that I *know* it, and that the *realization* of this act is in the thing. I refuse to identify *esse* with *percipi*; refuse to identify mind with things known; and do so by my reflective grasp of knowing as a unique originative response that finds issue in becoming aware of and understanding what is before it. This cognitive enjoyment of the object is precisely that: an act that is an achievement integral with the being of the knower and yet an enjoyment of something else; a matter mysterious to us only when we try to analyze it in terms inappropriate to it.

These inappropriate analyses are often put forward with the sound purpose of pointing to the intimate union between knower and known, which they emphasize by insisting on the *identity* of the thing known with the knower, in the familiar Aristotelian way, or by insisting that the whole being of the thing known (or perceived) lies in its being known (or being perceived). I here wish to preserve this intimate union by insisting that knowing is a functional act of the knower, the whole texture of which consists in the enjoyment of the known. But the intimate union of cognitive enjoyment does not depend upon an identification of knower and known, and is therefore not rendered suspect when we reject that identification. We are concerned with an understanding that is also an awareness, and neither of these aspects compels us to think in terms of identification. It is strange that what we are so familiar with, what so demands that we should accept it in its own terms, we should insist upon understanding in terms supposedly more ideal, but in fact a distortion of something that requires no such ideal. The postulation of that ideal of identification may well derive from the supposed obstacle presented to knowing by the physical gap that separates the knower from the common-sense objects of the world, an obstacle that could only be overcome if some constituent of the object could be disengaged from it to be united with mind, or if some reflection of the object could be received into mind. To reject identification does not of course end our troubles, for a whole swarm of equally stultifying alternatives present themselves: we think that if reason falls short of an identification with the object, it must instead operate by making, creating, or receiving something which it then subjectively enjoys— subjectively because what is enjoyed is then not that elusive independent entity which, despite all our confusions, we persist in thinking of as the ideal goal of reason. No doubt we have not been helped in all this by our readiness to begin any consideration of the knowledge problem by addressing ourselves to the status of ideas or forms. The presence of these entities as in some sort "in" our minds, and as constituting, as it would seem, something of the very fabric of mind, is presumably the cause of this—a cause closely related to the problem of the physical distance between knower and known.

We also falsify the intimate union of cognitive enjoyment if we attempt a complete interpretation of it in terms of causal influences that emanate from the knower and are incorporated in the very texture of the knower. This holds for doctrines analogous to Whitehead's doctrine of prehensions and also for the usual physiological accounts of sensation when these are advanced as a sufficient account of consciousness. In connection with these latter accounts there is a familiar argument—the starting point in some solutions of the body-mind problem—that the concrete experience of consciousness is something totally different in kind from a set of physical happenings in terms of which we might seek to explain it. My present point is equally concrete, although I am in fact making a stronger claim than that which concerns the irreducible character of consciousness taken as a datum.

In the intimate union we are concerned with, the known object (obviously a term that covers but a small range of what we shall be dealing with) functions simply by being what it is, and reason responds by a cognitive enjoyment of it, which, however imperfect and admitting of degree, demands that we should approach it in its own unique terms, and not in terms that conspire to make us think that what we so concretely know to be the case is in fact self-contradictory or otherwise impossible. It is a union the governing feature of which is the activity of the irreducible being of reason that brings it about. The accomplishments of this activity are as familiar as the light of common day, and the activity itself is rooted in myriad ways in the things of everyday that are in important respects different in kind from itself. Yet we do justice to it only when we dare to permit it to return upon itself. Then, beyond all perplexity and paradox, we see that intimate union of cognitive awareness for what it is. What we find in this reflexive activity is a "nature" of reason in only a very peculiar sense of "nature," for it does not have the perfectly determinate and set limits we associate with some senses of "nature" or "essence," but is present to us as full of possibilities it is struggling to realize. Yet presiding over all this is that character of the act that makes me speak of *radical* reflection; the self-knowledge is not the result of reason functioning at a level it has already perfected—we do not come to it as to something imposed, as my awareness of the garden below is in a sense imposed—but is itself an advance won by realizing some of the possibilities of reason by bringing about a cognitive awareness of reason at its work. Finally, and just because the radically originative character of reflection is complete, non-regressive, and pellucid to itself, we are aware of the advance in making the advance. The light of this reflective act plays over everything that I am now so tortuously expounding, and it is this, in the end, that allows us to see cognitive awareness in its own terms.

VII. *In going to the root of reason and experience we gain a certainty that is neither empirical nor rational; yet radically originative reflection gives us a matrix for all rational and empirical criteria, together with the autonomy to make use of it. As we produce this matrix, we enjoy something analogous to what we enjoy when either rational or empirical criteria are satisfied, but the empirical and rational components are now complementary and coincidental (presence and self-evidence march together). Presiding over the production of this matrix, and decisive in our acceptance and use of it, is the autonomy operative in radically originative reflection. In this sense reason takes up a position anterior to its own relation to experience without an illegitimate effort to stand "outside itself" or "outside reality" to do so.*

We misunderstand the present position if, looking for what is certain or otherwise reliable about radically originative reflection, we expect to find in it an analogue of the kind of certainty I possessed when I described myself as knowing, in a common-sense way, the garden below me and the bowl of asters on the desk. Our certainty about what radically originative reflection offers us is no such "empirical" certainty, nor any alternative "rational" certainty. We owe our findings to the release of reason's own creative response as it initiates fresh awareness and understanding of its own status. In this sense the autonomy that presides over this reflection establishes the quality of the certainty we now have recourse to: the act is a self-justifying one in which creative freedom gives us certainty in act, rather than the certainty of a "datum" or "truth." We appeal then to the very life of reason—an appeal that any other kind of appeal must assume. Let us be quite clear about this: it is not another appeal to "intuition" that is in question, but an appeal to a prior autonomy in which our responsibility for the vividness and content of any possible "intuition" is borne in upon us by the very exercise of that autonomy.

The realism of the present position is no doubt partly responsible for the dismissal of a regress of justifying acts and a consequent regress of self-doubt: it is reason *itself* that we come to know, and we are consequently able to take knowing seriously in its own terms rather than assimilating it to other functions. But it is the root of the matter that it is a realism illuminated and justified by the autonomy that presides over it: we realize our autonomy in employing it reflexively to know a reason both naturally reflective and naturally capable of autonomously bringing about a "realistic" awareness and understanding of what lies before it. We gain a certainty about the normal and habitual level of reason's activities that is prior to any certainties we establish within the framework of those activities, and that puts us in a position to surpass and deepen them.

It is the certainty in act of radically originative reflection that provides a standard for all empirical and rational standards of certainty. In section *II* this point was made by saying that in our reflective exercise reason elaborates a matrix for all rational and empirical criteria, from which it may then disengage with assurance whatever criteria are appropriate in the pursuit of interests of less concrete commitment. There the account of the matrix made use of the idea of Being; we may now enlarge that account by noticing that from one point of view the *content* of radically originative reflection is nothing more than the intimate union, at their root in the creative and responsble activity of reason, of empirical and rational criteria. We shall, however, proceed negatively, by showing how "pure" empirical and rational criteria fall short of the character of the matrix.

Consider, first, the notion of *empirical presence*, which has already played so large a role in the metaphysical, existential, and phenomenological strains in twentieth-century thought. It is a very plausible suggestion that the criterion for any veridical experience—whether of some quality; of some substantive entity considered in its own right, as one of these flowers before me, or some person to whom I address myself; or even of Being itself—is the presence of whatever it is we have under consideration. We might well think that we acquiesce in its reality because it is just *there*—I do not mean *there* in that impassive and stolid sense that an existentialist might have in mind as appropriate only to *things*, but *there* in its own appropriate mode, not excluding whatever active and responsible mode of "being there" we should think it proper to assign to persons—it is just *there*, and we are consequently in its presence, in defiance of any argument that should seek to set that presence aside as an epiphenomenon of some supposed more fundamental existence, or to annul it by some other mode of analysis. Yet plausible and indeed indefeasible as any such presence might be, it would not establish in itself the character of the matrix I have in mind. As one might well expect of any doctrine that finds the claims of any experience, however radically or concretely envisaged, inadequate to establish reason's best stance, radically originative reflection requires us to qualify our reliance on empirical presence.

First, in enjoying presence of whatever sort we are aware that the enjoyment of it is equally the enjoyment of the autonomy in which we bring it about; second, in enjoying articulate utterance in general, together with the self-evidence in which it sometimes seems to issue, we are aware that that enjoyment is a facet of our enjoyment of presence. The presence we appeal to is not *empirical presence* but *cognitive presence*. In this sense the matrix is as much a matrix for rational as for empirical criteria, and functions only in the atmosphere of autonomy. The standard of (empirical) presence taken alone would otherwise be self-defeating, since we should then be wary of our right to relate present items one to another and to appraise their importance. I attend to one of the flowers in the bowl before me and, as I do so, consciousness, ideas, sense data, qualities (as the bronzy tone of a petal), and that entity, the flower, are each in some sort present. How shall I settle the question of their relative importance by appealing merely to empirical presence? No sensory awareness however vivid, no experiential presence however persuasive, is an appropriate example of the kind of certainty that is coincidental with the exercise of the responsible autonomy of reason in radically originative reflection. As we shall see, no direct intuition of the real, no rational self-evidence is any more appropriate.

Finding them lying within the matrix provided by radically originative reflection, we are better able to evaluate the variety of empirical standards that we resort to so constantly. We are able to contrast them with their more concrete realization in the matrix and are therefore able to disengage them and use them independently with greater adequacy. We begin to understand the situation within which sensory evidence and other empirical standards are useful, and because we do, we begin to see how ambiguous these appeals are in themselves, and how helpless we are to remove the ambiguity by seizing upon some "pure" sensory evidence. We find sensory evidence no less persuasive, find especially the component of sheer contingency in it no less worthy of our submissive attention, but the way in which we employ it now undergoes a subtle alteration. We are no longer, for instance, prepared to offer some version of it as a groundwork for establishing the limitations of reason, or as a justification in itself for disregarding the claims of some putative mode of reality or of some other mode of experience. *That* something is "given" to us in experience is as irrecusable as ever; that the senses participate in our acceptance of what is given, no less so; but *what* is thus given, and *how*, remains problematic, for we now see that into the determination of these issues enters our creative responsibility for our very awareness, no less than for our understanding. The ambiguity of that which is given in sensation reveals itself as so complete that not even the mode in which the senses participate in our acceptance of it remains untainted. I may put this in a more positive way by noticing that radically originative reflection compels us to recognize the creative autonomy we exercise even in the habitual act of perception, no less than it enlightens us about less "primitive" aspects of cognition. Henceforward whenever we make a sensory appeal, we do so in full awareness of the autonomy and responsibility we bring to it, and in full awareness too that the *kind* of appeal must be appropriate to the interest that dominates us on the occasion in question.

If we turn now to the matter of rational standards, we find that they are no less ambiguous when taken in themselves. If we do not acknowledge that we find them lying in conjunction with presence within the matrix of radically originative reflection, and that they do us best service when, after we disengage them from it for whatever employment we have in mind, something of their origin still clings to them, then they will continue to afford us such perplexing diversions as the familiar debate about whether logic and mathematics are analytic or synthetic *a priori*. I may make my central point by drawing attention once more to the supposedly most "pure" standard, in this case the truths of logic, no less "pure" in the mode of *understanding* than any of the "pure" standards for *awareness* put forward in the history of empiricism. At least we find, in the effort to produce a fully axiomatized logic, a parallel to the search for a pure empirical standard. But our reflective act now permits us to see that the very situation that sanctions our employment of logical procedures sets limits on the "purity" of logical procedure in general and therefore on the "purity" of any system attempting to embody the laws of logic. As a sensory appeal purified of all rational and articulate presence claims was seen to be an illusion, so now we see that a logical truth so pure as not to have emerged out of the texture of some presence that we have autonomously won to is itself an illusion. This observation introduces what is an increasingly important theme in contemporary thought, namely, the consciousness of the limitations set upon all deductive procedures based upon axioms. These limitations can now be demonstrated in some technical detail, but I am now concerned only to make the point that radically originative reflection affords us a way of explaining their presence. It does so because it permits us to see that the construction of axiomatized systems of whatever sort takes place within a framework that that procedure invokes and presupposes in spite of all efforts to purify it of the need to do so. The construction and use of such systems is appropriate and justifiable within a framework, but for that very reason is of no significance in establishing the character of that framework. In the crucial case of logic, this does not mean that the emergence of articulate discourse and self-evidence from the enjoyment of a cognitive presence that establishes the framework of logic is also the emergence of a fully articulated logic; only that our efforts to articulate and systematize logic and, *a fortiori,* deductive procedures that presuppose it, rest upon a concrete act in which our right to *use* logic to do these things is grounded upon an autonomously-won presence of the real. A technical formulation of this claim might be given as follows: all our efforts to axiomatize ought to rest upon the recognition that we can not embody in any set of axioms all the assumptions on which we proceed; and this is true whether we wish to axiomatize a portion of some science, a branch of mathematics, or logic itself: in all cases the presence we cognitively attend to (something that varies with our interest) yields an irreducible component utilized in the development of the system, in logic this being the very inferential relationship that permits us to *use* logic in the axiomatizing procedure— the very root, as it were, of self-evidence, now seen to emerge out of presence as something that characterizes it.[6] All this means that even when we turn—as of course we can—to the construction of systems that we mean to devise in isolation from the presence that we intend to interpret by means of them, we have never really quite left presence behind: the articulation of any system is always in some sort the articulation of some presence.

Our matrix, then, is in contrast with the inadequacy of both "pure" empirical and "pure" rational criteria, taken by themselves. I spoke of it as positively characterized by the intimate union of empirical and rational criteria at their root. One may now clarify this claim by the device of isolating for a moment, and somewhat too abstractly, the "content" of radically originative reflection. In terms of this "content" an "intimate union of these criteria at their root" means that reason is seen to *creatively* produce its awareness and understanding, but only by submitting itself *responsibly* to the unique savor of what is before it and to the union of what is unique with what is common. The note of creativity issuing in the generality of understanding gives us the "rational" side; the notes of awareness and responsible submission give us the "empirical" side; that the creativity is *also* a responsibility gives us the inseparability of the two sides. But if we are to speak with any justice of a matrix, we want more than the inseparability of the two criteria. It is the *generality* of the act that permits us to speak of a matrix: it is the *general enjoyment* of creative and responsible autonomy that is at issue. And this point reminds us that we are no less concerned with a joint rational and empirical *satisfaction*—a *general* satisfaction—than with a generally apprehended theoretic content in which the *status* of rational and empirical criteria is seen to be one of union at their root.

From this matrix, and by virtue of a *right* that it endows us with, we can now disengage such rational and empirical criteria as we find appropriate to the level of attention at which we are engaged. It is a contrast with their more concrete realization in radically originative reflection that permits us to evaluate them thus. (We can also disengage criteria of mixed import. The world of common sense taken as a criterion for reality is a case in point, involving as it does a presence claim made articulate in language. So too would be the principle of sufficient reason, taken as a "self-evident" truth emergent from the patent and general presence of causal connections. These are put forward merely as examples: no attempt is here made to settle their status.) Our right to empirical and rational criteria, indeed, to self-evidence of all sorts, is always at issue. Here we are concerned with the grounds of that right. And the issue of our concern, as we shall see, is a sense of the variety of criteria that we can with right employ. In this sense we place ourselves, in radically originative reflection, anterior to all "empirical" and "rational" appeals, without however attempting to place ourselves "outside reality" to do so, and without any attempt to place ourselves "outside" the act of reason except in the unobjectionable reflective sense noted in section IV.

VIII. *Radically originative reflection begins in dissatisfaction with our habitual cognitive framework and goes on to a creative transformation of it, both the dissatisfaction and the transformation exhibiting reason's autonomy before all rational and empirical criteria. This transformation also affects the problem of reason and experience, for the interplay of "reason" and "experience" displayed by science and, indeed, by most human activities is now seen to take place within the framework supplied by our reflective act, and to have no appropriate use in determining the limitations of reason. The transformation gives us all the advantages one might hope to obtain by standing "outside" experience.*

One introduces a note of dramatic suddenness by speaking of radically originative reflection as an *act*. This is appropriate despite the many tentative beginnings and false turnings. There is an abrupt shift of focus, issuing in an access of self-knowledge; and this begins in a certain deliberation and resolution that reminds us of moral decision, and of that part of the artistic process that can be summoned consciously. This latter point makes it clear that this mode of knowing is inseparable from reason's capacity for *doing* and *making*. There is, then, an abrupt transformation in which reason, straining to see its own supposedly unseeable and ineffable nature, finds suddenly that it can both "see" and speak of what it sees. It sees that it is its task and power to originate an awareness and understanding of what lies before it, by deploying outwardly its own resources, so that they are resolved and completed in the enjoyment of what lies before it; it sees also that it has done just this in the reflective act.

The transformation affects also the problem of reason and experience, which now appears to us as having two chief aspects. The first and wider aspect concerns a framework that it would not be precise to describe as a framework of *experience* for reasons developed in the previous section: it is a framework in which we enjoy both "rational" and "empirical" satisfaction even as we elaborate it, and from which we may elicit rational and empirical criteria that will vary with the scope of our interests. There is no harm in calling it a framework of experience if we remember that "experience" is now used in a sense that can not fruitfully be contrasted with "reason," since it is in fact the creative and responsible autonomy of reason that establishes it. Second, there is the more usual contrast between reason and experience, which we must now think of as one properly made *within* this framework; consequently, the interplay of reason and experience, which furnishes the starting point for so much epistemology, must also be considered to take place within the framework and to be of no significance in determining the character of it. This was all implicit in the previous section, but it will require some rehearsal of the position to make this clear.

Reason begins its transformation with what may be described, depending upon our purpose, as an habitual mode of attention; as the everyday world upon which that attention is focused; as the symbolic, conceptual or linguistic framework in terms of which we apprehend it; or as experience in the widest sense—what I shall call, although always with the above qualifications, the framework of experience. Within this framework it wields with considerable power a variety of rational and empirical criteria for systematic, articulate, and well-founded knowledge, among which sensory evidence and logical order and system are significant examples. At the same time it feels a vague need for an ideal satisfaction—a satisfaction of reason in a wider sense than those rational criteria just mentioned. These vague demands it finds to be obscurely related to the framework of experience in that they are, whatever else they may be, evidence of a certain dissatisfaction with it; and this obscure relation fills it with puzzlement over the exact status of the more or less precise rational and empirical criteria that are employed *within* the framework.

From this position reason moves suddenly to one in which it realizes that it is autonomous before all rational and empirical (narrow sense) criteria, all "ideals" for reason, and all the empirical (wide sense) criteria inherent in our acceptance of a framework of experience, because all such criteria are by-products of the activity in which reason becomes aware of and understands anything whatever. Reason is, moreover, exercising in this very shift of position that same autonomy before rational and empirical criteria that is a chief part of the content of its vision from the new position. It now sees all empirical criteria as emerging from the very quality of its awareness of whatever "objects," whatever "world," it deals with; while it understands that this awareness is only won to and completed in an act that elaborates a whole network of conceptual structures, a whole web of rational order.

The conceptual web therefore develops initially *in* our penetration of the real in its coeval aspects of general and particular, and as a *result* of this penetration. If we suppose this secondary environment to be the sole environment of reason and contrast it with the supposed mere particularities of sensation, we make this interplay of "reason" and "experience" absolute, and are in danger of failing to see that the development of this conceptual web as a world of intellectual tools in isolation from its source is a highly abstract activity. And this is what leads us to use such "rational" criteria as coherence, consistency, simplicity and universality, whose dependence on a more concrete activity of reason we fail to recognize, in the construction of systems that we then regard as merely formal or merely analytic. On the other hand, when we attend to our sensory apprehension of the world in abstraction from reason's capacity to initiate cognitive awareness, we develop various "empirical" criteria, such as sensory objects, sensations, sense data, impressions, whose dependence on that capacity of reason we also fail to recognize. In either case we are *assuming* a framework of experience and searching out more precise rational and empirical criteria within it. But as the basis of that framework escapes us, we use these criteria, not just for the restricted purposes for which they were intended, but also to settle questions about the general capacity of reason, as well as other sorts of metaphysical questions. Such problems as the problem of induction are a legacy of this misuse.

On this view we reach a position of indefeasible certainty, not by settling upon a rational or empirical prototype for certainty, as has so often been done, but by seizing upon the source of certainties of all sorts, and by *using* this source to do just this. Rather than *consulting* either rational or empirical criteria in order to determine reason's best stance we are in the act of *elaborating* or *evolving* a matrix for all such criteria as we determine that stance.

We therefore have naturally all the advantages one might wish to obtain by an effort to place reason "outside itself" and "outside reality" in order to look back upon, and correct any deficiencies in, its normal function. Yet there has been no attempt to do what would rightly be condemned as self-contradictory in such an enterprise: to place itself outside itself and the world, and then, using its old mode of activity with all its inveterate confusions, to look empirically back upon and correct that same activity. Images of this sort, derived from everyday empirical observations, assail any reflective enterprise, and make it falsify itself, seeing itself as a kind of common-sense or scientific observation of something presented in experience. With it goes the image mentioned above, in which the situation of the body within a world that acts upon it, is assumed to give a legitimate and unqualified picture of reason within an experience, or within a language, that acts upon it. If, when it attempts reflection, reason remains dominated by these images, it destroys the spontaneity of reflection at root and cuts itself off from a proper awareness of the meaning of its own spontaneity.

Radically originative reflection is a creative act in the sense that it is a spontaneous response to an incitement that is purely internal, arising as it does not from an external stimulus but from reason's dissatisfaction with its grasp of its own situation. It is creative too in the sense that it quickens creativity, for reason now sees itself as everywhere responsible for even the most familiar savor of experienced things, and no longer supposes its own creativity to consist solely in a closer perusal of things combined with a more ingenious construction of conceptual webs to constrain them.

IX. *The claim that, in evolving a matrix for all rational and empirical criteria, we enjoy a satisfaction that is both "rational" and "empirical," is an elaboration of the earlier claim about the generality afforded by radically originative reflection. The most intractable resistance to this claim is offered by the empiricist view that a pure sensory awareness is the proper paradigm of empirical satisfaction. A re-examination of sensory awareness in the light of radically originative reflection reveals an ambiguity in it that is only resolvable if we suppose ourselves autonomous with regard to all empirical criteria.*

We have by now enlarged somewhat upon the theme of the generality afforded by radically originative reflection. It was expressed first in terms of the view that understanding is the completion and fruition of awareness, and was developed in terms of a complex tension between the One and the Many, in which the generality afforded by the unity of things was set against the uniqueness and particularity afforded by the diverse multiplicity of things. I claimed that this complex tension was exhibited both by what we attend to in our world and by the presiding autonomous and reflexive activity in which we enter into the secure possession of that world. We may put this in a different way by saying that it was exhibited both by the matrix for all rational and empirical criteria and by the presiding activity in which we produce and use the matrix. The association of awareness exclusively with particularity, and of an understanding thought of as devoid of direct awareness with generality, was of course repudiated: this was an important factor in our discussion of presence. The discussion of the status of self-evidence, and, more particularly, of the status of logic, afforded a further important example of a generality founded in cognitive presence. Implicit in all of the chapter so far is the claim that reason enters into a *general* self-knowledge grounded in presence, a claim which might be more traditionally expressed in terms of the presence of the "nature" of reason to itself.

Another way of putting some of these issues is to observe again that, if we regard ourselves as producing a matrix for all rational and empirical criteria in our reflective act, we must also regard ourselves as enjoying a kind of "rational" and "empirical" satisfaction as we do this. With regard to the "nature" of reason, we should then have to say that there is a sense in which we experience it. And although we need not offer a truly empirical groundwork for this experience—for that would defeat our main purpose, which is the establishment, not of an empirically validated stance, but of one from which we can understand and evaluate various kinds of empirical validations—we have still to quell the insistent demand that our "empirical" satisfaction should somehow approximate that so importunate paradigm of awareness, sensation.

Presumably my assurance that there is a garden lying below me is in some sort dependent on the sensations I have of it, and it remains stubbornly true that if reason's "nature" is present to me, and if the character of the real as supporting inference is present to me, I certainly have no sensations of them. But it is also true that this sensuous correlative, indispensable as it may be to ordinary empirical presence, is a curiously ambiguous thing, whose contribution to the authenticity of the experience it seems impossible to isolate with any precision. Thus, though it is easy enough to see that my ready acquiescence in the presence of the garden is dependent upon the *involvement* of sensation in my experience of it, it is hard to say just *how* sensation is involved in it. Attempts to isolate the contribution of sensation to an experience like that of the garden are familiar enough features of the empiricist tradition; they tend, as we know, to equate experience with whatever bare version of the sensory contribution is put forward, and in this sense deny any supposed "experience" of the garden as such. For our times these attempts culminate in the theory of meaning and the very narrow version of experience developed by the logical positivists. The extensive criticism these views have been subjected to—much of it the self-criticism of those who once urged them upon us—has brought it about that they are no longer widely accepted. The downfall of these doctrines tells us (if we really needed telling) that whatever the importance of sensation in an experience like that of the garden, it is impossible to isolate an exact sensuous correlative for what we mean by "garden," "tree," "leaf," and so on. The general temper of continental philosophy supports us in these views. Insofar as you can isolate the contribution of sensation —and who has done this in a convincing manner?—it seems insufficient to support the claim that you see a garden before you.

My point here is that you are in no worse case, with regard to an *exact* foundation in sensation, when you make claims such as I have made in this chapter, than when you make claims about experiencing leaves, trees, gardens. You may, it is true, make more indirect appeals to experience, as when linguistic philosophers speak of "occasions upon which one correctly uses the term 'garden' "; and, on some standard of correctness one may find that what I might here call the presence of the garden holds up rather better than, say, the presence of reason's "nature." But you do not in this way turn the point at issue: that sensation offers us no unambiguous empirical standard; and you thus leave open the question how we do settle upon such standards. If you justify much of what you assert about the world by appealing to the structure of language, you merely recapitulate with Wittgenstein the movement from Hume's position to Kant's; with this important exception, that you have not put forward a supporting doctrine of experience to match Kant's thorough-going anti-realist view of it. Certainly without reopening the thorny question of experience you do not seem able to strike down effectively such a claim as that in our reflective act the "nature" of reason becomes present to you.

Still, if we put all these difficulties aside, common sense, and many philosophical doctrines as well, will tell us pertinaciously that sensation is involved in some important way in our experience of the garden. However much we may find it hard to say just *how* it does so, sensation clearly supports my claim that there is a garden below me: in whatever mode I am aware of and understand the garden, sensation enters into that mode in ways in which it does not enter into my awareness of the presence of reason's "nature." To see that this fact in no way discredits the latter kind of presence, we have to look more closely at the way in which sensation is involved in the former.

And is the issue not precisely in this matter of the "support" sensation is alleged to give for some of our assertions? The word "support" suggests a distinction between the evidence and the assertion that we do not seem able to sustain. Sensuous evidence for the truth of any proposition is always an articulated evidence in which the *involvement* of sensation is just as inscrutable as we saw it to be in the case of the garden. The truth of the matter is apparently quite simple: we assess with our sensory faculties real features of things, but

features that are more salient in some modes of the real than
in others. Sensation, widely interpreted to include our sense
of subjectivity (in so far as that can be tied to an internal
bodily sense), puts us in touch with a wide variety of important features of the world. Chief of these are space and
its correlate location, and time and its correlate change, which
I shall later, adapting a usage of Whitehead's, call *extensive*
features; but these are themselves available to us only as bound
up with weight, resistance, warmth, color, texture, and so on.
And not only is it questionable to think of some of these
qualities as secondary and others as primary, it is also questionable to think of the whole collection of them as sensuous
data to be used as raw material for the construction of our
common world, or as raw material for correlation in the
theoretic constructions of science. My point is that in assessing
the world with our senses we really do assess it: we grasp real
features of it. There are more difficulties here than in most
topics, but it seems safe to say that while we have given much
attention to the way in which sensation sets a limit upon the
aspirations of reason, we have not adequately noticed the sense
in which it affords us riches that would be missed by a purely
intellectual intuition.

Speaking from a point of view that takes the concrete
activity of reason seriously, we may say that sensation opens
up channels to real features of things, focusing or directing
our powers of awareness upon them. More accurately, it *is* our
power of awareness, so directed and focused. It is part of our
own confusion that we allow what it thus puts us in touch with
to infect our view of all our knowing, so that we think we must
demand sensuous "correlates" to "support" judgments about
all realities, including those in which the features accessible
to sensation are no longer so salient as they are in the judgment
about the garden. It may be quite true that we cannot know
at all without sensation, and that all our knowing must be imbued with the features of things it makes accessible to us, but
we have no warrant for saying, as Kant does, that articulate
understanding, emerging as the fruit of awareness, must be

"built up" out of some primordial *sensory* awareness; indeed, what such an approach leaves out is precisely our awareness of the *real* as *having* features accessible to sensation. Our thought is imbued with sensation in quite another and more concrete way: we are creatures in some sense subject to those very features of things that sensation makes accessible to us. Were our sensory channels quite disrupted, we should be quite disrupted as the creatures we are, but this in no sense calls in question the presence of beings and Being; neither does it call in question the presence of the "nature" of reason, working through these channels *to bring about* a sensory awareness—working to assess, that is, real characteristics of its situation. This is to recognize our *need* of sensation, but it is to do so in a way that repudiates the image of consciousness as a complex relay and switching circuit. However such images enlighten us about some features of mentality, they leave out what is most vital: that *we become aware of* the features these channels afford us, and become aware of them *as* features. So here I become aware of all the sensuous variety of the garden, and aware of it *as* the sensuous variety of that garden.

Many of our difficulties about sensation probably arise from a faulty conception of our awareness of particulars: because memory and our command of concepts allow us to talk of some particular item of experience in its absence, and because this is a mode of understanding, we suppose that the presence of the particular thing in sensation is a sub-rational presence *to* our senses, not a presence to reason. This view is presumably reinforced by our ability to give sensory evidence for rational conclusions of a different order. In all this we do not do justice to sense-perception itself. If our linguistic forms represent an achievement of the race so habitual that we take it for granted, the power of sensation, being something we share with the rest of the animal kingdom, we take even more for granted. Yet it is an achievement continuous with those of reason, and shares the structure we recognize in reason. It has, even while it is our channel to multiplicity, variety, and particularity, its own proper mode of generality. While in some respects it furnishes the raw material for certain types of thinking—especially those that depend upon our power to construct theories and the like—it is itself a way of knowing, directed to its own proper "objects."

It is a common theme in rationalist thought, first systematically expressed in Aristotle's doctrine of the formal character of the sensible object, that sensation is continuous with knowing. We separate sensing and knowing by such devices as the distinction between percept and concept, but it is perilous to suppose that they belong to totally different realms. There is a generality inherent in any perception of color, for instance, that is independent of the generality that supervenes when we name it by a name like "red," as indeed it is the reason why we may correctly do so. Sensation is a way of assessing something that is unique, but unique in only a limited sense. When we see a certain color we are aware of more than what is unique to the situation in which we see it: just seeing it *as* a color is a mode of generalizing. And beyond this, there is in sensation the generality inherent in a rational acknowledgment of presence, which we are quite unable to separate from some supposed mute, inarticulate presence to sensation *tout court*. Efforts to isolate the pure contributions of sensation, being in the nature of the case self-contradictory, end only in the postulation of bare sense contents, which are in fact mere abstractions from a different mode of attentiveness and are in any case rationally acknowledged. We try to confine ourselves to such acknowledgments as "this green, now"; better, we try to attend to that patch of green with a totally mute receptivity; but even then language looms in the background, together with all it elaborates for us: we plainly understand at least this, that we are aware of a patch of green. Most of the time we are quite aware that sensation is as it were a way of selectively focusing the attention of reason, as when I say "See how fresh the green of the chestnut is after the rain," and thereby understand what I sense to be of such and such a sort, in such and such a context, and moreover implicitly acknowledge the mediation of my eyes. Mere sensory awareness, a wholly sub-rational presence *to* our senses, is for us an abstraction, whatever it may be for the rest of the animal kingdom.

We may now return to another species of generality—that of the matrix provided by our reflective act. The standard we disengage from it for some particular purpose may require us to look for particularity and uniqueness, as when, for instance, we feel called upon to consult just *this* nicely discriminated sense datum for some of the many purposes of science or common sense; yet, *as a standard,* it is something general that we are concerned with, for it is a *mode* of experience, and not some particular item of that mode, that confronts us as a standard: we consult the *item* because we find the mode a desirable standard. And this generality of the mode is just a reflection of the generality that infects both the "rational" and the "empirical" aspects of the satisfaction we find as we produce our matrix.

There is another way in which sensation is involved in that possession of the world in which radically originative reflection confirms us. Our reflective act permits us to acquiesce in the common-sense world, in which, puzzled by philosophical perplexities, we first moved to better reason's stance. In so far as we were involved in sensation in that world, sensation is also compresent with our reflective act. And, if we make our interpretation of sensation broad enough, we can say that the garden, the desk with its bowl of flowers, my own body inhabiting this place at this time, are all compresent with reason's "nature," and indeed in one sense form the background in which we apprehend it. That "nature" is therefore something perfectly compatible with the sensory situation in which it finds itself. It is indeed but one of the ontological features that, taken together, constitute an enrichment of the sensory world. What gives us that "nature" also gives us the *being* of that world with all the brilliance and immediacy of it unmarred by the philosophic doubt that so often assails the "intuition" of Being. The vividness and immediacy of the here and now, which we rightly associate with sensation, is complemented by a vividness and immediacy of another order, which it is a chief task of this essay to elucidate. There is in fact an interesting inversion here: we set out to describe what in this reflection is analogous to an empirical appeal, and we have ended the train of thought by suggesting that an empirical appeal—or at least the common-sense version of such an appeal—depends upon what we become assuredly aware of in this reflective act to authenticate it.

X.   *It becomes clearer that presence and articulated self-evidence are complementary when we recapitulate the viewpoint of radically originative reflection in terms of* recognition *(here understood as a technical term); this permits a fresh approach to such traditional contrasts as* a priori *and* a posteriori, *analytic and synthetic, idealism and realism.*

At the root of every act in which reason is implicated, from our most inarticulate and transient acts of awareness to those most advanced and complicated deployments of reason that issue in systematic knowledge and art, there is a common activity I shall call *recognition*. The parallel with Plato's *recollection* is intentional, but there is an important difference of emphasis. While Plato's *anamnēsis* suggests the recovery of something once possessed inviolate, in *a priori* isolation, the word *recognition* suggests that the real presence of whatever reality or complex of realities is before us is an incitement, not to our remembrance of something else, but to our very awareness and understanding of what lies immediately before us, which we then accomplish from "within" by unfolding powers fitted for just that exercise.

We must respect the intricacy of the extensive manifold that lies before us because it is an indispensable element in what we are trying to possess: the everyday objectivity of "becoming" in things and any deeper objectivity we suppose them to have challenge us alike to win to an awareness and understanding of them. What is recognized lies "without" in the sense that its very impingement upon reason is necessary for reason to become articulately aware of it and to assess it. This is not a physical impingement of the sort we have in mind when we think of the stimulation of nerve ends and the transmission of those impulses to the brain. As the brief discussion of sensation in the last section should have made clear, radically originative reflection does not require us to minimize the importance of these channels; it only requires us to think of them as focusing our powers of awareness in a way appropriate to important features of the subject matter. So here we may acknowledge the importance of impingement in the physical sense without neglecting another sense of impingement: the sense in which what we are aware of and understand impinges upon the responsive powers of reason *merely by being what it is.* This latter sense is enigmatic enough, but every attempt to deal with the body-mind problem that is not totally indifferent to the "mind" side of that problem must take account of it. This is because the correlate of that impingement is the creative response of reason, which we now give its full concrete weight.

What thus impinges upon reason need not necessarily be a physical object, a sense-datum, a real duration, a "life-world," a living being, or Being as such, although it might well be any one of them or an articulated structure involving all of them. The idea of impingement may be expressed by saying that what we are aware of must be, in its own terms, a causal factor in our awareness of it. Yet, as we have rejected every image of passive recognition, mirroring, representing, or becoming identical with the "object," it is plain that it does not wholly cause our awareness and understanding of it. Taking the act that issues in awareness and understanding in its own terms, we think of it as an achievement won under the stimulus of this impingement. The potentialities of reason are resolved outwardly in the enjoyment of its object by the exercise of a responsible spontaneity or autonomy. Reason *acts* in coming to know and in this act disburdens itself and completes itself *in* the enjoyment of what impinges upon it. Coincidental with this is the function of reason that has so often been dealt with in terms of the expression *a priori*. We may also adopt it here, under a limitation that will soon appear. Reason unfolds its own nature in this act, and this is prior to experience in the sense that the having of experience depends upon it. Philosophers have in the past marked the *a priori* by pointing to concepts, categorial schemes, principles, forms —any or all of these will serve here—the very content of which, or the patent truth of which, could not have been derived from experience. These have often been understood as in some sort the products of reason, but with a different emphasis from the present one. It has sometimes been supposed that reason is constrained within the *a priori* bounds of a categorial scheme that is no less inflexible for being a product of reason itself; its only freedom seems then to lie in rearranging the less ultimate features of the scheme under the stimulus of experience. Sometimes the scheme is held to be flexible, in that reason can develop it further under the stimulus of experience. The ways in which the present approach differs from such views, as well as from Plato's view, will appear from the following six principles, in which it may be summarized.

1] All "forms," ranging from single words, through the complex articulations of natural and artificial languages, including therefore all categorial schemes, theories, and principles, are *a priori* in the sense that they are products of the spontaneity of reason at work in bringing about awareness and understanding. This spontaneity is neither exercised in an isolation that leaves reason "empty" or "ungrounded," nor does it develop under the stimulus of experience. An exception to this latter claim is dealt with in (4) below; but, in the root sense of experience that is at issue here, experience is the product of reason's spontaneity.

2]   We elaborate these "forms" initially as we enjoy what impinges on reason "by being what it is." They are *products* of this enjoyment, and the articulate awareness that accompanies the elaboration of them is the completion or fruition of this enjoyment. This principle is not intended as a defense of this or that solution to the universals problem; but when we do eventually turn to that problem we shall be able to do so free of any obligation to suppose that an investigation of knowledge must begin with the existence of ideas in consciousness.

3]   The claim that the spontaneity of reason is not exercised in an isolation that makes the root work of reason necessarily empty or ungrounded depends upon the claim that we elaborate these forms initially in and with our enjoyment of what impinges on reason "by being what it is." This yields us a sense in which these forms are synthetic, although it is a sense quite different from Kant's. What is at issue is not the role of sense perception, which, in the present view, is considerably different from what Kant had in mind. It is rather that the development of our *a priori* forms requires nothing less than the *being* of what is before us, since it is in the act of unfolding its powers in the enjoyment of this that reason gives rise to these structures.

4]   These *a priori* forms, although they are the completion and end product of the act of awareness and understanding, also stabilize our enjoyment of the various possessions of reason, and enable us to recover our insights in memory and to communicate them. As such they also become objects of attention and can be developed in many ways. From one point of view we construct new complexes of them; from another they seem to develop in accordance with internal laws that we merely discern. A chief motive for developing such structures is to deal theoretically with experience in order to interpret and control it, and this gives us a sense in which the development takes place under the stimulus of experience. This sense of "experience" is the exception mentioned in (1) above, and it is obviously less fundamental than the root sense of experience that was at issue there. We therefore have a juxtaposition of reason and experience that is less fundamental than the one I had in mind in speaking of going "to the root of reason and experience." But when we attend to our *a priori* structures without keeping this in mind, we are troubled by their status. The problems that arise in this less fundamental juxtaposition are familiar enough to epistemology and methodology and I shall not rehearse them here, except for one especially relevant matter. This is our tendency, even though we notice the stimulus given by this kind of experience to the development of some of these structures—as we must do if we are to use them in science—to neglect their roots in our concrete enjoyment of the real, and to erect the impossible ideal of the empty analytic, pure and contentless, yet mysteriously able to suggest some of the lineaments of the real world. We learn many interesting and useful things when we do this sort of thing, but when we use the supposedly pure nature of such structures as a premise in efforts to establish the true status of reason we produce only confusion. This is only to observe that, although the less fundamental juxtaposition of reason and experience has its proper use within a background defined by the more fundamental one, we are in the wrong when we try to use the former to establish the best stance of reason. Consequently, although there is a perfectly useful sense of the expression "analytic *a priori*," its usefulness depends upon our acknowledgment of the limitation under which we use it. Our enjoyment of these structures is faulty if we do not understand that we elaborate them initially only as we enjoy something else, and that something of their origin clings to them however we use them.

5] The application of the term *a posteriori* is also modified. It follows from (1) above that none of our knowledge is *a posteriori* in any absolute sense. This is of course not to suggest that our obligation to the particularity and uniqueness of things is any less real. The garden lies below me at this moment with a particularity and uniqueness that requires that I wait upon it, and there is no disposition here to minimize that aspect of things: the extensiveness of things requires that we survey them if we are to know them. But the useful distinction between *a priori* and *a posteriori* that arises in this way functions appropriately *within* the framework established by radically originative reflection: it has no place in an attempt to establish the best stance of reason. When we do so try to use it, we introduce an absolute sense of *a posteriori* for which there is no justification. It is part of the consequence of invoking this absolute sense that "awareness" and "understanding" are drawn into the orbits of "*a posteriori*" and "*a priori*" respectively; we then tend to neglect the continuity of awareness and understanding, and come to think of the first as concerned with that which is wholly particular in experience, and the second as concerned with what is general in it, if indeed we do not with Kant identify the one with the matter and the other with the form of experience. We then reach the deceptive image of the total receptivity and passivity of reason before this absolutely *a posteriori* feature of things. Against all this, I have already suggested that the particularity of anything that lies before us is never absolute, but displays also something of that generality that so many doctrines of the *a priori* are concerned with. On this view the particularity and generality—the aspects, that is, of Many and One respectively —are alike in incitement to the spontaneity of reason and therefore both come under the heading of *a priori*, in the sense set forth in (1) above.

6]   Recognition is itself recognized in radically originative reflection and this enables us to trust the complementarity of presence and self-evidence (or awareness and understanding) that is so fundamental to it. A tension between the One and the Many pervades the reflective act in which reason recognizes its powers, the use of those powers in attaining its "objects," and the "objects" themselves. The act is general or uni-

versal (One) in any particular and unique realization (Many) of it and knows itself to be so; the "object" of whatever sort exemplifies a unity that is general or universal (One) and a particularity or uniqueness (Many) appropriate to it as an individual, both characteristics being necessary to it *as* an "object." It is within this tension that the act of *generalizing* is authenticated, and this applies to the proper application of general terms, to the articulation of general truths like those of logic, and to the articulation of the whole structure or "logic" of any natural language. It is only in a restricted sense that generalization is a movement from the wholly particular to the general: that all swans are white is something we must test by observing swans, but we properly assume a prior contrast of general and particular as we do this.

If we see reason's activity in terms of recognition, we see it as winning to an awareness and understanding of what it is confronted with by deploying outwardly its own "nature." We may say that reason discovers, discloses, reveals; but these words falsify a little, for there is no obstacle lying in the way of vision—there is only a deficiency in reason itself, together with the encumbrances of its own habits. The vision, moreover, is not something that supervenes on the uncovering, but is in fact identical with it.

All these images are associated with views described as realistic, as I have already acknowledged. This is intentional, but the word recognition is also intended to concede what is surely an important insight of various idealisms: that reason seems to find something of *itself* in what it is aware of and understands. This has often been noticed in connection with our elaboration of conceptual schemes in which the *a priori* component is important. But it also appears in very many idealist accounts of perception, and of our knowledge of the world about us. On the present view this is reinterpreted to mean that, while reason does realize *itself* and does this *in* what it is confronted with, it is not then necessarily confronting *a priori* forms or categories itself has made, except in the sense that as

it produces these forms it is putting itself in the presence of, or enjoying, whatever in the real it is concerned with. Recognition is an originative act in which reason expresses itself, but the whole purpose of this expression is to acquiesce in something it has not made—that is the realistic note again, and the note of responsibility as well. It thus resolves its need, expresses its nature, unfolds its potentialities, but does this *in* what lies before it, making that *available* to itself which would not have been so except for its agency. That "making available to itself" is what I meant when I spoke earlier of reason bringing its object "to the fruition of awareness and understanding."

It is an ungrateful task to try to preserve the insights of two doctrines that are usually felt to be quite at odds with each other, as I have tried to do in the preceding paragraph. It is hard to retain the nice balance we need here without tumbling over into the paradoxes that seem to tell us that what we know to be so can not be so. I turn now to a discussion of the realistic side, in which the idea of presence will play a considerable role. A reminder about my use of the word "presence" is in order before beginning. That the appeal to presence is an appeal to experience is so plausible a point that I must say again that it is not the point I wish to make. As we begin in our reflective act at a point anterior to empirical and rational standards, it can not be some sheer empirical weight, some primordial persuasiveness, that makes us acknowledge what is before us. It is not *empirical* presence, but rather the reflective exercise of reason's responsible autonomy as it wins its way to *cognitive* presence that is at issue. There is a component of generality in all presence and a corresponding rational satisfaction in the acknowledgment of it. We are *before* the opposition of reason and experience and notice that, when this legitimate opposition arises, it does so at a less concrete level of interest and attention than that to which we aspire. Here we begin neither with experience nor with self-evident truth taken separately, but with both as twin outgrowths of the responsible autonomy of reason. I am therefore concerned, in invoking presence in the next few paragraphs, only to state the realistic side of the

position as clearly as possible, and in such a way as to show that it is compatible with the insights of idealism I have just mentioned.

Consider first how such words as "awareness," "presence," "independence," "objectivity," and "support" supplement each other. I have, for instance, already contended that the foundation of the act of awareness and understanding lies in the enjoyment of what lies before us, which thus supports, clothes, or gives substance to the act. The act is completed in or resolved in what we are aware of: its whole living tissue is the cognitive enjoyment of what we are aware of. Yet the sense of support is part of the enjoyment, which is incomplete, muddled, and inadequate if it does not include the acknowledgment of independent existence we make when we use the word presence. Awareness is something won to: a kind of satisfaction in which we acknowledge that what we are aware of is exactly such and such; but part of the satisfaction lies in the acknowledgment that we are not then attending to a modification of consciousness, but to something independent of that; or we may say that part of the satisfaction lies in the acknowledgment of its objectivity. Yet though the words supplement each other indeed, they do so in a new situation, and if we do not manage to place ourselves in the new situation, we find that we stumble over their very familiarity; so that if we are not persuaded by one of them, we are hardly to be enlightened by turning to another. And there is always the temptation of the other side of our terminology: we say "the whole living tissue of the act is the cognitive enjoyment of what we are aware of," and are thus tempted to consider the mind as identical with the object, or the being of what we are cognitively aware of as identical with the act of awareness itself.

What is it then, that our words converge upon? It will be clearer if I begin with the earlier claim that what we are cognitively aware of is a causal factor in our awareness "by being what it is." I can then go on to observe that what is thus a causal factor divulges to us not only *what* it is, but also *that* it plays a role as a causal factor in the act. If we now apply this to presence we may perceive two aspects to it. It is, in the first place, always presence *of a certain sort* that we have to deal with: what is present may be present *as* an external world, present *as* an essence, present *as* another person, perhaps even present *as* Being as such. But besides this aspect of *what* is present to us, which differentiates one act of awareness from another, there is a common strand running through all of them, namely, the fact that something or other is present. One could carry out a similiar exercise with "objective," although it is an overworked word that brings in too many traditional overtones.

The common strand running through all acts of awareness, establishing them all as members of the same family, suggests that the problem of error is not such an obstacle to a defense of realism as is generally supposed. A reason that is in considerable confusion on the issue of *what* that which is present is present *as*, is rescued nevertheless from solipsism by what is common to all presence. It is tempting to say that "support" and "independence" stress this feature of our position, since they can be construed to mean that even when in gross error we are not the entire creators of what we are aware of.

But it is questionable whether the whole issue can be made clear without invoking Being in all its unity and variety. The various words I have been using—"presence," "objectivity," "independence," "support"—are merely ways of stressing, more vividly than one can at first do with the ancient word itself in its present condition, the various roles played by Being in our cognitive awareness. We do not do these words justice if we do not take this last step: they are pointers only, and remain notably deficient if we hesitate to invoke that which completes them. We may say then, that in awareness we enjoy always the *support* of the independence of *Being,* so that even our most trivial and muddled act of awareness is not a solipsistic one. The common strand in presence belongs, on this showing, to the unity of Being, and the differences summed up in the expression "present *as*" belong to its variety. Yet so to put it is to court the fundamental error of considering that this common strand—the most vague thing in awareness of presence—gives us in itself what philosophers have intended by such a phrase as Being *qua* Being. For if we apprehend the latter at all, presumably we then apprehend somewhat more than what will barely rescue reason from solipsism. The common strand in presence may indeed depend upon the unity of Being, but, if we are to deal with the latter more than vaguely, we can not then avoid that difficult double character of presence: the fact that in any state of awareness that is more than trivial we have also to deal with presence *as* of a certain sort. That was why, in my earlier list of examples, I included "present *as* Being as such."

One difficulty in seeing the compatibility of realistic and idealistic insights is surely our obsession with sense perception conceived of as a physical transaction; a corollary of this is a limited view of the idea of independence, derived from taking the external world as its paradigm. Independence seemed to involve a physical separation or gap, which we were called upon to bridge in order to effect a proper knowledge. *Here* the subject, *there* the object; the knower *here*, the world *out there*, in inviolable integrity that mocks our efforts to remain *here* and yet reach *out there* to share in its being. The expedients of idealism aside, there seems something forever unattainable in that being; a thought that is reinforced by the conviction that we should not in any case *really* attain it did we not somehow manage to share just the integrity it possesses. And as its integrity is mute, inarticulate, dark, that of something that abides forever in itself, reason's efforts to attain to it seem both self-contradictory and deficient in the dignity that belongs to that being. It does *not* seem at all to detract from the soundness of these observations that empiricist scepticism intervened to show that the "natural" view, which gave rise to these prejudices, is indefensible; it still established the framework for the ideal that the various desperate expedients of idealism were aimed at salvaging. Some of these expedients repair the gap only at the expense of the independence in the object that first caused the idea of the gap to arise. In different ways this holds for the *esse-percipi* doctrine as well as for the doctrine that reason must somehow create what it truly knows. Other solutions acknowledge that the gap is irreparable; Kant, for instance, holds that universality and necessity (as well as other cognitive ideals) come from "within" and cannot possibly really characterize what lies "without."

We are, in radically originative reflection, driven to no such unnatural identification of knower and known, because we were not initially perplexed by the physical separation that our dependence upon sense perception makes so salient a feature of the knowledge problem. Nor did we feel the corollary obsession with the inadequacy of knowing, *just by being what it is,* to that reality upon which it was directed. That obsession amounts to a conviction of original sin that leads those victimized by it to try to turn cognitive awareness into an inarticulate mode of being that imitates the pristine integrity from which it has supposedly declined. In taking cognitive awareness "in its own terms" we point to the independence of what we know by describing it as a causal factor that *supports* the act of cognitive awareness in which it is present to us. What we know is not an *ingredient* in reason, but a factor in the *exercise* of the basic *function* of reason, and a terminology that requires that what is a factor in this sense must also be an ingredient in some other sense destroys what is important in the act—precisely the cognitive *awareness*—in trying to save it.

That something should thus be a factor in an act of cognitive awareness, even though in its sensory aspects it is separated from the knower, and that *it* should be a factor in a sense not entirely elucidated by considering "messages" transmitted by light reflected from its surface, is a matter we are not called upon to explain in terms less concrete than those in which we know it. The structure of radically originative reflection itself is the structure of what in this section we have been discussing in terms of recognition. Our reflective act brings about cognitive awareness of the support given us in awareness by the presence of the "object"; or we may say that we *recognize* that support in the technical sense here advanced. Nor are we involved in any regress of "supports" as we might be if we sought to ground presence empirically.

Just as the satisfaction or achievement that is cognitive awareness involves an assent to presence that is assessed in radically reflective terms, so also there is an assent to presence in the *dissatisfaction* that accompanies every act of reason. What we are aware of supports the act of awareness and in doing so yields a sense of presence, but it also resists us and here too yields a sense of presence. Recognition is always partial, and if the discontent or restlessness of reason in the face of this comes from "within" it is also, like the satisfactions of reason, realized in what lies "without." We feel that we do not fully comprehend what lies before us: it is present to us even in those regions of it that balk our efforts to bring it into view, present indeed *as balking* our efforts at insight. We are never confronted with a presence of which we are aware *tout court*, but what is present is always present as an incitement to a more ample awareness. Both as to its unity and variety there is something deficient even in a cognitive awareness brought about under the guidance of radically originative reflection, and this deficiency I realize *in* my grasp of what lies before me, which in this sense taunts me even as it partially satisfies me.

*XI. Radically originative reflection permits us to intro-
duce some organization into the varied cognitive
interests of reason: within the framework of a central
"concrete" interest that issues in radically originative
reflection itself, we dispose other interests of a more
"abstract" character. The central interest is characterized by its concern for a coincidence of awareness and
understanding; the others, by a deliberate diremption
of awareness and understanding. This diremption
gives us a fruitful contrast of reason and experience,
which is not fruitful, however, in establishing the
limits of reason. The central interest, which is present, though vaguely, before philosophy, when further
developed issues in metaphysics.*

The word "concrete" has been used in so many ways in our
time as to require delicate handling to be of any further service.
The concreteness of the intent that leads to radically originative reflection is defined initially by the very ample complex
of subjective forces from which it springs; although it was our
intent to deploy the fullest resources of reason, it was a reason
rooted in the full subjectivity of the person that was at issue,
and one whose fate depended upon the proper realization of
that subjectivity: we were moved by a cry *from* the heart that
was also a cry *for* the heart. There are, to be sure, other claims
on the word "concrete," and it could be said that every attitude
has its own standard of concreteness, and that not all attitudes
bear upon the fate of reason so directly as does the present one.
When I. A. Richards spoke of poetry as our "completest mode
of utterance" he was surely urging upon us a claim about the
concreteness of poetry. I have no quarrel with that, but one
might add that it is only when we settle upon what is *concrete
for reason* that we find ourselves able to make pronouncements
with any authenticity about the relative concreteness of poetry.
This, of course, emerges clearly enough from the side of our

reflective act that makes us autonomous before modes of experience—the act gives us some grounds for asserting that philosophy is, in Whitehead's words, the critic of abstractions, and it therefore has strong claims to concreteness.

Besides the amplitude of its roots, besides the autonomy with regard to standards of concreteness in which it issues, our reflective act may lay claim to an authenticated grasp of Being, which manifests itself as an apprehension of both reason's "objects" and reason itself. The basis of this claim has already been laid in our discussion of the emergence of articulated understanding as the fruit of direct awareness, as well as in our discussion of generality. We may now formulate it by saying that an utterly general understanding that is also a direct awareness necessarily involves Being, whatever else it may also involve; and that, set over against this mode of understanding, any mode that cultivates a diremption of awareness and understanding is "abstract." It is none the worse for that: some of the most important activities of reason turn precisely upon a rejection of the coincidence of awareness and understanding. Indeed, the present amplitude and diversity of reasonable activities depends upon a constructive power in which reason turns precisely *away* from what it is directly aware of in experience in order to produce conceptual structures—languages, theories, systems—that eventually enable it to understand better what it is directly aware of. Any "concrete" view of reason that avoids this issue (and many of the existentially oriented versions of "reason" in our time have seemed to avoid it) must end by repudiating much of what reason has achieved and is achieving—must in fact repudiate the whole scientific tradition of the West, and more particularly, the explosive expansion of scientific understanding that is the salient feature of this century. The abstractness of these activities of reason is in fact their glory, and the only objection from the point of view of radically originative reflection is to an abstract activity that takes itself for the concrete one. The best stance of reason is one in which its various activities are recognized for what they are; and it may surely be supposed that any activity carried on in ignorance of its real status will exhibit serious failings *in that mode*. One mark of such a confusion in science itself today is the continued effort to settle the methodological problems of science while remaining stubbornly within the framework of the scientific method itself: satisfactory accounts of induction, of probability (as distinct from the mathematical techniques of statistics), of the foundations of mathematics, are still wanting, and it is hard to see how they are to be supplied by the mode of knowledge that is in question. The issue is already implicit in Hume's conclusions, just as his distinction between Matter of Fact and Relations of Ideas states clearly a distinction between awareness and understanding that is assumed by science and taken for granted in much of the formal inquiry of mathematics and logic.

In speaking of the diremption between awareness and understanding as a characteristic of all "abstract" activities of reason, I oversimplify. The experience or direct awareness that reason turns away from for theoretic purposes is itself complex, involving sometimes a coincidence of awareness and understanding, and sometimes a distinction between them. Even at a common-sense level we now directly articulate our awareness in concepts, now turn our attention away from it to move in a world of concepts—usually to elucidate this world of sensory awareness. But since we are always capable of treating any mode of experience as raw material for a further conceptual interpretation carried out in some independence of it, the point still stands. Although it is often appropriate to speak of "reason experiencing," it is always open to us to make, in the pursuit of some interest or other, a radical distinction between reason and experience.

As to the abstractness of all reasonable activities that depend upon a deliberate diremption between awareness and understanding: that diremption itself defines abstractness initially, because we then take for granted (as an object in the traditional sense) whatever it is that we are aware of: reason suppresses its own status as an ontological expansion responding to Being, and in doing so suppresses important characteristics of Being itself. The controlling image here—a common-place of the empiricist tradition—is the passivity of reason before experience. We take seriously the given character of experience and the constructive power of reason, and some-where between these poles we lose what we wish to find. It is not wholly an overstatement to say that what we understand in science is our conceptual structures, and that there is more of control than of understanding in our dealings with what is directly present to us.

Beyond this feature, one may correlate abstractness with the character of the interest involved, even as I did a while ago in the case of concreteness. The cry from the heart that is a cry for the heart is suppressed in this activity and must find its outlet through other channels. Once again, who would object to that, so long as our subjective dynamisms found somewhere an appropriate expression and satisfaction in all their ampli-tude? But if we deny them their appropriate role in the onto-logical expansion of reason; if we deny them a potential status as the Eros that Plato had in mind, as the Dionysiac energy in the service of Apollo that is our greatest lesson from the Greeks, as the Love bent on understanding that is the theme of Dante, then they become what in our failure of control we permit them to be: a dark world of feelings divided from reason and divided one from another—a chaos of drives an-swering to that chaos of clarities (to borrow a phrase someone once used of Voltaire) that makes up so much of our intel-lectual life today. Once we have done so we can, legitimately enough, take them as the subject of a purely scientific inquiry —that is the paradox lying at the root of so much of the psychologism of the century. Yet the cry from the heart per-sists, and drives us, when we do not understand it, to one of the well-meant irrational versions of reason that proliferate in our time. I must repeat that a position like this one is in no sense opposed to the real diversity of our interests: that there is profit and pleasure in geometry, even if it should also be true that we are geometers only by chance, is part of the diversity of our world, and our reflective act is intended to enable us to enjoy this diversity. To put it this way is to anticipate an issue that will be taken up in the next chapter, namely, the association between abstractness and an interest in extensiveness as such.

It was the point of radically originative reflection to understand reason's powers as they really are, not as we think they ought to be. In that sense it is the object of this reflective enterprise to change nothing whatsoever. Yet the shift of focus is a fundamental one, for we move from a situation in which we understood (with varying degrees of adequacy) in the multifarious ways of common sense and science, yet did not understand *what* we understood or *how*, to a situation in which we begin to grasp this. We therefore transform the *object* of our knowledge, the *self-confidence* of reason, and the *ambitions* of reason. This (if true) must permeate all the concerns of common sense and science, even as, in a different way, ordinary language philosophers would claim that analysis of the logic of language leaves everything as it was, yet profoundly alters our grasp of our world. A change in reason's self-knowledge must resound through all its activities, transforming all of them, not restoring an old and too naive composure, but establishing a new one. We can say that we change nothing whatever only in the sense that a distinction between our *concrete* and *abstract* activities is already present, though vaguely, in the common-sense attitude that dominates so much of the life of the ordinary man, and so much of the working life of scientists and philosophers as well. With regard to concrete interests and activities, as I shall claim, even now understanding and awareness coincide. Against this background other activities depending upon a diremption of understanding and awareness go on, but the background is not attended to, remains vague, and is therefore denied. After the act of radically originative reflection not only does our sense of concreteness become clearer, but we also become aware that the abstract activities go on *in* a background, and our understanding of these is enriched: we find that we understand more clearly *what* we are doing and that this clarity depends upon a coincidence of understanding and awareness with respect to the background.

Consider first my attitude to the garden that lies below me. I am aware of it in a way that involves my senses and, as I can speak about it, presumably I have some understanding of it. It seems at first glance easy to separate my understanding from my awareness. As I speak about it I invoke the whole structure of our language, together with the range of categories that binds together at least the group of languages with which we are most familiar. I use the word "categories" only as an example, and the categories of Kant or Aristotle may be thought of indifferently here, or even the flexible and pragmatically oriented categories of C. I. Lewis. I invoke, in any case, language structures not made explicit in any single utterance such as mine about the garden. We very readily then suppose that my awareness is of—well, whatever brute fact is out there, while my understanding is of the categories or concepts we normally employ.

It is especially easy to do this because sensory awareness is habitual and continuous, even when our attention is elsewhere. The breeze rolled through the treetops just now, making a watery movement of light in the room; I noticed it and speak of it to illustrate a point, but the same thing has often happened while I have been thinking of something else, and how natural it then was to think of myself as concerned with a web of ideas, while the world stirred about me in some subrational presence. Clearly, did my simplest utterance about the garden not invoke the whole panoply of language, I could not either understand it or communicate it. Therefore, even setting aside a naïve epistemology that should say that what I understand is always *ideas,* is it not true to say that what I understand is something general, if only general in the sense in which what today is called the "logic" of a language is general; while what I am aware of is as incurably particular as just this garden before me, just that watery movement of light? The separability of awareness and understanding makes the difficulty persist even in face of the fact that *I* at least seem to understand this very garden that I am aware of and the fact that *you*, in understanding what I say invoke (however vaguely) the memory of experiences that furnish an imaginative surrogate for the garden.

Yet against this we find that, even in our common-sense understanding of our world, we are aware of, as well as understand, something general, and that the awareness of and the understanding of what is thus general tend to coincide. We are not very clear about this at a common-sense level, but many if questioned would say that they are aware of and understand "reality," "being," or "the world." The vagueness of all this makes the word "general" not quite applicable here, but it would surely be correct to say that we are aware of what is before us as set in a background of which we are also aware. This room, this garden, this occasion can each of them be a background for a more minute observation, but these themselves appear to me as set in a background that is much more extensive. Whatever is the object of attention qualifies its background, but we do not think of the background as a mere assemblage: we think of each thing we can isolate as in and of a background, and we are aware of making an abstraction when we lift things *from* this background. And—what is perhaps more important—the concepts (or linguistic structures, categories, symbolic forms) that we employ in speaking about this room, this garden, this day, also stubbornly refuse to be separated wholly from a background. I cannot attend to them at all, cannot perform any act of understanding with them, without invoking this background, and, even when I wish to say that I understand and *am aware of* precisely these concepts, they insist on appearing to me as qualifying a background of which I am also aware. Let me operate with symbols however formal, and I still think of what I come to understand (perhaps some theorem in logic) as an aspect of this vague background "world" or "reality." Moreover, this background is in no sense different from the background we are aware of when we are aware of the garden before us. Common sense may often be muddled and vague about Reality, but it never supposes that there is no Reality, only realities.

These observations apply no less to the activities of science than to those of common sense. There are, however, more difficulties in the way of seeing this. Speaking again of the garden, we may say that the problem of an adequate scientific understanding of it is the problem of erecting *a priori* structures of more specialized intent, which a more specialized (and frequently more fine-grained) observation of the garden could be shown to invoke, and which would tie these observations to many other partially similar and partially different observations, even as a common-sense observation of the garden is tied by common-sense categories to many other observations. Just this constructive power is a difficulty, for we seem to have not a coincidence of awareness and understanding, but a deliberate effort to turn away from what we are aware of to construct conceptual systems, and these systems then seem to be *what* we understand. (We are, then, it is true, aware *of* what we construct, and this in a different way from our awareness *of* the categories of language, for we have not deliberately constructed the latter.) Yet important parallels remain with the common-sense condition: we find our fine-grained observations *in* a vague background just as we found our common-sense observations in a vague background, so that, though we are aware *of* what we observe, we are aware of it as qualifying a background of which we also are aware: and we find our constructed systems also in a vague background which they qualify, so that, however much we like to think of them as "pure" constructions, we seem also to get through them an awareness of characteristics of that background. Again, the two backgrounds of awareness and understanding tend to coincide. Even systems that turn out to be logically coherent but otherwise inapplicable seem to tell us something of that background; we may wish to think of them embodying mere relations of ideas, but it takes an act of high abstraction indeed to do this.

The truth is that even before an act that should place us

in a more adequate possession of reason's powers, even now, when reason wields so many powers without being able to give a clear account of what it is doing, we can make out a case for saying, at least of our grasp of the wider framework within which we discriminate particulars, "no awareness, no understanding." To explain why it often seems otherwise, we have only to point out that awareness and understanding have many layers and that a mixture of vagueness and clarity runs throughout them. There are layers of attention, shifts of emphasis; in some moods (say that of an epistemological enterprise) we concentrate so intently on *some* of what we are aware of in the act of understanding, that we forget what in other moods we are prepared to recognize: we detach things from the background and deny the background. Or again, we are skilled at developing our understanding in and with systems, but are never quite clear about what we are doing when we do this; we understand and are aware of something, but are not sure what it is we are aware of.

In connecting what I have here called the background with a concrete interest, I have been expounding an approximation. We might sum it up by saying that when we pursue our concrete interest there is a coincidence of awareness and understanding with regard to reality, vaguely understood; and that when we pursue abstract interests we construct systems that are objects of understanding and can be used to deal with what particular items we then think ourselves to be *merely* aware of. The approximation lies in the fact that the background I speak of is not a *merely* general framework: it is a framework constituted also of particulars, for common sense, though sure enough about Reality is equally sure about realities.

I do not suppose that the foregoing account of a concrete background in which there is, even in the pre-philosophic state, a vaguely apprehended coincidence of understanding and awareness will produce philosophical conviction. But I suspect that there is no one who in *some* mood (perhaps more or less habitual) has not accepted this kind of coincidence, even if he has denied it when engaged in what he takes to be a more reliable analysis of the situation. In radically originative reflection we do not take refuge in a mood, or indeed in habit, neither of which can give us an ultimate standard for what is present to us. We make instead a philosophic decision that leads to a recognition of both reason's powers and the possessions already gained by those powers. In this reflective act, then, the concrete interest emerges into self-consciousness and is justified; after which it can pursue its own bent further and distinguish itself from more abstract interests. It is here that we can expect to find the most important of the changes in the life of reason foreseen at the outset of this section; but I suggest that we shall also find, as was also foreseen, that much in reason's activity as we now know it will remain unaltered except for an access of self-consciousness that may remove some of our present confusion about these activities.

Consider first the further pursuit of the concrete interest. It is important that the emergence of that interest into self-consciousness is very far from being the complete satisfaction of it; for, though we awaken to reason's powers and its possessions, we have by no means then entered into an unqualified and complete possession of the real. It is not only, as I remarked earlier, that there is always a partial dissatisfaction that accompanies any of reason's satisfactions; beyond this, the very character of our recognition puts the better possession of the real before us a task, and one that is within our power. In that recognition we saw the root of all understanding in the *production* of an awareness, or, as we may also say, in the *making accessible* of presence, out of which articulation and discourse emerge as the fruit. We cannot therefore assume that the task of awareness is already at an end, and that we have only to theorize about what we are thus aware of.

The successful issue of such a developed concrete interest is metaphysical knowledge, and the sense in which that knowledge is independent of experience (as ordinarily construed) is the sense in which philosophical questions are distinct from those of science and common sense. In the interplay of this developing knowledge with more abstract interests lies one chief task of reason the governor. But it may well be that the main outcome of such an interplay would lie in the justification it would give us for recognizing these other tasks as abstract. I do not mean that we should have settled anything merely by successfully establishing the abstractness of these activities. What we require is to see *how* each activity is related to concreteness, and this in turn is simply to understand these activities more adequately than we now do. We may hope to understand *what* exactly it is that we understand when we engage in these activities; what methodological problems are worth pursuing and what arise out of a faulty starting point. We may hope to decide how far we are justified in thinking of the theoretic structures we employ in science as *constructed* entities, and how far in thinking of the elaboration of any such structure in terms of the *recognition* of some *aspect* of the real—may indeed hope to find out what exactly we mean or ought to mean by an aspect of the real. It may well be that a heightened sense of the concrete would suggest new approaches for theoretic constructs and to that extent help remove some of the impasses of science; on the other hand, it might turn out that the nature of the real dictates that in the approach by way of theory there must always be a certain proliferation of theories that supplement one another without being susceptible of unification. But in all this there is no reason to suppose that radically originative reflection would alter that diremption of awareness and understanding that the building of systems and the testing of systems in science seems to require; this of course corresponds to the restricted distinction between reason and experience developed in section X.

I do not mean, of course, to restrict the term abstract to the proceedings of the empirical sciences and to the less systematic use of reasoning in going about our ordinary occasions. The construction of "pure" systems can also be approached in such a way as to raise some at least of the expectations considered above; to these we might add whatever clarification of the status of these systems we should gain from a fresh approach to the problem of universals, and to the problem of the status of the ideals that govern our framing of such systems.

More important for our present purpose is the status of our common-sense apprehension of the real. If radically originative reflection issues in an awakened concrete interest, presumably we have an obligation to describe our pre-philosophic common-sense knowledge as also abstract. Yet there is, as I noticed earlier, a "vague" concreteness inherent in common sense from the beginning. At this point the present view makes common cause with Husserl's conception of the life-world and with some insights of the ordinary language movement. There *is* a sense in which common sense is indefeasible. At the same time it *is* vague in the pre-reflective state and demands, if not the correction of science, at least the deepening that reflection makes possible. The difficulty is, though, that the world of common sense is ambiguous, its significance differing according as we see it as the correlative of different activities. With an awakened common sense we have no quarrel; indeed our reflective act claims to be that awakened common sense, and to give us adequately just that world of the garden. This world we are indeed sure of much of the time, though timorous of our right to be sure of it. What is *really* abstract, and this time in a pejorative sense not intended in the case of science, is the simulacrum of common sense that arises sometimes from poor philosophy, sometimes from a misunderstanding of scientific conclusions, sometimes from our tendency to think of what we find in the world as only a collection of obstacles to, or instruments for, the attaining of our ends.

5

PHILOSOPHICAL KNOWLEDGE AND
THE SPECULATIVE-EMPIRICAL CYCLE:
PREPARATION FOR METAPHYSICS

I.   The new composure of reason established by radically originative reflection is merely the beginning of a philosophical knowledge directed upon Being. In dealing with traditional objections to the development of such a metaphysical knowledge the responsible autonomy uncovered by radically originative reflection is of the first importance.

This investigation began in an obscure groping towards a self-realization in which reason should preside, the whole movement being governed by the presentiment that without this concrete emergence of reason the various other powers of the self—powers of doing and making—would find no adequate outlet. And, because the self too remained problematic while reason remained so, the whole movement was directed towards self-knowledge, even as philosophy itself has been from the beginning. This peculiarly concrete mode of self-knowledge was conceived of as inseparable from our knowledge of the world: our whole effort was, in fact, to recognize our world in and with the light in which we recognized reason itself. But our first efforts set us only at the portals of an adequately concrete knowledge; we must now press on with this topic.

Our starting point leads us to more than a simple composure of reason that allows us to go about our various reasonable occasions with confidence, and more than a dumb acceptance of the concrete that rids us of neurotic self-doubt. I think of it also as a liberation to a task recognizably metaphysical, and as such capable of revivifying many of our other pursuits. We are interested in more than a secure possession of the world of the garden: we wish also to set that world in a web of systematic completeness embodied in the general theoretic utterance now largely discredited in the West except for purely scientific theories. Not that we would know it scientifically; it is simply that an order of which science is but one exemplification, rather than the prototype, must be attainable if our approach to the concrete is to yield us more than the mute *rapport* with things that some varieties of existentialism seem to offer us. Reason's affinity with its "objects," and its ability to realize its nature in apprehending *them* rather than simulacra of its own devising, we may hope to have shown, but surely we need in a truly philosophical knowledge more than an inarticulate savoring of things, and more indeed than the articulate savoring of things that is one part of the poet's task.

There were of course many intimations of all this in the preceding chapter, for the point was frequently made that radically originative reflection must bring us also to Being itself. It was not appropriate, however, to make this issue central where we were concerned first of all to establish the composure of a reason uncertain even of its most basic rights. Had I begun directly with the old problem of metaphysical knowledge in all its intricacy, it would have been all too easy to lose sight, in the dust this old controversy always raises, of the chief good a starting point in radically originative reflection affords us: a secure command of reason's responsible autonomy. But in this chapter the topic of Being will finally become central, and will then dominate the discussion in the next.

Before it can do so, however, we must traverse again, though with a somewhat different gaze, some of the ground we have already been over. That is because, in attempting to make the full issue of our reflective act clear, we at once call into the field some of the traditional objections that were avoided earlier.

But as a preliminary to this I must emphasize again the condition that governs our whole approach to Being. Once we understand it we have the end of a thread that will guide us through a labyrinth of traditional difficulties. Consider first the topic of generality. If the awareness of presence issues in an articulate understanding, if the understanding is itself an enjoyment of presence, then presence is itself general. I marked this by speaking of cognitive presence, and we may speak here of cognitive awareness. Not that it is *only* general, being as it is continuous also with sensation, which focuses our awareness upon the multiplicity of things, so that the whole activity exhibits a tension of general and particular, of One and Many. I have suggested that the cognitive presence of any individual entity of this Many is inseparable from the presence of something that is One—the presence, that is, of Being. The generality that emerges with understanding is therefore the utter generality of Being, which is coincidental with our ability to recognize discrete individuals. If we turn now to consider our reflective act, the situation is much the same: it encounters both the diversity of a world of discrete individuals (it is *your* reason and *my* reason, in any one moment of its exercise) and the unity of Being (it is *reason* in you and me that is at work winning its way into its own *general* dimension). There are other aspects to generality that were dealt with in the previous chapter and need not be rehearsed. Suffice it that this complex satisfaction of reason, which I spoke of earlier as producing a matrix for all rational and empirical criteria, is from the first a satisfaction in beings and Being. The governing condition of this approach to Being is, however, the secure exercise of reason's creative and responsible autonomy. It is the root work of reason to bring beings and Being into cognitive awareness, and to enjoy in this act an archetype of rational and empirical satisfaction; it is the achievement of reason in radically originative reflection to initiate a like cognitive awareness of its own being at its work, and to see its fitness for that work and for that reflective exercise. This achievement is an archetype of rational and empirical satisfaction that authenticates the first one, for part of it is nothing but the secure exercise of responsible autonomy.

This governing condition means that we do not merely claim that we need only open ourselves to a knowledge of Being as I once looked down on that English garden, and as I now look down the vine-clad flank of the Alban Hills to the plain below. Even if I were to go further and make the claim that in enjoying what now lies before me—the children playing in the vineyard, the hill towns of Cori and Roccamassima standing out on the olive-silvery hills across the long slope, and the Cape of Circe in the distance, its visibility, my hostess tells me, a sign of a change in the weather—I enjoy a cognitive awareness of Being in which all this reposes, I am little better off. Every version of experience, every version of self-evidence, is questionable. Why should the combining of these satisfactions in the doctrine of cognitive awareness fare better, unless reason's right to it is also established? If we lose sight of the gains of radically originative reflection, our investigation loses its impetus, and we relapse into the very doubts and confusions we are trying to escape from. Holding to it, we exercise reason's autonomy upon itself, confirm its fitness for a penetrative reflective exercise, and win our way to the exercise of reason's autonomy throughout its dominions. I therefore rightfully exercise it to give me all the variety of this moment in the Italian landscape, and all the unity of it in the Being that is compresent with it.

Thenceforward, the capacities of the direct and reflective components in reason's life develop together. We may now go on to deepen our cognitive awareness of Being, but without ever supposing that it is merely the simultaneous enjoyment of "experiential" and "rational" satisfactions, grounded upon that Being, that brings this deepening about. It is the reflective autonomy that is crucial, so that the deepening of our command of Being is also the increasing of the adequacy of the reflective component. As we do not wish a version of Being imposed by an habitual level of attention, so we must always work at an improvement of reason's self-consciousness: it is the release of reason's powers in Being to bring about a deeper cognitive awareness of it that is at issue.

II. *When we seek a systematic metaphysical knowledge in which articulate understanding is the fruit of awareness, we demand the simultaneous satisfaction of two ideals posed by rationalism and empiricism respectively. Despite everything that has been said in the previous chapters, these ideals appear to be in conflict: the completeness proposed by the rationalist ideal seems irreconcilable with the extensiveness and incompleteness of experience.*

When we demand a systematic metaphysical knowledge, we are demanding the simultaneous satisfaction of two great ideals for reasonable activity that have haunted every effort to establish its bounds. They are in fact ideal forms of the rational and empirical criteria that we met in the last chapter. The first ideal is that of systematic completeness, which may be summarized by saying that we require of the articulate formulation of our knowledge that it exhibit unity, generality, and order. The ideal requires further specification before it applies with exactness to any particular philosophic or scientific ideal: we can alter the whole sense of it, for instance, according as we construe order in terms of a formal deductive system or in terms of some such teleological image as that of the great chain of being. That, however, is part of the point. I mean to describe an ideal that can be discerned in the rationalist side of a great many philosophic and scientific outlooks. The following are only some of the forms it takes: Plato's description of ideal knowledge in the *Republic*; Kant's concern both with the constitutive universality and necessity he thought he found in synthetic *a priori* judgments, and with the systematic completeness that the Ideas of Reason, as regulative principles, propose as a goal for reason; the intuitive-deductive ideal of Descartes, and, *mutatis mutandis*, of Spinoza; the ideal of classical physics from Newton through Einstein's final efforts at a unified field theory; various modern efforts to unite logic and mathematics in a single deductive system; and Whitehead's conception of speculative philosophy as the effort to frame a coherent, logical, necessary system of general ideas.

The second ideal is that all knowledge must be of or about what is in some sort present to a subject (or a knower, a consciousness, an awareness, a mind, a reason) independently of wish or will. What is known must be present to us; what can be known must be capable of becoming present, or, at the least, our knowledge must be capable of being reduced to, resolved in, or grounded upon, such presence. As one recalls the ambiguity of presence, which must have been patent in the distinction made in the preceding chapter between what something is present *as* and the fact *that* something is present, it may well be protested that this is an unhappy approximation of the empirical ideal, which was after all intended to provide us with a foundation in some utterly reliable experience. Why not put forward instead some version of that most persistent factor in empiricism, sensation? Or, if some more general word is wanted, why not simply "experience"? But an appeal to experience, while it is surely intended to be an appeal to the incontestably certain, is as ambiguous as any appeal to presence, as the history of philosophy readily teaches us; while an appeal to sensation, although more specific, can yet be taken in many ways, ranging from Hume's impressions to whatever it is sensation offers us when we appeal to it on a common-sense level. But beyond this *tu quoque* the use of the idea of presence, as defined in part in the preceding chapter, allows me to deal fairly with the empirical aspects of the issues I am now raising, and yet to do so in terms compatible with the fresh approach to the problem of reason and experience that our reflective act affords us. We thus prepare in advance for the objections that still remain to be developed.

More specifically, the advantages of posing the second ideal in terms of presence are these.   FIRST, the attractiveness of the appeal to experience results in part from the assumption that there is something brute and uncontrived about experience, not only in the sense that it is independent of our wish and will, but also in the sense that there is something sub-rational about it. What we really experience we do not experience by means of reason but by means of something more primitive and incapable of general utterance. This is in part what authenticates it, as we might authenticate what is evident to sight by appealing to the evidence of touch as being independent of it and more basic. So experience is thought of as the touch of reason, supposedly different in kind, more basic, and because of this, more trustworthy. The use of the idea of presence allows us to suggest, without in any way impugning the appeals to sensory evidence we make in science and in common-sense activities, that the sub-rationality of such appeals requires the kind of correction outlined in the discussion of sensation in the preceding chapter.

SECOND, by invoking the idea of presence we are able to put the disagreement between rationalism and empiricism into proper perspective. It is not sufficiently recognized that rationalisms make appeals analogous to empirical appeals. Empirical philosophers object to rationalist metaphysics because knowledge claims are made there without either any direct experience of the supposed reality to which they are intended to apply, or any grounding in experience that would make them tenable by inference. Yet it would surely be unfair to many of the great rationalists to say that they have no interest in the kind of groundwork that experience is supposed to provide. There is hardly a rationalism of any influence that does not have a high regard for experience in the wider sense of presence. Thus

Descartes' first argument for the existence of a Perfect Being in the *Meditations*—surely an extreme example of the rationalist approach to metaphysics—rests on the supposed presence to a thinking being of the idea of a Perfect Being, that presence having something in common with the presence of all ideas (it is presence *as* an idea), and something distinctive too (it is the presence of just *this* idea that is at issue). There are many other prominent examples. To Plato the Forms and their interrelations are present to intelligence in a way in which the passing ingredients of the world cannot be; and even the Form of the Good, different as it is said to be from the other Forms, is held to be ultimately accessible to *nous,* and in that sense capable of becoming present to us.

THIRD, we are able to see that the empiricist's judgment of the significance of the rationalist ideal of unity, generality, and order depends upon his assessment of the presence of systems of ideas exemplifying it. If the presence of the ideas seems to be derivative from another and more authentic presence, so much the more problematic is the status of that ideal. Thus Hume's claim that ideas are faded impressions establishes a framework within which the truth of systems conforming to the ideal appears to be analytic, its usefulness obvious when tied to observation, but no less a puzzle for that.

But despite any help the idea of presence may eventually give us in reconciling the two ideals, the objections are formidable enough. It has generally been thought by most scientists, and by many philosophers, including not a few who are metaphysically oriented, that the ideals are not to be satisfied simultaneously in a perfected philosophical knowledge, and that the most we can hope for is to bring those certainties gained in the pursuit of unity, generality, and order into harmony with those gained in the pursuit of presence. We must, to revert to a more common terminology, ground our theoretic efforts in experience.

Our difficulty is not just that there is something brute

and given about experience, a quality of simple *occurrence* that takes no account of wish or will; it is rather that there is an extensiveness to it that seems to forbid our complete survey of it. If we return to one of our earlier formulas, and speak of reason *experiencing*, we remember that the whole point of this activity was said to lie in our winning our way into the presence of what is in some sense *there*. And if I now regard my apprehension of the vineyard sloping downhill below the terrace as an achievement of reason, I must remember that it was once an English garden that furnished me with an example; and as for the vineyard, it might have been something else, it alters subtly as I write, and, though there have been vines here since the Romans, it will eventually pass away. Was it not just the close observation of this aspect of experience—an aspect that persists however we reinterpret it—that disabused men long ago of the ancient folly of reason's boundless dominion? It is in fact what Kant called the *matter* of experience that is at issue, and we do not expect to find unity, generality, and order there. The concrete, so understood, is what it is, and . . . what it shall be; besides, much of it is "elsewhere"; we can neither survey it totally nor anticipate all its surprises. Kant's statement of the problem is of course classic: there being no wholeness to experience, how can we expect to satisfy all of reason's aspirations there, even if we cannot help using these aspirations to guide us in what is within our reach? It is also very much to the point that when he thought he found in the texture of our common experience a generality suited to the demands of a deterministic science, he at once concluded that we do not deal in our common experience with the concrete (or, as he would say, the thing in itself) but with something whose form is a product of the understanding.

Reason wants unity, generality, and order, and our passion for this, as somehow bound up with the full realization of the self in all its affective intricacy, moved us to look again at the possibility of philosophical knowledge. But how can a philosophical reason expect to find this ideal in a concrete understood as something to be experienced?

The other side of the difficulty becomes plain as soon as we consider the effort to give the conceptual structures established by reason in the theoretic pursuit of unity, generality, and order a proper foundation in experience. At once we think of reason and experience as *separate* realms, and express this in several commonly accepted contrasts: reason deals with *sense data*; it supplies the *form* for a *matter* given by the senses; it deals with *ideas*, which bear an obscure relation to *things*; we think in *concepts*, experience involves *percepts*; in experience we confront the *concrete*, but reason deals with *abstract* things that are surrogates for the concrete. And when, in the interest of some more direct and "absolute" apprehension of things, we try to make reason itself descend into the arena in which the concrete can be confronted, we find it hard not to do what Bergson has seemed to so many to do: to reduce reason to a sub-rational *Gefühl*, buying the sinuosities of the concrete at the expense of the generality we rightly cherish in reason itself.

Reason wants the real, the concrete, what is there, what is the case. How can it descend to it without losing unity, generality, and order? How can it descend to it, indeed, without losing that very articulation that we have been supposing all along to be inseparable from understanding?

III. *But the objections to philosophical knowledge arise from too abstract a setting, in which we misconceive the extensiveness of experience. Abstractness is now defined in terms of the speculative-empirical cycle, and this cycle is now seen as taking place within a more concrete frame, defined by a more concrete activity of reason: reason as (responsible) originator of the frame is contrasted with reason as the inhabitant of the frame.*

These are formidable enough difficulties, but they become less so when we notice that we cannot even formulate them without assuming a setting that is not the appropriate one for determining the limits of reason. It is an inevitable setting for many of our problems, but as soon as we take it for reason's only setting we find not only that we cannot give reason a metaphysical scope, but besides that we cannot even see how we have the right to go about solving the problems for which it *is* the appropriate setting.

The setting is one in which the extensiveness of experience, with which I was so concerned in the previous section, is overwhelmingly clamant. We see ourselves as experiencing an intricate diversity of things spread out in the "dimensions" of time and space, and we suppose that our experience extends only to a segment of what is so spread out. If we find or establish an order as we think about that segment, we have only one reason for supposing that it also characterizes what lies beyond, namely, that in the past we have been successful in moving from any limited extensive range to a wider one. It is therefore more appropriate to think of ourselves as *harmonizing* a unity, generality, and order reached in conceptual thought *with* our experience, rather than as *finding* it *in* our experience. The methodologist is at pains to clarify the various complicated means we use to produce this harmony, but it is surely clear that a deductive process, terminating in an interpretation that ultimately furthers our control of experience, is at the root of the matter. There are to be sure less fastidious moments, in which we take it for granted that the conceptual order we progressively articulate marks our progressive control of a "reality" that, however incompletely revealed to us, is yet all of a piece. But it is just the point of this setting that, when we ask ourselves questions about our right to attach this or that significance to the order we discover, we find ourselves compelled to think of this less fastidious attitude as a faith.

If we wish to transpose this description into terms of presence, we must say that in taking this setting for our ultimate one we have simply assumed that all organized knowledge rests on a speculative movement that begins in presence, departs from it (perhaps into a realm of derivative presence) in pursuit of some version of the rationalist ideal, and returns again, by way of deduction, to an accounting in terms of that presence. But the intrusion of the term "presence" is hardly legitimate here. The concern for our right to the procedures of the setting brings out another feature of extensiveness that is decisively at odds with the idea of presence. I have been concerned so far with extensiveness in the sense of a manifold whose boundaries, if they exist, we can never reach: there is always more experience than we can compass. But experience is also subject to extensive division: we can think of ourselves as contracting the temporal and spatial span of attention indefinitely, and, to the degree that a commitment about a wider span seems more difficult to support than one about a smaller span, we suppose that we approach closer to certainty as we do this. The tendency is just as strong as our tendency to think of the extensiveness of experience as its defining characteristic. In practice, though paradoxically, attention to this aspect of experience is what lends plausibility to an atomistic doctrine of sensation like that of Hume, and to the positivistic preference for data expressible (if at all) in such terms as "this green now." Yet could we sharpen our focus so as to limit the extensive span still further, we should presumably get still simpler impressions. Ideally a simple impression is one of minimum extensive import, as well as one of qualitative simplicity.

What is really at issue is that in this setting we find it impossible to accept the presence of entities that *embrace* an extensive span; that are present *throughout* an extensive span, and present there just because extensiveness is but one feature of their presence. This is that old familiar, the denial of the possibility of our apprehending substance, although especially here we do well to use the original Aristotelian word "entity" (*ousia*), whose place, through circumstances I need not go into here, is so often and so inappositely pre-empted by the word "substance." If it is possible for an entity to be present to us, then it is present throughout the extensive range given by its parts and its history, establishing parts *as* parts, and phases *as* phases; but it is precisely this that we boggle at when, in surveying the extensive divisibility of experience, we find it more plausible to say that we experience a sense impression than that we experience an entity. The macroscopic side of the extensiveness of experience seems to forbid systematic completeness; the microscopic side seems to forbid the presence of entities. Yet, touching the latter side, what we are dealing with is only what I described earlier as the ambiguity of presence, and this gives us no more warrant for speaking of the presence of an impression (which has some extensive range, however slight) than for speaking of the presence of an Aristotelian entity. Our unreflective moments present us with no such puzzles; our everyday world is, speaking loosely, a world of Aristotelian entities and of qualities having some reasonably extensive span, just as it is a world in which we suppose that the theoretic order we find in the world of concepts characterizes "reality."

Remembering, then, that the problem of extensiveness, which is so salient in this setting, is a complex one, and that it introduces a fundamental ambiguity into the idea of experience, let us call this cycle of experience—speculation—deduction—experience the *speculative-empirical cycle*. On the one side lies sensation, impressions, or our everyday apprehension of our common world—in short, experience, however interpreted; on the other side ideas, theory, conceptual thought. The cycle characterizes many of our common-sense activities, it characterizes science, and, according to some authoritative testimony, it also characterizes science and metaphysics taken jointly. For Aristotle and Whitehead, for instance, once an extreme unity, generality, and order have been reached in a grasp of "first principles," there is the possibility of a deductive interpretation of the experience from which the departure was made. (In such metaphysical traditions there are hints enough of another ideal, already mentioned, in which the grasp of first principles is also an entering into a direct presence that makes all deductive return to a sensory experience unnecessary. But in so far as this is both a scientific and a metaphysical ideal, in which some deductive relation between metaphysics and science is assumed, the need to return to sense experience to interpret it persists.) We have met the cycle as a setting once before, since it was a prominent feature of the situation we were attempting to escape from at the start—the situation in which the exact role of experience troubled us. In our present encounter with it we find that if "experience" is understood in terms of the common-sense world, then the setting is characterized by a movement between that world and a world of theoretic order, and by the problem of macroscopic extensiveness, which, even if no other considerations intervened, forbids a metaphysics aiming at systematic completeness. If "experience" is understood in a way that calls this world in question, the problem of extensive divisibility then comes to the fore, and becomes so pressing that we have then no reason to trust even the minimal versions of sense-experience put forward by positivists. The first version of the setting is comfortable if we do not press it too far; the second gives rise not only to the difficulties for metaphysics described in the last section, but besides to the question whether the cycle itself can be rationally justified, even in its use in science and common sense. Problems associated with it persist: the problem of induction, given this setting, has resisted all efforts to solve or dissolve it; the analytic-synthetic argument goes on, despite many fresh and ingenious assaults upon it; nor is it even clear that solipsism, that so persistent threat to the peace of mind of empirical philosophers, has really been overcome.

Within this setting there are many glimpses of wider vistas. Kant, in claiming that reason is responsible for the form of experience, suggests to us the possibility that it is also responsible for the framework within which the cycle goes on. Yet the framework is for that reason factitious: we do not, in regarding it, attend to something that might rescue us from the reign of extensiveness—a world of *beings*, perhaps—but merely to a structure that the mind has imposed upon a raw material. And it is this failure to subdue extensiveness on this level, except in a way that is of only subjective import, that makes it necessary that, in aiming at systematic completeness, reason should also be defeated by extensiveness, and should have to content itself with being guided by ideals it can never attain. The contemporary ordinary language movement also tantalizes us with such glimpses. We may construe its doctrine to mean that we need not necessarily turn away from presence to find a theoretic order, but may already possess, in the very logic of our common language, an order that is also the order of what is present to us in common experience; we should then be possessing directly a level of reality correlative to our habitual level of attention. But the panel slides to, like the panel that once opened to reveal a tranquil landscape to the troubled Marius and then closed again; we find ourselves back again in the mere *acceptance* of our common world.[7]

But although the extensiveness of experience, conceived of in terms of the setting, is indeed an obstacle to a philosophical knowledge based upon the continuity of understanding with awareness, we need not take the cycle as our setting, and need not therefore take the extensiveness of experience as an absolute and unqualified one. We awaken to a more concrete framework when we confront reason's autonomy in the real, and when we do so, we see that the cycle takes place within that more concrete framework, finding there its ultimate empirical and rational grounding in this sense, that the empirical and rational criteria employed in the cycle now appear as limitations of what we enjoy in the more concrete framework. This was the sense in which, in the previous chapter, radically originative reflection was held to furnish a "matrix" for all rational and empirical standards. The cycle continues to dominate much of our everyday life, and much of the work of the scientist, since the extensiveness of things is ineluctable; but extensiveness being but one important feature of our new framework, we have transferred the argument to a quite different setting.

The speculative-empirical cycle constitutes but one mode of knowledge then, the other being coextensive with a more concrete framework, as it is coextensive with the responsible autonomy in which we bring the more concrete framework about. In one mode reason inhabits a framework and works within it; in the other it is aware that it has responsibly originated the framework. The more concrete mode, being not completely realized, has therefore not played its proper role in relation to the speculative-empirical cycle, which in turn has fallen short of some of its possibilities. If there is one central thesis to this book, it is that the life of reason is still incomplete, and that it is the job of philosophy to help complete it.

Our reflective act justifies us in *placing* the mode of the speculative-empirical cycle within the frame of the more concrete mode simply because the more concrete mode now comes into full and self-conscious play. In the preceding chapter I described our new starting point by using examples drawn mainly from common sense: radically originative reflection was represented as permitting us to see ourselves as bringing the garden to our cognitive awareness within the "world," which formed the indeterminate boundary of our apprehension, and which was itself brought into cognitive awareness. We thought of reason dealing with various items—the trees, the woman on the bench, the children playing, and so on—not only as simply given to it, but also as achievements in its creative initiation of its own awareness and understanding. But reason's autonomy was held to extend not merely to the garden and its contents, but to the total framework of all of these. The framework was not simply the widest spatio-temporal framework we can envisage—an extensive world that is an extrapolation of what we are familiar with—nor yet a categorial scheme furnishing a formal structure that we impose on something that either lacks one or possesses in itself a quite different one inaccessible to us; but instead, that framework, a puzzle since antiquity, in which the Many are apprehended as One.

But the idea of a framework is itself deceptive to some degree, bringing with it Kantian overtones that make it difficult to attend to the point I wish to make. It is not merely a *formal* structure establishing by its dominance certain formally general features of our apprehension. In the first place, our frame is characterized by all the concrete presence I have tried to emphasize in talking of awareness: we are not merely aware *within* a frame, but the frame itself is both inseparable from all our awareness and is itself an "object" of awareness. The latter point is best made indirectly. As we initiate an awareness of an entity and complete this awareness in articulate understanding, we overcome an extensiveness "internal" to that entity; *if* the entity is present to us, it is present in virtue of an aspect of it that is non-extensive, for who can survey any entity in all its extensive intricacy? To overcome the extensiveness is to apprehend the being of the entity; or, more appropriately, it is to apprehend extensiveness as the extensiveness of a being. But so to initiate cognitive awareness of an entity is also to initiate cognitive awareness of the frame, and thus to overcome an extensiveness "internal" to *it*. This is to apprehend Being, and to apprehend extensiveness in general as a feature of Being. The two operations are inseparable: we overcome the extensiveness internal to an entity only by overcoming the extensiveness internal to the frame; or we may say that we apprehend an item in the Many as *one item* only in so far as we are capable of apprehending the Many as One. In the last chapter we saw the generality of our frame, and indeed the generality inherent in the act of radical reflection itself, to be inseparable from this fact. Universality or generality, wherever we find it, always involves the gathering of many into one, and we invoke the same feature of things when we gather the extensiveness of an entity together in understanding it to be one entity and when we gather the members of a class under a class term—or indeed when we articulate any structure that we organize hierarchically in terms of increasing generality. The contrast of the One and the Many is diverse and intricate, yet everywhere the same. We think of ourselves as producing a cognitive awareness of beings in and with a cognitive awareness of Being, and as suspending within this living tension of the One and the Many all acts of generalizing whatsoever, and therefore all the intricate world of "universals" as well.

Our frame then *is* this contrast of the One and the

Many, but each of this Many possesses its own inner contrast of one and many; which is only to say that when we attend to our frame we attend also to the *being* of whatever it is that is immediately before us. But it is a frame that we responsibly and creatively produce in an act that exhibits and realizes its own contrast of one and many. In one sense our framework is Being; in another it is the reflective expansion of the being of reason itself. Our secure possession of responsible autonomy overcomes the extensiveness of experience, and we are not troubled, as we contemplate our responsibility for the frame of experience, with the same doubts that troubled us when, struck with the extensiveness of experience, we still sought to satisfy there both our "rational" and "empirical" ideals.

It is in this sense that we are able to place the speculative-empirical cycle within the mode of cognitive awareness, which then enframes it, without, however, pre-empting its tasks. But just what are the tasks of the two modes of knowledge? It is a question one had best approach with respect, for it is all too easy to lapse into invidious talk of higher and lower, absolute and relative forms of knowledge. We shall first distinguish the two tasks in outline, and then, in the next chapter, exercise the more concrete mode of knowledge to bring the issue of Being more clearly into view.

IV. *The concrete, philosophical, or metaphysical mode of knowledge is concerned with the uniqueness of each being and therefore with Being in general. Extensiveness is seen as one aspect of Being, and this mode of knowledge consists not so much in an extensive survey, as in a penetration of what is everywhere present. It sees Being in terms of degree; and is unable to formulate in advance a complete definition of the order that would satisfy it or the interest that moves it.*

This discussion, as well as the discussion of the speculative-empirical cycle, is complicated by being in part normative and in part descriptive: we are attempting to describe certain features of the life of reason that are already present and also to permit certain still latent features to emerge.

Our concern in the philosophical mode of knowledge is to bring about a cognitive awareness of whatever entity we attend to. We are interested in its uniqueness as *this* particular entity, but find that that uniqueness is not available to us except to the degree that something else is available to us, namely, what it is to be a unique individual. Yet to the extent we are able to do this, we link our entity at once with all other entities, for what lies at the basis of its individuality lies also at the basis of the individuality of any other entity. We apprehend an individual as such only to the extent that we understand that its individuality means more than *mere* uniqueness. This does not mean that we do not attend to it for what it is in itself: our survey may indeed dwell on all the complexity of its development in time and its disposition in space; on the contrary, we are able to apprehend all this extensive intricacy as genuinely belonging to it only because our apprehension of our entity contains more than what an account confining itself to extensive features could provide. The superficial similarity of this claim to Kant's views on the unifying of a sensuous manifold should not deceive us. We do not pull together and give structure to what would otherwise lack coherence, and as we do so find universality and necessity in the operation; we see instead a unity in the multiplicity and passage *within* any entity only because we see that same unity in multiplicity and passage in general. Our categorial operations issue from this recognition and do not precede it as a precondition of its possibility; that is why our categories are capable of change.

Our cognitive awareness in this mode is therefore a kind of *penetration* of what lies before us, and the further development of it owes nothing whatever to any perusal of the extensiveness of experience that lacks this penetration. This does not mean that an extensive survey is irrelevant to this mode of inquiry; it is simply that an extensive survey that can contribute to it must not be conceived of as an *empirical* extensive survey. The proper significance of an extensive survey appears when we notice that in this mode we do not approach reality as an ungraded collection. If we attend to the uniqueness of what lies before us on any occasion, we find that there is simply more *there* in some cases than in others, and therefore the possibility of increased penetration is sometimes available, sometimes not. There is, then, an analogue to the progressiveness of the empirical side of science, with this important reservation, however, that whatever genuinely new we encounter demands of us an effort more than habitual—a recognition in the technical sense already established.

We have grown so accustomed to dwell upon the extensiveness of experience that we tend to think of it as an unqualified extensiveness: we observe *changing* things *in* time; we see *extended* things *in* space; and we suppose that to overcome these extensive features we have only such permanence as we can find in a world of conceptual structures. Yet the unity we find at the heart of any entity, a unity which, being not peculiar to it, binds it to every other entity in such a way that our apprehension of the individual is already the apprehension of the general, is quite outside time and space. It is not, however, an ideal, but the most concrete thing we can know, present in one sense *in* each entity, in another sense present as that *within* which the extensiveness of the entity finds place. Multiplicity and passage are not pure unqualified aspects of things, present to us *tout court,* no more than the uniqueness of any particular is present to us as a uniqueness *tout court:* we find multiplicity and passage *within* beings, and therefore within Being.

In this sense whatever we know in the first mode of knowledge does not depend only upon extensiveness and therefore is not called in question by the unsurveyed extensiveness of things, except in so far as the latter may conceal opportunities for further penetration in the dimension of hierarchy. In this restricted sense, metaphysics is universal and necessary.

It is to be expected that the conceptual structure in terms of which this knowledge is articulated will exhibit characteristics analogous to the systems that metaphysicians have put forward in the past. But this is very far from saying that one expects a return to systematic metaphysics, seeing that we cannot say in advance exactly what the expected order will consist in. I have deliberately spoken of unity, generality, and order in a sense broad enough to compass a variety of past metaphysical ideals, which are only shadows of what we are trying to establish. One expects to *recognize,* in the sense already established, the order appropriate to this mode of knowledge when we find it. We have already had intimations of how the generality we are looking for must differ from the universality and necessity of a purely formal system like that of the Kantian categories. It must be a reflection of the concrete tension of the One and the Many I have been expounding. The mode of order often called "coherence" must also spring from the same tension: we cannot think of it only in terms of a net of interlinked and mutually supporting concepts, except as such a network might result from the unfolding of our awareness. The most basic way of putting these points is to observe that this mode of knowledge, under the guidance of radically originative reflection, is exactly the mode in which the matrix for all rational and empirical criteria, discussed in Chapter 4, is formed. In one sense that matrix *is* the responsible autonomy of reason in self-conscious action; in another sense it is what that autonomy progressively articulates as it develops: the matrix is a living one. The ideals for systematic order that we establish to suit our various special purposes are properly, then, limitations of an order that we progressively define as we progressively articulate our knowledge in this mode. Thus the order we demand in axiomatized systems was represented in the previous chapter as a limitation of an order that emerges from our understanding of presence in the most concrete sense. The difficulties about the definition of an ideal rational order are of course the obverse of difficulties about final criteria for experience: we cannot know in advance the criteria for all modes of presence, although we can be sure of our responsible autonomy in dealing with them.

A corollary to our pursuit of an ideal order that we are as yet unable to define with any precision is our inability to attach any final general meaning to such key terms in metaphysical speculation as "cause," "essence," "freedom," "entity," "power," although in special and limited contexts we might define them to our satisfaction. They are words we are concerned to develop as we press forward in the exercise of reason's autonomy. The next chapter is devoted to some of these issues.

There are parallel difficulties with regard to the interest, the affective complex, the passion, that moves us to develop this mode of knowledge. We may tentatively speak of the general interest of reason, but, just as the character of reason's satisfaction (a satisfaction in "order") emerges only as this mode of knowledge develops, so the interest that seeks the satisfaction remains to a like degree opaque. The important point here is that, while we normally define an interest in terms of some accepted framework, we are here concerned in the very *development* of a framework: the development of a framework for all our knowledge, and the development of the whole person considered as a framework for all our activities. We do not know in detail what we mean by the integrity of the person; we have only approximations—approximations just as puzzling as the ethical disputes to which the formulation of one of them instantly gives rise; and, because we do not, an interest that seeks integrity must remain obscure. The difficulty is, *mutatis mutandis*, the one Kant met when, unwilling to define any impulse that moves us to the autonomous self-legislation of the categorical imperative as an "interest" in the ordinary sense of the word—a sense which, in his case, is correlated with the technical term "inclination"—he was driven to speak of our "*taking* an interest" in the categorical imperative. The action of self-legislation produced, as it were, a new interest; or at least made articulate what theretofore was latent. So here, in prolonging radical reflection in this philosophical mode of knowledge, we progressively articulate the character of the interest that moves us. And since that mode of knowledge is a progressive articulation of what it means to be an entity, it must also be an articulation of what exactly an interest is—of what role interests play in the integrity of an entity. We are dealing, in short, with an entity's interest in its own best integration; and since we define reason always in relation to this, we may speak of this interest approximately as the morality of reason.

A final word, which will be developed in the concluding section of this chapter: this mode of knowledge is self-sufficient and for its own sake, even as the ancients held it to be. It goes about its task integrally: we cannot divide its field in order to deal with it more efficiently; it gives rise in itself to no subsciences, although more specialized interests may cause us to view the field in a variety of other lights.

V. *The speculative-empirical cycle is abstract, first, because of its diremption between awareness and understanding, which makes it necessary to refer it to a framework to justify it; second, because it may subserve a variety of interests, which define a variety of aspects of things, more or less fundamental; third, because of a pervasive interest in binding one extensive region to another; fourth, because on its speculative side it is a mixture of construction and understanding. The proper use of the cycle requires an acknowledgment of its abstractness, i.e., an acknowledgment of the framework to which it belongs; but when that framework is the world of common sense, the cycle tends to subvert it.*

As in the previous section, the discussion of the second mode of knowledge is directed both to its status now, when it puzzles us all the while we use it so successfully, and to an ideal status in which, because supplemented by the first mode, it would serve us without perplexing us, and perhaps with a gain in efficiency. My aim is first, to free the cycle from the misemployment in which it is denied that its proper role is within an enframing mode of knowledge that it is unable to account for; and second, to make it clear that that enframing mode is itself capable of development, which in turn has consequences for the cycle. We shall have to return again and again to the role of common sense, seeing that the world of common sense is our usual framework before radically originative reflection. In Chapter 2 we saw that the acceptance of our common-sense world was by no means an unvarying feature of what I there called our "situation"; but in recurring and important moods within that shifting situation the common-sense world is our working framework, being both what we attempt to elucidate by means of the cycle, and the empirical pole of the cycle as well. That it is at best an ambiguous framework is merely a reflection of the operation within it of impulses, both "philo-sophic" and "scientific," that aim at either perfecting it or setting it aside.

Although a fully developed philosophy of science would require a thorough consideration of the speculative-empirical cycle, it would be inaccurate to think of the cycle as coexten-sive with science. Its writ runs much further: we make use of it not only in the highly sophisticated activities of science, but also in all dealings with the everyday problems of life that rise above the level of instinct and habit. The most interesting and problematic features of the cycle turn up, however, in its use in science, and it is natural to dwell on this side of it. A preliminary way of defining it is as a movement between what we are aware of in common-sense terms and theoretic con-structions by means of which we bind together features of the common-sense world. By theoretic constructions I mean not only such obvious examples as Newtonian mechanics, rela-tivity theory, quantum mechanics, alternative geometries, the periodic table of the elements, and so on, but also such de-scriptive structures as are used in the classification of animals and plants or in the analysis of social organizations.

The most fundamental feature that justifies our calling the work of the cycle abstract is that *what* we understand when we utilize the cycle is not precisely the common-sense world but rather the theoretic structures that our awareness of that world incites us to construct. I shall defer a full discussion of such construction in order to develop first some other features of the cycle. But if it is true that our understanding is an *understanding of our constructs*, and true also that the cycle is the prototype for all articulate knowledge, the foundation of that knowledge will be in question. We shall then tend to-wards thinking of knowing in terms of the production of in-struments that, when we understand them, and when they are suitably related to our world, enable us to control it; and we shall wonder whether we really understand the world that we thus control. The possibility of propounding another mode of knowledge within which the cycle operates is the possibility of justifying what in itself resists justification. As we saw, the common-sense world itself, articulated in our common language, imposes itself upon us as our proper framework in some moods, and to the extent that it does so, it offers us not just an empirical pole for the cycle, but an *alternative* to the cycle. But it is doubtful that it enables us to *justify* the cycle, seeing that so much epistemological reflection upon the relation between our common-sense knowledge and knowledge considered in terms of the speculative-empirical cycle has ended in rendering them both suspect. But here I am only concerned to point out that the chief feature making for abstractness in the speculative-empirical cycle is the diremption between awareness and understanding that characterizes it: what we come to understand is not precisely what we wanted to understand. There is, to be sure, another sense in which awareness and understanding coincide in the speculative-empirical cycle, for we are, after all, *aware* of the theoretic constructs that we also understand. That, however, does not alter the point just made.

The proceedings of the cycle are also abstract with regard to the interests that move us in employing it and the subject matter the interests are directed upon. Consider the latter first. We now think of our world as a given *field*, within which we select aspects of things that we are moved to study. What is an aspect? If we do not press the matter too far, no question could be easier. We have only to single out the subject matter of any recognized discipline: economics, psychology, biology, and physics are each of them concerned with aspects of things that are of fairly wide import; monetary theory, learning theory, embryology, and electronics, respectively, with corresponding aspects of narrower import. And we know that as our awareness of the ramifications of things increases, and our demand for control grows more exacting, we can discriminate aspects of very narrow import indeed. Seen from another viewpoint, the question grows more complex. Even where an aspect corresponds to a class of entities, as when we study ornithology or lepidopterology, our discrimination of it is an act of generalization; and in the singling out of many aspects—aspects in the more usual sense of a feature that might be shared by a wide range of entities, as for example labor, behavior, life, or simply "the physical," in the sense of the subject matter of physics— we are both generalizing and "abstracting" in a very usual sense of the latter word. On the view I am trying to express, one would have to say that we *recognize* such aspects, in the technical sense developed in the last chapter: that is, we initiate our awareness of them, and bring this awareness to completion in an articulate understanding. In distinguishing our two modes of knowledge I am not suggesting that there is not one life of reason pervading both of them. Our recognition of aspects has, however, a different intent from our recognition of what I called the tension of the One and the Many that characterizes our matrix, for we recognize them, even before radically originative reflection, *as* aspects, and after it, find them suspended *within* what we apprehend as we develop our matrix. Our *right* to them *as* aspects derives from our ability to see the complex satisfaction we take in recognizing them as a special and limited case of the satisfaction we take in the matrix itself.

These aspects do not constitute a democracy: we often judge some to be more "fundamental" than others—the aspect I call "the physical" is the most obvious example; and on other occasions find some to be "higher" than others—life and mind, for instance. These judgments are often in conflict and vary from mood to mood. Each aspect exhibits an order appropriate to it, even as any entity or Being itself exhibits an order as we recognize it in the first mode of knowledge. In our first mode we were concerned with the depth of that reality, and thought of it as providing the "proper" unity of what was before us. In the next chapter the problem of order is taken up at a more concrete level and is related to this issue of unity. In the speculative-empirical cycle there is a unity and consequently an order that characterizes any aspect we choose, and a unity and order that we look for in our theoretic constructions, but it is not precisely *the* unity of things, without qualification, that then concerns us. We may say that in the various aspects of things we find the various aspects of unity and order, as, for instance, in finding nature amenable to measurement and numeration, we are also (whatever may be the final verdict on the relation between mathematics and experience) finding, *in* the "physical" aspects, a quantitative unity and order. The point is that we must qualify our use of "unity" and "order" in these connections, and that we must not permit any mode of order so discriminated to define order in general for us.

If we ask further about the interests that move us in our various projects that make use of the speculative-empirical cycle, difficulties at once arise. Can we, for instance, correlate a variety of *abstract interests* with the discrimination of a variety of *abstract aspects?* It is surely only by virtue of a restriction or limitation of the full subjective dynamism of the knower that we are able to single out and dwell upon an aspect as such, a restriction that surely distinguishes the impulse to study, say, thermodynamics, from the kind of complex impulse, discussed in Chapter 3, that moves us to philosophy. Yet even within the framework in which the speculative-empirical cycle occupies us, aspects do not, as we saw, form a democracy. Although a variety of aspects are real enough for the common-sense attitude in which we first meet them, the economy of the cycle draws us towards preferring some of them as more fundamental than the others; thus, that aspect of things dealt with in mathematical physics has held a commanding position for over three hundred years. One is tempted to think of the interest that moves us to physics as correspondingly more fundamental. But it is strangely crossed by the interest we take in life or mind, an interest that it is often hard to distinguish from the concrete interest in self-integration, which leads us, as I have claimed, to radically originative reflection. We cannot settle this kind of conflict here, and must be content with pointing out that this latter interest might, even before our reflective act, and as an unauthenticated concrete interest, adumbrate the first mode of knowledge: an interest in mind that does not take mind to be "merely" a function of the physical may be in effect an interest in Being. But surely this kind of conflict, which is a commonplace among scientists investigating such matters—one has only to think of Sherrington's or Schrödinger's writings on the body-mind problem—makes it difficult to say that there is an abstract interest that we may correlate with the study of *any* aspect of things.

But there was, after all, something in the suggestion. When we speak of ourselves as "interested in" botany, or psychology, or history, or evolution, or even in something so specialized as the physical basis of consciousness, it is often true that our interest has very little ontological import. We take the aspect for granted in a reality we also take for granted; it is "there" or "given" to us as that same reality is "there" or "given" to our habitual attitudes. Reason, not being struck with the exercise of its own being as it attains to the aspect of being that lies before it, to that extent diminishes or attentuates what lies before it. The aspect, as known, is isolated from its roots, and because of this, it has a completeness and self-sufficiency it would not have had, were we to attend to it and to its roots as well. In our reflective act we apprehend the uniqueness of any individual thing, or of any aspect of things, as a uniqueness springing from common roots; as, in fact, an exemplification of the resources of what is common. Any order thus apprehended appears as an *achieved* order, attained to by an act of reason that is itself an *achievement*: the one echoes the other, and both spring from common roots, so that the achievements of reason are congruent with whatever achieved order happens to concern us. The involvement of the self under reason in what we apprehend is, on the other hand, minimized when we are simply "interested in" some entity, or class of entities, or some aspect of things, and consequently the interest is the more clear-cut and manageable. We may thus be "interested in" even the problem of mind in a way different from that quasi-ontological interest I spoke of a while ago. We then tend to think of ourselves as particular items set in a common-sense world made up of other particular items that are wholly external to us, and that have aspects bearing upon us in a variety of ways important for our survival and well-being. What this well-being might be, what patterns of interests *it* might require us to satisfy, can then, if we wish, be studied in the same way, and with a similar diminution of ontological import. All study of man in terms of a complex of drives would fall under this heading. I am, of course, making the picture clearer than it is in practice today: it is, as we saw, part of our current situation that we waver between a straightforward employment of the speculative-empirical cycle and a demand for a more authenticated stance for reason: hence the ambiguity of the problem of mind.

But it now becomes possible to say that the manifold "interests" correlated with the variety of things we investigate, can themselves be brought under a pervasive interest in *control*. It may well be that we are "interested in" a variety of things in just this spirit only because we are also interested in controlling our courses in the world.

There are ample precedents for regarding everyday knowledge and science as in substance pragmatic, but it seems to me that this is a mistake, in which we separate, more nicely than they are in practice separated, a theoretic and a practical impulse. There is, I believe, a pervasive interest that makes for the refraction of the philosophic one into a variety of interests in a variety of things and aspects of things; yet it is not an interest in control, but an interest in the extensiveness of things, where "extensiveness" includes also diversity and variety. The first mode of knowledge, it was maintained in section IV, concentrates on the unity of things, although without losing sight of extensiveness; the second mode concentrates on extensiveness, and concerns itself with unity in senses appropriate to the aspect of things that, at the moment, dominates its extensive concern. Thus it is the proper job of mathematical physics to give us the underlying quantitative unity of the physical extensiveness of things—where "physical" means, whatever else it also means, "measurable." It is concerned to permit us to range from one extensive region to another, by allowing such regions as we are acquainted with to suggest formulas that will apply to all, or at least to more than we are acquainted with. Once again the ideal of unity is clearly allied to the ideal of generality, but we do not claim to find either the unity or the generality of our theoretical structure *in* what we are directly aware of when we experience our world of particulars. We relate *this* particular to *that* particular, and it is the formula or the theory that *has* the generality, which consists indeed in its *applicability* to a range of particulars. This concern is not confined to mathematical physics. Wherever we fit particulars into interpretative schemes that will enable us to deal with similar particulars encountered elsewhere, we may be said to be dealing with extensiveness; thus ornithology, anthropology, or anatomy have also an extensive concern.

This feature is intimately linked with the most basic feature of the speculative-empirical cycle: its intended diremption of awareness and understanding. What we are aware of is conceived to be some particular or complex of particulars in our common-sense world; what we understand is the theory, the formula, the conceptual or symbolic structure, which we conceive of as "applying" to a range of particulars. The unity or generality proper to the aspect we are dealing with is another matter, clearly related to what we find in our theoretical constructs, but it remains outside the scope of the cycle, and is a permanent problem for epistemological theory. I have suggested its real status by claiming that we apprehend such general aspects by means of recognition, and this suggestion will be brought forward again a little later in connection with the role construction plays in the development of our theoretical structures.

Clearly control is closely related to a concern with extensiveness. Clearly too, in some of our extensive concerns we are more interested in control than in others: as we move from theoretical physics through psychology and economics to engineering, our interest in control presumably grows. Yet all these disciplines may be pursued not to control our world but simply to understand features of it; and all of them, on the other hand, can be directed towards control. It is indeed hard to think of any discipline that belongs to the speculative-empirical cycle that could not conceivably subserve our interest in control: not lepidopterology or archaeology can completely baffle our ingenuity in this sphere. The real issue, I suppose, is that all the disciplines belonging to the cycle are concerned to bring together the relevant features of one extensive region with those of another; their interest in generality is an interest in displaying the uniformities germane to the aspect under consideration that extend through all extensive regions. This can well be construed as a theoretic interest in the details of extensiveness; but it is obvious, first, that such an interest *can* be directed towards control, and, second, that a latent interest in control may move us to find theoretic employments within the cycle interesting.

All of which is enough to suggest that it is an oversimplification to suppose that we can distinguish the concrete mode of knowledge and the speculative-empirical cycle as theoretic and practical respectively. And the intermingling of theoretical and practical we find in the second mode has its counterpart in the first. I spoke of knowledge in the first mode as, in effect, "for its own sake," but if we regard the production of the integrity of the self as "practical"—as it surely is in the classical sense of that word—we cannot interpret that "for its own sake" in merely theoretic terms, and can only say that when we apply it to the first mode we mean that we are not concerned there with control of our environment.

There is another complication about control. Some disciplines bear so directly upon action that we can hardly pursue them merely theoretically even if we wish to. They are the disciplines that deal in whole or in part with the springs of human action—such disciplines are economics, sociology, psychology, and history. Probably all theoretic observation conducted within the cycle disturbs to some degree the context observed, a fact that it is sometimes possible to neglect, and sometimes not, for instance when we deal with very small events. In these disciplines, however, we are concerned with human action, which is clearly altered to a remarkable degree as men come to understand it: to the extent that there are "laws" regulating business cycles or the fluctuations of the stock market, studious investors will intervene in new ways that alter the pattern of events and consequently the "laws"; study of the marks of class or caste produces behavior that quickly renders those same marks ambiguous; and investigation of the springs of passion often destroys it. These matters are infinitely complicated, seeing that it is not only theory that is more or less "true" that can produce these curious effects, and seeing also that it may often seem to be to our advantage to behave in ways that *produce* what the theory purports to predict, rather than in ways designed to avoid it. Without in any way questioning the claim that there are unconscious roots for much of our behavior, one may suspect that the persuasiveness of Freudian and related psychological theories owes much to this effect.[8] The general lesson for psychology is, of course, the inadvisability of supposing that the effort of self-knowledge must go forward only within the confines of the speculative-empirical cycle. There is a general ambiguity here that any theory of human action, including, of course, any attempt to explain it more concretely than in the cycle, must face: our understanding of action, in whatever mode of understanding one chooses, must further certain possibilities of action and hinder others.

The final feature of the speculative-empirical cycle to be considered here is the role construction plays in its speculative side. I shall deal with this by way of a closer examination of the role of the world of common sense as a framework for the cycle before our reflective act. The class of things or the aspect of things that we deal with in the cycle belongs to this common-sense world; the movement from one extensive region to a wider one is a movement within this world, however much some of our theoretic concerns should require us to think of, say, time and space in ways very remote from a common-sense one; certain very important features of the theoretical constructs of the cycle—I am thinking of the use of models in the sciences—are given in terms of the common-sense world; and, finally, it is on the outcome of action and observation within that world that the "empirical" side of the cycle depends. For this last point a simple illustration will suffice. We deal with a general aspect of the common-sense world when we think in terms of energy, mass, charge, and velocity, all of which we take to be measurable, but our measurements are given in terms of the reading of instruments that are for the moment as much a part of the furniture of the common-sense world as this pen I write with. In this sense the speculative-empirical cycle is a cycle *between* the common-sense world and theoretic constructs, these latter being in part given strictly in terms of the common-sense world, and in part having only whatever connection with it logic and mathematics may have.

Yet as we know the cycle before radically originative reflection, or before any other philosophical assessment of it, the role of the common-sense world is ambiguous. It is sometimes both the framework of the cycle and its empirical pole, as in the ordinary working mood of the scientist and the man in the street. But sometimes we pursue the cycle in such a way as to call in question whole tracts of reality to which common sense, left to itself, accords a healthy, if vague, respect. There are two principal factors making for this ambiguity. The first is the wish to unify science by holding up to all scientific investigation the ideal of mathematical physics; the second is the prevalence of epistemological theory that is in part based on the claims of mathematical physics to be a model for all knowledge and in part designed to further those claims by clarifying and justifying procedures that are as yet to some degree obscure.

The effect of these factors is complex. In the first place, while we continue to return to the common-sense world for the empirical grounding for the cycle, we no longer take that level of experience as a standard of reality. The realities we are aware of and understand we think of as less basic than the world as we know it in terms of the scientific version presented by the speculative-empirical cycle. Consequently even a scientific treatment appropriate to such common-sense realities as intelligent life and consciousness seems to fall short of an ideal unless it excludes notions, like purpose and consciousness, that would be inappropriate in mathematical physics. Instead of aspects of a common-sense world, each dealt with by a speculative-empirical cycle appropriate to it, we have only one aspect, to which we try to reduce the others.

In the second place, these factors alter the way we understand the cycle itself. A] All empirical confirmation takes place within the world of common sense; yet, since our apprehension of the frame does not conform to the ideal for knowledge that the cycle suggests to us, we come to distrust it. The point is, of course, related to the one just made, yet it is not now a question of merely distrusting our normal assessment of the realities of the common-sense world, which we could do while continuing to suppose that our experience must nevertheless be given in such terms, but of looking instead for a more authentic experience behind the epiphenomena we take ourselves to be confronted with. I have already described this as in part an effort to narrow our extensive range until it should yield only the "dancing colored spots" a positivist would accept, embodied in such reports as the one we have already met—"this green now." B] As for the speculative side of the cycle, although the theoretic constructions we employ in it bear the mark of their origin in the common-sense world—even in matters very remote from common sense we hear of electron *orbits*, electron *shells*, electron *spin*; of electromagnetic *waves*, *bundles* of such waves, and so on—and although we insist that our constructs of whatever sort should possess some operational consequences that ultimately bring us back to our ordinary world, it is nevertheless a widely held belief that we should be able to derive our working theoretic constructs as interpretations of formal deductive systems that do not in themselves bear the marks of the real world. This is the search for what I earlier described as the empty analytic, pure and contentless, yet somehow capable of yielding us, upon interpretation, laws in terms of which we can correlate one extensive region with another. Having produced these empirical and rational ideals by deliberately attenuating our common-sense knowledge, and by dividing awareness from understanding, we should not be surprised that we are left with problems about the status of analytic knowledge.

All of which is a reminder that the common-sense world, although a framework in which the understanding embodied in our common language emerges as the fruit of awareness, is itself a kind of abstraction: what the world is like if we live in it with as little reflection as may be. It is therefore subject to the seductions of a too-hastily imposed intellectuality. One envisages a happier role for the common-sense world, in which our reflective exercise would deepen our command of it. The least consequence of failing to see the depth of what we possess in common-sense experience is that we lose sight of the whole point of the cycle, and take it as a fully concrete knowledge, or simply as knowledge, without qualification. But the cycle itself is also impoverished, since we are then incapable of seeing just what it is we are dealing with by means of it. So it is that in attempting to understand as much as we can of life in terms of physics and chemistry—a thing unobjectionable in itself— we fail to grasp the most important matter of all, namely, what exactly it is to be a living entity, what exactly we mean when we say that life has evolved. It is not that the speculative-empirical cycle cannot produce explanations of some importance in this sphere—biochemistry and genetics have done wonders, especially in point of control. It is simply that there will always be much that is obscure and unsatisfactory about such explanations when they are put forward as complete, and as archetypes of explanation.

Any extended discussion of the problem of evolution in neo-Darwinian terms will afford abundant examples. The underlying thesis is that the evolution of life is to be explained in terms of random mutations perpetuated or erased by natural selection, with the origin of life itself being explained by an analogous interaction of random combinations with environmental conditions. It is not improbable, we are told, that the introduction, though not the perpetuation, of any new function or organ is "by chance." The appeal to chance is itself obscure, for if it is clear enough what "chance" means in some well-defined set of circumstances, it is not at all clear what it means if we take it to designate some general principle that operates in nature. In practice, this kind of appeal to chance is expanded in terms of some such metaphysical assumption as that all possible combinations, no matter how complex, of basic "particles" must eventually come to pass. "Possible" combinations are, of course, such as the "laws of nature" tolerate, which introduces the further obscurity that some laws of nature—and there are impressive voices telling us that this is true of all laws of nature—appear to be gross regularities emerging from the summation of multitudes of irregular (chance?) small-scale happenings. Moreover, there are grave difficulties in interpreting the statistical reasoning used to support the claim that it is not improbable that life has evolved in this way. For one thing, an adequate account of probability (as distinct from the mathematical tools that we employ in reckoning probabilities) is still wanting. It is not possible to go into this matter in any detail here. Nevertheless I venture to suggest some broad principles. All probability reasoning rests upon: A] our recognition of order and of the efficacy of order; B] our recognition of conditions tractable to the display of that order, and for this reason exhibiting a different order of their own, which is no less so for all that we often describe it as random; C] and our ignorance of some of the conditions in question. There is, therefore, something paradoxical in using a probability calculus to determine the relative probability of the evolution of species by chance, for we are then appealing to the efficacy of order to suggest that order can arise without that efficacy. All these obscurities are compounded by the common practice in neo-Darwinian theory of resorting to anthropomorphic expressions of a teleological cast when the explanation would break down without them, and then rendering them inoffensive by cautioning the reader that he is to take them in some Pickwickian sense.[9]

When the speculative-empirical cycle works at its best, either now, in that recurrent mood in which the world of common sense forms a framework that is not subverted by mistaken epistemology and reductionist metaphysics, or later, when radically originative reflection provides a new framework, it exhibits a curious mixture of understanding and construction. There is initially, as we have seen, an articulated understanding of some class of things or some aspect of things of which we are also aware. But the vast articulated structure of the sciences and other disciplines does not spring from this awareness with the same directness and immediacy. It is rather something constructed or produced, and under the stimulus of two quite different factors. One is an imaginative brooding upon the aspect of things that we are concerned to understand theoretically, an aspect that varies in importance according as our scope varies in ambition. It will presumably always include the "logical" feature of things, which I spoke of in Chapter 4 as supporting the inferential relationship, so that it will never be completely free, or, as one may say just as readily, completely empty. The other factor is the world of theoretic order as it is already given to us in our inherited culture-world, which comprises the symbolic forms not only of science, but of art, religion, and morals as well. This complicates our exposition, because, on our assumption, this world itself must be the result of a mixture of understanding and construction: any account of man dealing with him in his capacity as *homo faber* can hardly neglect the influence upon him of what he has already made. We may perhaps here neglect the remotest origins of our power of production. At any rate, our understanding of the received world of theoretic order marches with our awareness of it, an awareness that is different from our awareness of the world about us, although in interplay with it. We need not suppose that theoretic understanding requires total awareness of theory, since some features of the structure we are concerned with will be more basic than others. The important issue, however, is that our understanding of the world of theory is primarily an *under-*

standing of a construct, and only secondarily, and in so far as that construct is appropriately related to our world, an understanding of that world.

But I am not so much concerned with the character of our understanding of the world of theory, as with the way it enters into a function I described as a mixture of understanding and construction. This understanding of the world of theory combines with our direct understanding of some relevant aspect of things, and with an understanding of what we require by way of a relation between theory and experience, but the new insight that may follow is not *just* an insight: in part the advance is by way of a new creation, construction, or production, and *what* we then understand is precisely that new structure. This production takes place, to some extent, in accordance with rules that can be imparted, but this is by no means the whole story: in any important advance the creative autonomy of reason, which is my main theme, plays an important role. No more than we can for the arts can we lay down for the world of theoretic order a set of rules governing the ultimate form it should take. The activity in which it grows and develops is indeed more like the activity of art than is usually admitted: it is stimulated by the world as we know it; it is stimulated also by past works; it shapes partly in accordance with standards it finds in past works, and partly in accordance with standards that only become fully articulate in the course of the shaping process itself; it draws on the resources of feeling; and it transforms the world of feeling as we take satisfaction in productions that it is no mere flourish to call beautiful. Yet the imaginative constructions of theory are less an end in themselves, less a prolongation and completion of our own nature than are works of art, because however shapely, orderly, and satisfying to the mind that creates them they may be, they must be brought back at last and justified by the increased amplitude they lend to our extensive grasp.

So to insist on the constructive side of the speculative-empirical cycle, and to claim that *what* we understand is our construction, is of course to neglect precisely what entitles us to describe knowledge in terms of the speculative-empirical cycle as *knowledge of our world*, namely, the mysterious congruence of theory and fact that we are capable of attaining. Within the framework provided by radically originative reflection the congruence is less mysterious. It is, in the first place, the same reason that establishes the framework that here inhabits and explores it. The empirical tests that we find satisfactory, the systematic order that we demand in our theoretic constructs, are both recognized as formed in the matrix for all empirical and rational standards that radically originative reflection provides. The very power of recognition displayed in our first mode of knowledge is an analogue of reason's productive power; or say, rather, that the power that is in the one instance directed towards recognition, is here directed towards production.

6

PHILOSOPHICAL KNOWLEDGE:

THE PROLONGATION OF RADICALLY

ORIGINATIVE REFLECTION

I.   *A review of the position so far assures us that a prolongation of radically originative reflection will permit us to satisfy in Being itself the two great ideals
for reason that dominated the last chapter. A striking feature of our new beginning: we are dealing not
just with reason's right to any subject matter whatsoever, but also with its highest subject matter: reason
itself, taken as a mode of being in the course of fuller
emergence.*

The claims made in this chapter are tentative, as the enjoyment of reason's creative and responsible autonomy is not.
But they are tentative only in the sense that another effort
of the same order might displace them, and not in the sense
that they are subject to the methods of the speculative-
empirical cycle.

      Even in the first intimations of radically originative
reflection we were already dealing with Being. What reason
initiated awareness of was a vast variety of beings and Being

itself, which is their common root; what reason understood in bringing this awareness to the fruition of articulation was again beings and Being; and the creative and responsible autonomy that reason came to enjoy as it brought itself under a reflective survey of the same order was the autonomy of a being that in acting for itself acted also for Being. I expressed this in Chapter 4 by calling our reflective exercise an ontological expansion, and I developed this theme in terms of a concrete contrast between the One and the Many, which had several aspects: a] the unity of any entity as contrasted with the multiplicity of its components and the multiple phases of the process in which it completes itself;   b] the unity of Being as contrasted with the multiplicity of interdependent beings and with the process that is part of that interdependence;   c] the unity of reason as contrasted with the many here-and-nows in which I am aware, with the many phases and factors within any here-and-now in which I am aware, and with the many reasonable consciousnesses of which I take my own to be one. These several contrasts were held to be *many* aspects of *one* contrast, which was, finally, enriched by our finding the unity proper to reason to be common in the sense of being hospitable to society and discourse. I spoke of this as the reflection of multiplicity back into the underlying unity of things, which was therefore no mute and stolid Parmenidean unity. In Chapter 5 these matters were pressed further in the discussion of extensiveness, which was taken to comprise the various aspects of multiplicity: temporality, spatiality, variety. There the problems set by extensiveness to an outlook like the present one were dealt with by suggesting that the proper way to regard extensiveness is to think of it as *within* any entity, and *within* Being in general, whereupon it becomes the extensiveness *of* something that is not exhausted by a purely extensive account.

One may turn confidently to Being itself in order to satisfy there the two great ideals for reason that dominated our last chapter, for we shall then only be prolonging and deepening what we began in our reflective act. An expository difficulty persists: the word "being" has had a long career, and has led so often to stultification that the reader may be unwilling to attend to it in yet another setting. There are good reasons for persisting in the use of it, as the character of our effort, which is to bring more sharply into view what the word has always been applied to, should demonstrate. Once the creative and autonomous power of reason is released to its responsible task, there is no turning back: we have only to make more fully present what was in some sort present as soon as we began to realize the autonomy; what has been indeed tantalizingly, because vaguely and inauthentically, present through much of the history of philosophy. The claim is nothing less than that a mode of being emerges now with more definiteness than heretofore and establishes itself firmly in the enjoyment of the autonomy that has been my main theme; and with the full emergence of that mode of being, Being becomes more authentically present to us.

The consequences of this last claim are important but easy to misunderstand. We are dealing simultaneously both with reason's highest subject matter and with its right to any subject matter whatsoever, so that the pattern of our investigation must bring us back again to reason itself—only, however, after we have made it clear how it is that access to that highest subject matter illuminates any subject matter whatsoever. Our new beginning is not, then, merely a primitive and bare certainty upon which we are to build a new superstructure, but is itself an affirmation of graded order, which, as common sense has told us for so long, characterizes the world before us. What might have been put forward as a "foundation" is from another point of view a pinnacle, and attaining it gives us at one blow that most mysterious and puzzling feature of things: a directed order *in the making*, a universe not only embodying value, but besides directed upon value not yet embodied, a universe with a *telos*, although a *telos* that calls out for explanation in other than anthropomorphic terms. The production of cognitive awareness is an *achievement*, answering to the *achievement* we find in any entity whatsoever; yet the full release of reason's autonomy in radically originative reflection is again an *achievement*, and one that certifies for us that the resources of Being are concerned with bringing about the achievement of the potential. We put ourselves in a position to understand such a fact as evolution by means of an act that shares in the character of evolution itself. I do *not* mean that we use our understanding of consciousness as the foundation for an analogical understanding of nature; our recognition of entities, including their order, is direct, and is merely authenticated by our reflective exercise; I mean only that what awakens in this exercise—such is the significance of the generality permitted by our pervasive contrast of the One and the Many—is recognized as the same power that displays itself throughout nature, here exerting itself in a positive advance. One runs the risk of sounding presumptuous, but it is questionable whether any attempt at coping with the present situation in philosophy can avoid a presumption of this sort. Something of this kind, surely, is the significance of philosophy's long and inconclusive preoccupation with the old adage "know thyself." Here we make common cause with what I suspect to be the best impulse in contemporary existentialism: not its preoccupation with faith, with the inarticulate, with the dark side of things that resists formulation in terms of essence, but its concern with existence as an unfinished business, in which the decisions we take are genuinely formative of reaches of finite reality that might not otherwise have come to pass. In this sense the philosophic effort is "existential," and, under this restriction, I trust that the present approach has an existential significance.

The authenticity of this point is, however, only as great as our ability to grasp *any* level, *any* mode of being, and we have still to make clearer the intimations of Being we have already had. This prolongation of radically originative reflection will enable us to look at several traditional issues of metaphysics in a new light.

II.   The presence of an entity is a presence in extensiveness but not entirely of extensiveness. A consideration of the non-extensive side of individual presence leads to the general aspect of individual presence and therefore to Being.

To make these claims more definite, I shall now take up the topic of generality again and enlarge upon the points made in a rather compressed way in Chapter 4. In the earlier exposition the topic of generality was introduced directly; here we come at it by way of the topic of non-extensiveness. I shall claim that the non-extensive side of beings comes close to defining their presence, and especially the *general* character of it.

In the last chapter we met two aspects of extensiveness. The first was the unsurveyed extensiveness of experience: the fact that it exceeds our reach and that any pronouncements about the whole of it are to that extent questionable. The second lay in the possible dissolution of any presence in the face of an extensiveness glimpsed within it. The first was the aspect of macroscopic extensiveness; the second, of microscopic extensiveness, or extensive divisibility. We found them to be overcome as problems when we recognized that our proper framework gives us a concrete contrast of one and many both with regard to Being itself and with regard to any entity. In this sense we claimed to find something non-extensive in all presence. We must now look at this issue more closely.

When we acknowledge the cognitive presence of an entity, and take it seriously *as* an entity, we are acknowledging *that it makes use of an extensive range in order to be present.* If we consider any reasonably complex entity, this becomes clear enough. Its presence is extensive in this sense, that it is also the presence of a large number of subordinate entities that enter into its structure; it does not matter whether we consider the entity at one moment in its history or survey it as a process. But its presence is extensive only because it *makes use of* an extensive range; so that if we consider it as an entity, rather than as an aggregate or complex of entities— consider it, for instance, as an animal rather than as a complex configuration of molecules—it is just as illuminating to say that it *supervenes* on an extensive complex, that it *makes use of, presides over,* or *unifies* an extensive range. The components of the entity, spread out in space and time as they are, we nevertheless find to be the extensive pattern of the entity: we cannot give an adequate account of some component simply by relating it to its neighbors, even if our account should comprise the whole extensive pattern. *What* we know is genuinely extensive; there is no claim that it is "out of" space and time. Yet to be an entity is not to be merely an extensive pattern. To claim that this is so and that when we are in the presence of an entity we are in the presence of something that has a non-extensive aspect, is not to pretend to some wholly transcendental knowledge; all that is at issue is that extensiveness is not self-sufficient: we can only comprehend it as the extensiveness *of a being* or as the extensiveness *of Being.*

An account of such an entity as a man must in great part be an extensive one. The extensive description would if complete comprise all the sub-entities (organs, cells, molecular structures, and so on) and all the processes in which these interact and develop; it would properly also include all the gross physical characteristics and all the humane characteristics that common sense recognizes. To the extent, however, that such an account (which is in any case endless) is an account of an assemblage or a configuration, we should have *missed* the definiteness of the entity, for part of that, part indeed of what makes an extensive description relevant, lies in the fact that the extensive components are components *of* an entity. However intricate and complete we make a purely extensive description, and it is of course part of the naturalistic program that this should approximate an ideal description in terms of physics, the vital bond is missing—*Fehlt leider nur das geistige*

Band. The unity of an extensive span embraces the whole of it: it is present in all of it, yet we cannot localize it and cannot identify it with the whole of it. From the conceptual point of view it is a *way* of taking the whole of it, a fact that we notice when we observe that concepts are in some sort removed from time and space; we are here simply claiming that our faculty of conceptualization is grounded upon a feature of things that is present to us. The point may be summed up by saying that when we take an entity to be wholly an extensive complex, we are in fact in danger of dismissing the entity and attending instead to its components; and that if we attend to the components in the same spirit, then the same difficulty will arise about them.

We have to deal then with a presence that is a presence *in* extensiveness, but that is not entirely *of* extensiveness. That Being is in part exempt from time is a theme that the Platonic tradition has made a commonplace, but in that tradition it has been supposed that its formality exempts it from passage. Here I claim rather that the ordinary beings we know in the world about us, dwelling in a network of subordinate entities, having their being *in* them, subject therefore to passage and multiplicity, are themselves still partakers of a non-extensive mode of existence; and that when the entity is truly present to us, this non-extensive element is also present. This indeed is what is meant by the *unity* of an extensive entity. Where else should we look for the unity? If we call it the unity of a *pattern*, of a *configuration*, of a *law*, we have surely done nothing more than recognize, and from a non-extensive point of view, that same formality; we have certainly not avoided a non-extensive commitment. In our reflective act we try to see that non-extensive element for what it really is: a fundamental feature of the presence of an individual entity.

But it now appears that what is thus non-extensive is also common; philosophy must always make its peace with the Platonic insight. If we reflect upon any group of such supervening, presiding, dominating, unifying presences, we are quite unable to suppose that the non-extensive side of them constitutes a bare plurality. This is a consideration independent of any resemblances we might find between these entities. None of them is wholly individual in its non-extensive aspect, even though it is precisely non-extensiveness that confers individuality upon it. If an entity is present to us, presiding over its extensive range, then Being is also present, presiding over *its* extensive range. Non-extensiveness has a unity that is peculiar to it *qua* non-extensive, even though it is also diversified by virtue of the extensive entities that share in it.

III. *The common or general aspect of non-extensiveness is the foundation of all our contrasts between universal and particular, including our contrast of a level or degree of being with an individual that exemplifies it. This is in contrast with the Platonic and Kantian approaches, and makes possible a new treatment of the Aristotelian doctrine of essence.*

The non-extensiveness we find in individual beings is the non-extensiveness of Being; so long as the one is present the other is too. There is nothing mysterious about this. What is really mysterious is that anyone should wish to make extensiveness self-sufficient, thinking of entities as *in* and *of* time and space in some unqualified sense. And when we reach this point we have a concrete contrast of the One and the Many that displays itself in several ways: A] Being as contrasted with beings. B] Any individual being as contrasted with its components, phases, and factors; more generally, any being set in contrast with *any* extensive analysis of it. As a component of a being is a being of a different order (the cell is a component of the organism, the molecule of the cell, and so on) this contrast in turn displays itself on many levels. c] The unity of Being set in contrast with the inner diversity of it that belongs to it by virtue of its sustaining the beings that participate in it.

This very *present* contrast of the One and the Many, in

which the unity side is present in terms of non-extensiveness, gives us a foundation for any contrast we might wish to make between the universal or general and the particular or individual, and furnishes the source of the timelessness that we associate with universals, whether we understand them as Platonic Forms, Aristotelian Essences, or Whiteheadian Eternal Objects, or understand them in some other sense. In the first place, the inseparability of the presence of beings from the presence of Being assures us that each being will have *something* in common with every other, and that what is thus held in common is non-extensive. In the second place, we are given common *levels* or *degrees* of being, which owe their common character to their non-extensive root. The point is an elusive one. That there are levels is hardly to be disputed, but their significance, and especially what I am calling their common root, is another matter. Consider the extensive range over which any entity presides, and which is a condition of its presence. This range may be viewed in terms of those entities in it that are immediately contributory to the presence of the presiding entity, as when, for instance, we think of the immediate components of some relatively simple organism as cells; or we may go on to deal with these contributory entities in the same way, attending to them in terms of the entities that make up *their* extensive span. This gives us an obvious sense in which there are levels. Now each entity in a given level "belongs" to it in that *with* the other entities at that level it contributes to the order of the presiding entity: their action is "in common"; each functions (whatever its individual contribution) in the "same" way; each contributes as one of many that taken *together* form a subordinate level. The contrast between a presiding entity and its subordinate entities is a contrast between one at the presiding level and many at the subordinate level. We may now complete our exposition of the point by recalling that all of the entities now under consideration owe their unity, hence their very status as entities, to the common unity they exemplify, share in, or participate in. It then appears that any presiding unity exhibits a different degree of the *same* Being exemplified in its subordinate entities.

We may say, then, that to belong to a level is to belong to a degree of being. This is not only to participate in the common unity of Being but to do so in a *way* that is common by being exemplified in others as well. I do not mean to suggest that the idea of a level or degree of being is something inevitably exemplified in a group of individuals; towards the end of this section and again in section *VIII* this issue is amplified. But even in the present exposition there is justification for grounding the status of universals in the non-extensive aspect of the presence of beings and of Being.

"Degree" is to be taken in somewhat the traditional sense: some levels are "higher" than others; they contain "more"; they are foreshadowed by their subordinates, which in turn find their fulfillment in them. We are, of course, using "subordinate" only in the sense of "component in an entity," and no political or social meaning is intended. The justification for such hierarchical claims is the very character of our recognition of presence: recognition, in attaining the individual, attains individuality in its common roots; but it also attains the individual as a degree or level of being, and grasps as well the many levels that are to be found within an individual. Recognition is a valuing activity, and value is of course here given an ontological status. This will be expanded somewhat later in our discussion of order.

Whenever we speak of a class (e.g., living beings), which we name with a common name, thus raising at once the "universals" issue; whenever we speak of a general mode of being (e.g., motion, life, consciousness), thus intensifying the issue by seeming to speak not so much of a group of particulars as of a general *mode* in which individuals might participate; we have in fact merely invoked three aspects of presence. A] The unity by virtue of which individuals have their character as entities is common. This is Being, functioning as the principle of individuation, and participated in or shared in by whatever possesses individuality: the primal uni-

versal character is the possession of the character of entity.
b] The common character of Being is available to participation in terms of degree. Degree may be exemplified by many
individuals with no loss to their individuality, or may, on the
other hand, be exemplified *in* any individual as a feature that
does not belong to it uniquely. c] The non-extensive feature
of Being is the root of its common character.

It is important that a *degree* of being is something
grounded in concrete presence. Degree has its positive side:
it is an achieved order, a reality with definiteness; it has its
negative side as well: we are dealing with a *limitation* of what
is common. The presence of an individual is the real presence
of a *degree* of being, and because it is, it is the "partial"
presence of Being. The presence of an individual is also the
real presence of a *common* degree of being, and because it is,
it is the "partial" presence of something that is *common* while
acting as the principle of individuation. The idea of the *common* character of a degree must be stressed in order to make
it clear what is present to us when we turn our attention not
to the individual entities of the world, but to realities that
already exhibit, in whatever presence they have, their common
or general nature: I mean, for instance, what I have called
modes of being—life, reason, motion, change, indeed extensiveness itself. There is a pervasive importance of individuality, in that the basic contrast of the One and the Many is
tied to individual presence; but, as we have seen, individuality
itself can be considered a mode of being: Being is not *merely*
common, and individual entities are not *merely* individuals.

This line of thought may be summarized as follows.
The relationship One-Many is grounded in terms of concrete
presence, in which it appears also as the contrast of the non-
extensive with the extensive; this in turn is a two-fold contrast:
of Being with beings, and of any being with the extensive
sweep of the beings that contribute to it; and this, finally,
is a contrast of what is common with what shares in the common, for Being is common to beings, and any being is common with regard to the subordinate entities over which it

presides. The idea of the common, general, or universal is thus associated with non-extensiveness, where non-extensiveness is taken as a feature of concrete presence. Also associated with non-extensiveness is the idea of degree as applied to that which is common: a higher degree presides over a lower extensive range and in its presiding there is something non-extensive. All this is a way of articulating or understanding presence, and in such a way as to make unnecessary the usual posing of the problem of universals.

From the beginning philosophers have frequently contrasted the extensive and non-extensive. That which is exempt from time has been called eternal; it has been thought to have an absolute unity (e.g., God, the Form of the Good, etc.) and an internal diversity exempt from time and space (e.g., the realm of Forms or Essences). Yet the permanance of ideas that has been the model for this has been quite unsatisfactory. There has been a strong temptation to think of ideas as abstract, and to take the non-extensiveness they exemplify as a mere exemption from the erosions of time rather than as the source of the concrete individuals of the world. I am here taking non-extensiveness seriously, not as a hypothetical realm deduced from the quality of ideas, but as part of the presence of any entity. We shall see in the next section that the act of recognition is a response to the non-extensiveness we find in all beings.

I have contrasted the present viewpoint with that of Kant at several places; some heightening of the contrast at this point will make the association between universality and the non-extensive more vivid.

The use of the word "entity" would not have been appropriate where the presence of an individual, taken to be coincidental with the partial presence of a common non-extensive Being, was dubious. The use of the Kantian "object" or some metaphysically neutral variant of it, would then have been more appropriate. "Object," as Kant uses it, conveys no immediate coincidence of the unity of the object with the unity of the nature of things, and is thus compatible, for all the universality Kant finds in it, with his later contention that the latter unity, if it exists, is not cognitively accessible to us, even though it may function as a cognitive ideal. If we were dealing with *phenomena* in a Kantian situation, rather than with what I am calling entities, it would appear that reason performs, to produce each of them, a unification of what I am calling extensiveness, a unification that in Kantian terminology is the unification of a sensuous manifold; certainly in such a situation we should not speak of presence. There is, then, a vital difference: we do not deal with phenomena, but with beings that are present; we do not *unify*, but recognize in entities a unity that is part of their presence. Not the unification of extensiveness, but a present unity *in* that extensiveness is our theme; more strictly, we find extensiveness *in* that unity. Setting aside this difference, there is still in the present approach something akin to what Kant was after in his consideration of objects. He saw that the judgment that gives us any one of them, gives us at the same time every one of them, for we exercise in the case of any one of them a synthetic *a priori* judgment, which must by definition extend to all. We find in our own view that there is this peculiar property of those entities into whose presence reason wins its way, that the non-extensive unity of any one of them is not *just* the unity of just *that* entity, but also a common unity that is the unity of Being. What we claim is a coincidence of universality and presence.

We are now in a position to make some preliminary observations about the problem of essence. The setting of twentieth century metaphysical philosophy has on the whole been especially hostile to the Aristotelian version, which was founded upon the obvious stratification of nature, and on our supposed ability to grasp this with our reason. It has been felt by Bergson and by some existentialists that if the definiteness of an entity derives from the formality of an Aristotelian essence, then such limits are set upon its achievements as make its significance as an individual suspect. The freedom and creativity of *existence*, or of the *élan vital* have thus been invoked as a counterspell to the domination of the species. From the present point of view this objection is based on a misunderstanding, not of Aristotle, who does indeed pose just such problems, but of the problem of the definiteness or order that an individual may share with others. In interpreting this, I appeal first, to the *common* character of the unity of individuals. This gives us already a definiteness or order (if only that of being an individual entity presiding over an extensive range) shared by a multiplicity of individuals—indeed by all. Second, there is the degree manifested in the definiteness or order of a particular individual. Whatever differences between individuals might exist at a certain level— and these might be considerable at some levels, negligible at others—so long as we have a *number* of them *at* a certain level, and are able to view this level as a level *of* what is common, we have all we require for the conception of essence. To possess the definiteness of a certain degree of being is no more at variance with the possession of individuality (with whatever freedom and spontaneity should belong to it at this or that level) than the possession of individuality is at odds with the existence of other individuals. The question becomes in any case less important if we notice that any entity of a certain degree of order exhibits many layers of subordinate order, and that we may think of any one of these layers as both one and many: one in that it is the same level of order wherever exhibited, many in that it may be exhibited in many individuals. It is also pertinent that, in any supposed creative advance in which an individual should go beyond the order held in common with entities that share its "essence," the new order that emerges is also common, seeing that it may be participated in or shared in by other entities yet to come. Perhaps, however, objections to any doctrine of essences arise mainly from an interpretation of essence in terms of Form and a consequent view of formal and final causation that seems destructive of freedom. This topic is taken up again in section VIII, which deals with causation.

IV. The prolongation of radically originative reflection is now directed upon reason itself to reveal it as a degree of being exemplified by an entity presiding over an extensive range and rooted in the common or general aspect of non-extensiveness. The act of recognition therefore answers to the structure of what is recognized, and in the realization of this reason comes to preside more fully over its extensive span. The common character of reason is, however, of a special sort: it is concerned with the general, is societal, and reflective, and, because it is a degree of being in the making, these characteristics further illuminate the common character of Being. Climax of the topic of generality: Being is present to us as "common formative power."

We have arrived at some understanding of the common, general, or universal aspect of presence, and, in order to accomplish this, have been relying on the autonomous responsibility of reason *to bring us into that presence.* In that sense we are relying on the reflective act outlined in Chapter 4, but have not yet, in the prolongation and deepening of it that is the task of this chapter, made reason itself once again the subject of our attention. We have, that is, been concerned with the common as that is found in any entity whatsoever, and have been concerned with reason only to the extent necessary to ensure our right to acknowledge such entities. We are now, however, in a position to make our grasp of the issue of generality clearer by turning our attention to reason itself; we shall find that what is true of reason is inseparable from our understanding of Being in general. Our claim is that reason is a general function or degree of being that is, however, *concerned* with generality: any progress in our understanding of reason is a progress in our understanding of Being itself.

Whether we are dealing with the presence of an entity or of Being itself, we are dealing with something that presides over an extensive span by insinuating its order throughout it. The order is more than a pattern or configuration *of* that extensive span, for the unity of an entity is the action or deployment of the non-extensive *in* the extensive. Now it is only by virtue of a similar action or deployment that we are able to recognize the pattern or order of an entity. There is indeed something synoptic even in our discernment of order in the limited sense of pattern or configuration; for a spatial pattern, for instance, is not given by the mere specification of the location of the items that make up the pattern: we recognize it as a whole, and the symbolic terms in which we convey it, as for instance, those of a mathematical equation, specify a total unity. Beyond that, however, the pattern or order of an entity presiding throughout its extensive span is not simply the equivalent of its shape or configuration, not even if we take configuration as including an element of process. The Aristotelian idea of Form, which implies both a directed or telic development, of which the shape is only one result, and a common or universal character, is a parallel case in which order is given a partially non-extensive sense.

Noticing that the activity of reason that responds to the presence of beings and Being is in part an extensive activity, we may say that the power of recognition is a unifying or generalizing over an extensive range; but, as we saw, this involves some distortion, and it is more accurate to say that recognition shares in both the non-extensive and extensive sides of that which comes under its sway, and also that it exemplifies the principle of hierarchy or degree I have already noticed.

A] It takes place in a time range and makes use of the spatial organization of the body; it makes use of subordinate levels of being that in any rational creature echo phylogeny— that is, its use of the body's neural apparatus, and indeed of all the bodily structures we share with the animals, is a use of levels of being that contribute to its own being; it surveys with the help of its bodily involvement at least a segment of the extensive configuration of what is recognized; and it calls upon the whole complex of our affective natures—the subjective dynamism of Chapter 3, of which I shall be in a position to say more in section *VIII*.

B] Recognition is itself a feature of a presiding or supervening unity, a mode of being that is present throughout an extensive range, but does not belong wholly to it. This observation amplifies the account of the *a priori* in Chapter 4, section X: the resources of reason that are deployed as we initiate our awareness and understanding of our "objects" are in part non-extensive resources; this is the highly restricted sense in which ideas are "innate."

c] The non-extensive aspect of recognition answers to the non-extensiveness of what in the previous section was described as common. The power of recognition is a common power rooted in extensiveness. The common character of reason was of course one of the chief findings of our first exercise of radically originative reflection in Chapter 4. We now enhance our understanding of that common character as we see it in terms of an entity presiding over an extensive range.

It is well to pause for a moment, however, and recall just what it is that we now speak of as presiding over its extensive range. We have been talking in terms of the non-extensive or common feature of *all* entities, and are therefore talking of the common without the illumination that can be brought to that topic by noticing the unique sense in which reason is common. Reason is a level of being exemplified in individuals and, as exemplified, shares in a common unity that makes it clear that itself is something that may be shared in. Yet *this* degree of being is also *concerned* with the common. I spoke in Chapter 4 of how in our reflective act we step from the here and now—from any here-and-now—into the common atmosphere of reason, an atmosphere which was that of a potential society in this sense, that we understand our entry into it to be only one of an indefinite number of possible entries. The assurance we gained was a shared assurance, marked by the articulateness of discourse—the assurance of *consciousness* rather than of *my* consciousness. It was in fact the *common* atmosphere of a *common* concern for what is *common*, marked by a *common* or shared assurance. The seeming complexities are expository only, and we can refer them to a central simplicity by saying that we are dealing with a reflective consciousness, just as reflexive complexities disappear when we keep it in mind that reflection is native to reason and is to be conceived of in terms of a direct enjoyment of presence rather than a mirroring of an object.

Our reflexive recognition that reason supervenes upon an extensive range whenever it recognizes beings and Being is also a recognition that what supervenes has just the common atmosphere we have been discussing. At the same time it is a fuller realization of that same act of supervening or presiding. In Chapter 4 I spoke of radically originative reflection as an ontological expansion: this expansion now completes itself as we begin to see what the term means. Reason as a mode of being fully supervenes upon its extensive range as it understands that this is a characteristic of all beings and of its own activity as well, including its essential reflex activity.

We may conclude from all this that the non-extensiveness of the exercise of reason permeates its extensive life more fully than is the case with other entities: the life of reason is qualified, even in the active flow and internal space of consciousness, by what I have been calling its common atmosphere. Hence some of the paradoxes of consciousness, as for instance when Bergson describes it as a real duration having at the same time some of the attributes of eternity. The life of reason as we know it and dwell in it, the very movement of consciousness, is, for all its incommunicable uniqueness and privacy, colored by generality.

Here it is appropriate to recall the interpretation of essence put forward at the close of the previous section. We may think of an entity as exhibiting many layers of order, and may think of any one of these layers as both one and many: one in that it is the same level wherever exhibited, many in that it may be exhibited in many individuals. There is, in this sense, an essence of reason, although it is complicated for us by being reflectively *concerned with* generality.

The first movement of our reflective exercise gave us our right to any subject matter, including reason itself. Exercise of our right has pressed our understanding of Being somewhat further. This in turn helps complete our understanding of reason. But the influence is always reciprocal, and in this movement our understanding of Being is again heightened. The reflective character of reason, its societal character, its concern for the common, all of which enter into what I have called its common atmosphere, is a mode of being that "shares in" Being, which is in turn amenable to such participation. We are not dealing with separate modes of generality, one appropriate to things at large and one appropriate to reason, but with the generality or common presence of *Being*. It was this that led me to distinguish the unity of Being from a Parmenidean unity, and to think of it instead as a unity one of whose expressions is an internal ordered multiplicity of a non-extensive sort—for that is one way of characterizing the common atmosphere of reason. I said in the first section of this chapter that we were concerned both with reason's right to any subject matter whatever, and with itself taken as its highest subject matter. This was not to say that we have any right to an idealistic identification of Being with reason; I meant only that our concern for the life of reason— a concern that is at once a concern to *know* it and to *further* it—is also a concern for a fuller realization of what is a real though in part unexercised feature of Being. We know Being as susceptible to degree (as something that may be participated in) and we know life under reason as the highest degree accessible to us—a degree in the making. This is compatible with the claim that there are ranges of Being beyond us. We are never confronted with the alternative that some conceptions of the task of metaphysics taunt us with: *either* complete knowledge of Being *or* no knowledge of Being whatsoever, but only knowledge of phenomena (or knowledge of our categories or our languages). This matter is pursued further in our discussion of potentiality in section IX.

We consequently speak of Being as *common* for several reasons: it is the source at once of the unity of individuals, and of the unity of general modes or levels of being; and this unity, which is non-extensive, is also the source of the unity of reason, which in turn is characterized by a common atmosphere. We take the common character thus imputed to Being to be present in a way inseparable from the presence of any individual, and inseparable from the presence of reason, in all its autonomy, to itself. The generality we are concerned with is the most fundamental accessible to us: we may say that it defines the character of self-evidence for us, or that we presuppose it whenever we appeal to some more special mode of self-evidence. Thus the self-evidence of logic (which is general) and the self-evidence of the applicability of a "universal" to a particular (also general), together with any other mode of self-evidence we should advance, finds place within the self-evidence of a common or general presence. We may also say that the matrix produced by reason's creative and responsible autonomy, from which we detach all rational and empirical standards, has itself a general presence. The other side of all this is that the presence of individual things, although inseparable from diversity and multiplicity, can never be taken to be a bare multiplicity or a bare extensiveness: presence is always as much *common* as *unique*.

This summary runs counter to some usual ways of approaching the question of universality.

A] Because we deal with all this in a framework of language, it is easy enough to look to language as the source of the common atmosphere of reason, and therefore the source of any sense of "common" we have need to invoke. The generality to which reason awakens, we sometimes think, is perhaps simply the recognition that all its activities go on within language and are therefore all of them dependent upon the structure of language. Genetically this is true enough: each of us learns a language, which then becomes an environment inextricably bound up with the environment that is his world. Yet it is also possible to recognize the status of language as a product of reasonable activity, in which case the concrete awakening of reason to its own common power and to the common presence of Being will appear as the ground of the possibility of language, and indeed of alternative languages. We need not, that is, *deduce* the common or universal character of reason by noticing that we possess a language having a categorial structure understandable by others, and that we can enunciate propositions in it that must procure consent from all rational men. We may recognize instead the *source* of language even while our recognition completes itself in language.

b] Similarly, it is only part of the truth that in articulate consciousness we bring a number of particulars under the same general or universal term, categorial scheme, or theory. It is true that the universality of a universal consists in its applicability to a range of particulars that may be said to exemplify it, to participate in its unity, or to be correctly named by it. This fact has given rise to various difficulties. It is usual, for instance, to consider the universal as one and to distinguish its presence from the many individuals to which it applies; and this has led, by way of the assumption that whatever is present must be present as an individual thing, to our regarding the universal as—if real at all—a peculiar kind of individual entity, present in our situation alongside of other individual entities, although with a presence that has its own baffling characteristics. Just what status such a universal should then be accorded has of course been the "problem of universals." Generality, in any case, has been taken to be a *function* of a universal entity, rather than something that can be present precisely *qua* universal or common. On the present view, we possess, in our concrete contrast of the One and the Many, a very present universality or common character. This gives us an utter generality, which justifies and supports the relation between one and many that is so familiar in the application of universals to particulars. It is something we find *in* what we attend to directly, and only for this reason something that belongs to our universals.

The common unity of things is so striking after radically originative reflection that it is not too much to say that we *detach* things from it in order to attend to them. There is an obvious sense in which we detach things from a vaguely apprehended "world" when we attend to them in a common-sense way; now, however, the detachment is of beings from Being, or of aspects, levels, or modes of being from Being. The wisteria already in an Italian April past its height and fading in the sun; the vines sending forth their first shoots; the individual flowers and leaves of these; the children idly watching the ducks; the cypresses along the edge of the road; I can not attend to any of these, any complex of them, any contrast of vividness and vagueness, without lifting them out of an underlying unity. And I can not single out any component of these things—can not make any extensive analysis of them —without detaching what I attend to from the unity of its presiding entity. The two cases echo each other. I can only see the extensiveness within any entity as the extensiveness of something that is present with a unity that is more than just a pattern in that extensiveness, and I can not attend to the extensiveness of things in general without taking that to be the extensiveness of a unity that is more than just a pattern in that extensiveness.

All our encounters with generality, although developing different aspects of it, have been encounters with *one* generality, whose presence we gradually enter under the guidance of radically originative reflection; in that sense we are always deploying the creative and responsible autonomy of reason. If we now speak of Being as a *common formative power,* the sense "common" has in this formula should be clear. It remains to elucidate the sense given "formative" and "power," and to show, in the course of this discussion, what radically originative reflection can contribute to our understanding of order and causation respectively. The formula itself, however, is but another in the long succession of ways of characterizing Being, and there is consequently no reason to suppose that, if we take it to be equivalent to "Being," it will prove any more adequate than past proposals. It is not, however, put forward as an equivalent. We have always before us the task of bringing about more adequately the cognitive presence of beings and Being, which means articulating this presence more adequately in concepts.

V.   *The power inherent in the presence of beings yields us a sense in which the presence of beings is also the presence of the causal relationship. The category "entity" is, however, held to be more fundamental than the category "cause," and the limits of a theory of causation appropriate to philosophical knowledge are set by describing the supervening of an entity upon an extensive range in terms of ontic power, which is distinguished from the causal or conditioning power exercised by its subordinate entities in making their contribution to its presence.*

When one speaks of Being as a common formative *power,* one does so in the first place to avoid the persistent identification of Being with formality itself. What radically originative reflection makes accessible of Being does not permit itself to be identified with the aspect of form that we find so prominent in philosophies that, whatever their greatness, confuse the order and stability of Being with the linguistic or categorial forms in which we articulate our awareness of it. I have myself come as close to this mode of thinking as I suspect it is profitable to venture in conceding that all cognitive awareness, all genuine apprehension of presence, finds its fruition in articulate discourse; as well as in pointing out that the unity of Being is qualified in its common character by the common atmosphere of reason in which, among so many other degrees of being, it is exemplified. But the stability of our symbolic forms is the stability of all man-made contrivance—exempt in some measure from time, possible to contrive no doubt because there is also something exempt from time in Being itself, but causing us to misunderstand that exemption. Here the instinct of Bergson was right, and, even if he was over-concerned with the dynamic features of things—as he must needs have been, conceiving of intuition as he did in terms so closely tied to experience—he has still given us some classical criticism of form-dominated philosophies.

But besides this negative reason for insisting on the presence of power, there is in the presence of all beings and of Being itself a character that is well described by this troublesome word, provided only that we are careful to note that its physical sense is only part of what we intend. This qualification is developed further in the next section. Other words have been put forward with a similar intent, among them "process," "creativity," "duration"; and there is a like motive behind many of the uses to which "existence" is currently put. These, however, have the disadvantage that they ascribe the vitality of Being chiefly to its temporal span, in which things, with difficulty and against obstacles, evolve. This is indeed one important feature of what I here mean by "power," but it is an insufficiently general notion, which besides takes no account of the exercise of power that is, on the present view, the central one, namely, the presiding of an entity over the extensive span given by its components and its history. This exercise of power is the very birthright of an entity, and corresponds, *mutatis mutandis*, to Leibniz's idea of a monad dominating its colony: to be an entity at all is to dominate an extensive span within which other entities are subordinated by being constrained to contribute to the character of the dominant entity.

On this view, then, the influence exercised by an entity in presiding as the non-extensive unity of an extensive span is an exercise of power; while the entities that make up that extensive span themselves exercise power, in that the presiding unity is the unity of just *this* entity because of the contributions of *just these* subordinate entities. This at once introduces two fundamental aspects of the causation problem, in which certain classical difficulties appear in a somewhat different form. The only one that need concern us now is the difficulty of speaking of the influence of the presiding entity upon its subordinates without introducing such questionable expressions as "self-causation" and "self-creation": *what* is it, we may well ask, that exercises this influence, since it *is* not, does not *exist*, prior to the "exercise" of these "influences." What is it indeed, since it *is* not, does not *exist*, prior to the contributions of these subordinates? Questions of this sort have considerable force, and one does well not to forget it under the influence of the common metaphysical concern to uphold both the reality of freedom and the possibility of a complete causal account. But we really need not lay ourselves open to such questions. An account of causation need not be such as to make a complete causal description a sensible objective when we are dealing with an entity, however appropriate it might be if we were dealing with an event or happening: there are respects in which the category "entity" simply includes everything we might wish to articulate by means of the category "cause," and in which recourse to the latter simply blurs what we are trying to attend to. To say that an entity presides over an extensive span is to say that a subordinated entity is under influences it would not have been under were it not so subordinated; and it is to say that the other side of these influences is the successful insinuation of the presence of the presiding entity throughout its extensive span. It is not entirely inappropriate to say that it "emerges" throughout its extensive span, but it is more in keeping with the present position to say that it supervenes upon its extensive span. This supervening is not so much a power exercised *by* an entity as it is the power of *being:* the power, that is, of existing *as* an entity, rather than as an aggregate of components. This mode of power, which has a non-extensive side, to be related in section *VIII* to the *common* feature of our common formative power, I shall call *ontic power.* All power exercised *by* an entity is then held to be derivative from this. Of these multifarious derivative powers, I shall be most concerned with that which is exercised by an entity as it contributes as a subordinate to the character of a supervenient entity, and this mode of power I shall distinguish from ontic power by calling it *causal* or *conditioning power.* The intent is to sketch the outlines of an approach to the causation problem, and many derivative senses of "cause" will be ignored.

The suggestion is that there is a point at which the category "cause" gives way to the category "entity," and that it is more useful to think of subordinate entities as exercising *their* power by being causal factors in a dominating entity, than it is to speak of a dominant entity as exercising power over one of its components as a cause produces an effect. This restriction is intended as much to protect the integrity of the category "cause" as to protect that of the category "entity"; the suggestion is that we are capable of *knowing* causation only as a certain way of regarding beings and Being.

We may summarize this line of thought by saying that the Aristotelian four-fold approach to causation (a scheme already more informally present in Plato), while bringing out a real complexity in things, would have been more successful if the close alliance between "formal cause," "final cause," and "entity" (which Aristotle in fact acknowledges) had been exploited to bring out the different sense the word "cause" has in the first two cases from what it has in the expressions "efficient cause" and "material cause." As it is, much needless effort on the part of those who see some worth in the metaphysical tradition has gone into the enterprise of demonstrating, what is surely true, that causal accounts in terms of efficient and material causation are incomplete.[10] They must necessarily be incomplete in that they neglect the *entity* they seek to describe; any naturalistic or scientific account of the emergence of life or of consciousness will afford an example. The point here is that we ought not to try to complete them in some metaphysical sense by resolving, however ingeniously, the category of entity entirely into components of a telic or a formal sort. We thus express in our own terms the concern of so much existential thought to protect the *freedom* of *existence*.

Being concerned here with the first, or philosophical mode of knowledge, we are not obliged to give such an account of causation as shall be consonant with the needs of the speculative-empirical cycle. The abstractness of that cycle may call for a version of causation equally abstract, and equally restricted to the issue of a complete extensive description. Thus the interest of physics in causality is circumscribed in somewhat the way suggested by this definition of causality put forward by R. E. Peierls: "By the law of causality, one usually means the statement that the laws of physics determine the fate of a physical system completely, provided that all the information about it is known at one particular instant of time." [11] Professor Peierls goes on to make the qualifications that the indeterminacy principle makes necessary, noticing, what is surely true, that these difficulties about the observation of individual electrons make no difference to the absoluteness of the laws. Physics may be said to be concerned with a complete causal description whose perusal of extensiveness is only slightly divergent from that proposed in the ideal of Laplace. But what may well be an entirely reasonable pursuit within the dimensions of the speculative-empirical cycle is not only not obligatory but besides wholly inappropriate in our first mode of knowledge. In the one we may even leave the category "entity" out of account, in that we take entities of some sort for granted and focus instead upon the measurable conditions of the *events* in which they move, interact, combine and recombine, are transformed, and so on. In the other we are concerned to make entities present in their very character of entity. In the philosophical mode of knowledge the problem of causation, although central to our discussion of power, should perhaps be dealt with not by another *theory* of causation, but by allowing the character of our recognition of Being to suggest that we are in danger of an inappropriate abstractness when we press the issue of causation too far in our first mode.

On this view, then, the influence exercised by an entity that presides over or supervenes upon an extensive span as the non-extensive unity of it, is the exercise of power, although an exercise less susceptible to treatment in terms of causation than is the reciprocal influence of the subordinate entities upon which it supervenes. Even that reciprocal influence is, however, no reason for the exclusive insistence on temporal order that is so common a feature of theories of causation, especially those that are appropriate to the speculative-empirical cycle. The presiding unity that is present to us whenever an entity is present exercises power by supervening upon an extensive span that is *both* spatial and temporal; while the influence exercised by the subordinate entities in contributing to the character of the dominant entity is also both temporal and spatial. The claim that in their spatial order subordinated entities contribute a causal power is the denial of the claim that entities that are "simultaneous" can have no causal concourse.

VI. *Merely because we say that we feel certain modes of power, we do not mean that such power is not at the same time* known. *We know power through the mediation of the body and know also this mediation. Our reflective act permits us to see that powers so known are modes of a power whose more fundamental sense we capture in the expression* "ontic power."

In approaching the problem of power by way of the presence of individual entities, we have circumvented one common misconception. It is that power is accessible only to a pre-rational or sub-rational apprehension, such as Bergson's intuition of the *élan vital* so often seems to be. This prejudice is associated with another I have mentioned frequently: that all direct awareness has something sub-rational in it in at least this sense, that it is intractable to conceptual formulation. This prejudice is intensified in the case of power, which we think of as intimately associated with a wide and various mode of sensuous apprehension often summed up in the word "feeling." Even so convinced a rationalist as Whitehead seems to have supposed that this is the mode in which we apprehend power, a consideration which has surely much to do with his making prehension so central a category in his philosophy. The prejudice is a deep one, whose grounds are certainly strong enough. There is a clear association between our senses and at least the most clamorous kinds of power: the pull of gravity on our bodies, the shock of an electric current, the impact of a blow, the warmth of the sun; the exercise on our own part of muscular power in some physical game or task, or of nervous energy as we work at some intellectual task. And we cannot give a description of any power without invoking, at least metaphorically, powers like these. Even those powers we encounter when in the grip of emotion or when—a related but not identical matter—we enjoy a work of art, we speak of in terms that are rooted in these familiar powers.

Against this misconception it should be clear that we are *cognitively* aware of powers of many sorts, even if that awareness is bound up with the acknowledgment that it is mediated by this or that bodily faculty that goes back ultimately to sensory roots: I am thus cognitively aware, for instance, of the weight of my body, of the heat of the sun, of the taste of wine, of pleasure and pain, although I also acknowledge that these are powers that affect me through my body. The sanction given by reason's creative autonomy to our cognitive awareness of the presence of beings extends also to what is after all not something different and new, but a characteristic of that presence. Our grasp is also in this case a mingling of the unique and the common: we grasp just this *particular* power, grasp it as just this *mode* of power, and grasp it as *power*. A being in its unity supervenes upon an extensive range, but that supervening, both in its individual and its general aspects, is expressible as power. The full awareness of power, like the full awareness of anything whatever, finds its fruition in the articulation of discourse.

Yet we may still wonder whether the connection of the word "power" with the world of sense and feeling does not inappropriately color our apprehension of ontic power. To claim that there is a sense of power that is an important aspect of the very exercise of being would seem to be to use a sense-laden conception beyond the sphere in which sensation is possible. It is a difficulty somewhat like the one established for metaphysics by Kant when he claimed to show that our *a priori* categories are synthetic because they are bound to the sensuous manifold. We have, however, mastered the difficulty before, in our discussion of sensation. There we saw sensation not so much as a limitation as an avenue, for creatures situated as we are, to much of the variety of extensiveness. The approach by way of recognition allowed us to make an inversion: we did not so much come to beings and Being by way of sensation as we came to the nature of sensation by way of the recognition of beings and Being. The color given to our language by sensation persisted, but no longer deceived us because we understood its significance. So here, with the analogous topic of power, in which we come to recognize the modes of power that are closest to sense and feeling as precisely *modes* of a power whose root sense is more adequately captured when we speak of it as ontic power than when more usual senses are employed. Yet the echoes of the world of sense that the word "power" always carries with it are salutary: they remind us that we are not talking about something behind and quite different from our everyday world, but that same world as it really is. The common word merely begins to gain an unsuspected depth, even as do such words as "unity," "presence," "common," and even "Being."

VII. Power even as embodied in individuals has its common or general aspect. This feature, which is seen in the next section to have consequences for teleology, is in this one used to develop a sense of power analogous to the classical idea of matter.

We can now go on to speak of power as the influence of entities, remembering however that one of these influences is a peculiar one: not that exercised by an entity taken as a whole, but the "ontic" power exercised by an entity in order to be the entity it is. It was implicit in our earlier discussion of the *common* aspect of Being's formative power that the ontic power of an individual is a sharing or participating in it. The presence of any individual entity is also the presence of the common unity of things, and both the individual and the common presences manifest power. I said, in section *III*, that the layers or modes of being upon which a higher entity supervenes possess themselves, *as layers or modes*, a general aspect: the character of a subordinate level was not entirely captured by thinking of it as a mere assemblage of entities each making an individual contribution. This approach to the problem of generality will yield consequences for teleology in the next section, but here I wish to use it in order to develop a sense of general power analogous to the classical conception of matter. The point at issue is that whether we analyze an entity in terms of the causal contributions of its subordinate entities (causal or conditioning power) or recognize it *as* an entity (ontic power), we are unable to deal with it adequately in terms of purely individual presences, but must look at individuality itself in terms of both particularity and generality.

We are often able to attend to the exercise of power by a given entity taken as a whole: this complex molecule in the cell nucleus is associated with such and such gross characteristics of the organism; a certain friend influences me in a difficult decision; just this man cuts back the vine in the vineyard below. Much of the time, however, our attention is not discriminating enough, and we are concerned with the power exercised by large groups of entities whose identities are lost: an animal in the course of a day consumes this or that quantity of a certain protein molecule; we are penetrated daily by I know not how many bundles of energy from the electro-magnetic spectrum. Few would quarrel with the examples except perhaps to point out, first, that an exact scientific description of all these transactions would take a somewhat different course, leading us rather far from what can easily be construed as an account in terms of Aristotelian substances; and, second, that the obviousness of such "power" transactions has been in dispute at least since Hume. To the first, it need only be said that we are now concerned to mark the presence of certain modes of power, not to give a quantitative account of their deployment; an answer to the second has, of course, been given several times in the course of this book. There are other powers that do not fall in either of the classes just considered: they are not exerted by individual entities, nor is it appropriate to think of them as merely the summation of the contributions of large numbers of individual entities. Space and time are thus general powers in the sense that they estab-lish conditions for any entity inhabiting them. It is true enough to say of space that it is a way in which entities are together, but if space were not more than this, we should leave open the possibility that the entities we know might somehow exist "without" space; and plainly these are entities *fitted* for this mode of being together: they are precisely spatial entities. By this I mean only that being together in this mode is not some-thing extrinsic and accidental to them. Being fitted to be to-gether in this way is to exemplify a general level or mode of being. We may think of space, then, as having a general char-acter that gives it a unity of its own rather than the unity of an aggregate. So too with time. It is tempting to think of it as merely a way in which entities are together—the togetherness of entities looked at somewhat differently from the way that yields space. We cannot, however, expunge temporality from the character of any *one* entity that we should consider: these are entities *fitted* for that mode of togetherness that we call time. If there is no time without individual entities, there are no individual entities without time: these are temporal entities, and being together in the mode of time is not something extrinsic or accidental to them. Both time and space "belong" to each individual entity, yet there is more in these powers than the aggregation of these entities will explain. They are not merely *phenomena bene fundata*, whose foundation consists in the mere plurality of entities, but themselves modes of being, having their foundation in a common formative power, which supports individuality as well. The idea of a common formative power implies more than just a contrast of the One and the Many, in which these stand respectively for the *collection* and the *plurality* of the items collected; generality itself —the *sharing* of many in one is part of what we mean. What is general or common in the sense that many may share in it may also be shared in by modes of being that are themselves common. The world we recognize is a world of individuals, but the common power that supports all of them manifests itself also in powers that are in some respects general powers.

This means only that the "world" has a unity of its own, and is not simply an aggregate of entities each of which happens to have a common root. The manyness or diverse multiplicity that I have been calling "extensiveness" has a unity of its own. The unity of each individual entity is one in which a *being* insinuates itself throughout an extensive span, a being whose components are *beings*, and to which the aspect of extensiveness is not something extrinsic. Nor can it therefore be extrinsic to the common formative power that is at the heart of all extensive entities: our grounds for refusing to think of an entity as a merely extensive pattern are equally grounds for recognizing that extensiveness itself is a mode of being, sharing in the common formative power of Being even while remaining the principle of diversity and multiplicity.

The topic of the general powers that act *on* an entity, and that are reciprocally made use of as it presides over its extensive range, is one aspect of the problem of power. But matter does not appear only in the guise of such general powers as time and space, gravity, and energy. Any complex entity does, it is true, supervene upon such powers, and also upon layers or modes of being that are present as a multiplicity of individuals (as an organism supervenes on molecular structures) and that therefore exemplify another aspect of matter; but it supervenes besides over layers or modes that, although they *could* be embodied in individuals, are not so embodied in the case in question. Thus man's highest mode—the mode of rational self-consciousness—supervenes on a general layer of animality, which is elsewhere exemplified in individuals of a lower rank, but is here simply a subordinate mode in an individual. It is a mode embodied to be sure in organic structures, but these form for the supervening individual a layer or mode which, although it is indeed *its* animality, has no status either as an individual entity or as a collection of such but exists precisely *as* a level *in* an individual.

Matter thus understood as a general power is always matter in a relative sense: a degree of being, which in turn could be regarded as a supervenient level. Pressed far enough, however, as in the discussion of extensiveness just above, it is the topic of *prime* matter that is at issue: not some particular extensive complex over which a new entity presides, but the mere fact of extensive multiplicity, taken now as something that possesses a generality of its own. So understood, the influences of matter are pervasive and ambiguous; as much so as the barely real factor that Plato called the Receptacle—something we characterize only at the risk of falsifying it. From our point of view, extensiveness itself is thought of as a general power, and as such an expression of the unity of the common formative power, though not in itself a unity in that sense. Its only unity is that of a pervasive medium, and in this sense it is a power that is prior to any particular embodiment of it.

VIII. The dispute between naturalisms and finalisms cen-
ters on the question of the force that so orders causal
powers as to permit new ontic powers to supervene.
Once more ontic power—this time that of the com-
mon formative power—is invoked: the common form-
ative power, as the presiding unity in which successive
layers of supervenient power share, is, by virtue of this
same fact, that ordering "force."

The approach to the problem of causation by way of the
distinction between ontic power and causal power is so far
incomplete. If we suppose an entity supervenient upon the
causal contributions of its subordinate extensive complex, and
think of that supervening as an exercise of ontic power in
which these contributions are levied to its needs, we have still
to ask how it comes about that the subordinate entities are so
ordered that the supervenient entity is able to supervene. Just
here naturalistic and metaphysical outlooks are most at odds,
especially when the question is posed in terms of the evolution
of life. What sort of account is to be given? Are we to restrict
ourselves to a program based on a doctrine of causation suited
to the interests of physics? Or should we attempt an account in
terms suitable to our persistent, although doubtless muddled,
concern for the problem of purpose? I shall develop an answer
predicated upon the right intent and value of our interest in
purpose, which I take to be congruent with our interest in
Being itself. It is an answer given, however, in full consciousness of the muddle that usually accompanies telic theories, and
with no pretense of escaping muddle entirely. Nor do I intend
to deprecate our continued efforts to press naturalistic explanations of such matters as life as far as we are able within
the limitations of the speculative-empirical cycle. Such explanations at the least give us something that we are deeply
concerned to know: causal or conditioning powers in all their
intricacy; and we need hope for no further restriction upon

them than that they should be pursued in consciousness of their limitations.

We begin by noticing the success of naturalistic explanations and the difficulties this poses for any attempt to defend a telic view.

The periodic table of the elements illustrates the dependence of the properties of chemical elements, and consequently of the compounds they will form, upon their atomic structure. A proton as nucleus and an attendant electron form the ordinary hydrogen atom; a combination of eight protons and eight neutrons as a nucleus, and eight attendant electrons forms an oxygen atom; two atoms of hydrogen and one of oxygen form a water molecule. The story thus simply begun can be continued systematically through more complicated non-organic and organic compounds until we reach the complex protein molecules that make up the chromatin material in the nuclei of living cells. The arrangement of this material in sets of chromosomes in reproduction, the structure of these sets in different species, and the structural behavior of these sets in the formation of new individuals, can be studied in ways that bear important resemblances to a study of the combinatory characteristics of elements. The principle that the determinants of distinct gross characteristics in the organism are local structural properties of the molecules making up the chromosomes is unquestioned, even if the details are only beginning to be understood. Mutations are clearly structural changes in complex molecules, and these changes can be subjected to the same sort of quantum analysis as can be brought to the study of structural changes in elements and simple compounds. This last point qualifies my otherwise over-simple account in terms of an easy assortment of integral items. But with this qualification, the way would appear to be open in principle to a causal account of life and its gradual development in terms exclusively of combinations of simpler entities. In the present terminology, such an account would deal only in the causal power of the component entities, treating what I have called the ontic power of supervenient entities as merely a function or epiphenomenon of these. There would consequently be no need for any nearer approach to the telic issue, and we could content ourselves in matters of evolution with some version of the neo-Darwinian approach, which I discussed briefly in Chapter 5, section V. I do not mean to suggest that the category "causal power of an entity"would have any very appropriate place in the speculative-empirical cycle. I am also ignoring the fact that there is reason to suppose that the simplest entities that are ingredient in things are not individual entities but familial sequences of individuals, each of which might be thought of as having an extensive span, although not one analyzable in terms of subordinates. In passing, however, it might be observed that the view of presence made tenable by our reflective act is quite hospitable to this latter interpretation.

By stating the root idea of the naturalistic program in just this way, one emphasizes a strength that no modified telic program need be loath to concede to it: causal or conditioning powers are real powers, and no complex entity can either exercise its ontic power to supervene in their absence, or escape an alteration in its own constitution if the conditions established by the causal powers alter. This should not, however, conceal from us the fact that, as concerns higher entities at least, no one is presently in a position to press the matter beyond this concession—we are surely dealing with what is still a program only. In simpler spheres one has only to produce the conditions, that is, suitably conjoin the simpler entities, and the more complex ones will result: igniting a jet of hydrogen under ordinary laboratory conditions will inevitably produce water. But in so complex a sphere as life we can only say that alteration of the causal or conditioning powers produces alterations in the living entity; we cannot say that the conditions *produce* the entity, for we cannot isolate all of the conditions and consider them *before* they are already inextricably *conditions of a living entity*. The structural behavior of chromosomes is as much an *effect* of life as a *cause*, and we cannot consider them apart from the role they play in the development of entities. Some of the causal powers that play a role in an entity can indeed be considered apart; but about the totality of them we can say only that it is possible to describe in some detail the effects that are produced within the living entity by altering them. Nor is it at all clear that we should have made very great headway towards completing the naturalistic program if we were able to produce some form of life artificially in the laboratory, seeing that we should then have had recourse to the efficacy of our own living purpose.

But beyond these difficulties, the greatest obstacle in the way of the program is the question of the principle that brings about the juxtaposition of causal powers in such a way as to produce "higher" entities, or, in the present terminology, to permit them to supervene. We have already seen the great obscurity surrounding this question when it is approached in naturalistic terms, an obscurity that has helped foster a widespread interest in alternative approaches even among many writers whose frame of reference is by and large science rather than philosophy. But telic interpretations of the principle are equally obscure, and frequently self-contradictory, in that they seem to defeat the very freedom that it is one part of their purpose to defend. The struggles of Leibniz, of Whitehead, and of Bergson with the problem of freedom offer a case in point: it is not at all clear that the first two have escaped what Bergson called radical finalism, nor does it seem that Bergson's revision of finalism escapes the voluntaristic difficulties of his nineteenth century forebears. On the present view there is indeed a *telos*, but only in the sense that [A] the exercise of ontic power has its non-extensive side, and [B] ontic power is more fundamental than causal power. This claim will now be discussed in two fairly extended stages, in which themes already stated will be developed so as to display their relevance to the problem of causation. The real *defense* of the claim is simply our power of recognition as authenticated by radically originative reflection; I hope however, that the obscurity of both naturalism and the current forms of finalism in dealing with such a matter as life will make others more receptive to yet another attack on this so familiar problem.

In the *first stage* we deal again with an entity as displaying layers or levels of order, as well as with the interpenetration of individuality and generality in real presence. As we recognize any complex entity, as for instance a man, we recognize levels of supervenient power, which may be alternatively expressed in terms of levels of supervenient order, or simply in terms of levels or degrees of being. It is the presence of an order *making use of* other and lower levels of order that strikes us, and both the *fact* of presence and the *stature* of it are authenticated by the responsible autonomy with which recognition proceeds. If the reformulation of finalism is to become clear, one must insist that the extensive span upon which a higher entity supervenes cannot be understood merely as a multiplicity of subordinate individual entities, but must also be taken as a series of levels or degrees of being that are, taken precisely as levels, general or common. The point at issue is this: whether we analyze an entity in terms of the causal contributions of its subordinate entities (the causal or conditioning powers entering into it) or recognize it *as* an entity (its own ontic power), we are unable to deal with it adequately in terms of purely individual presences; individuality itself, whether it is that of a supervenient entity, or that of one of its component entities, is never "pure," but itself is always a mingling of the unique and the general.

In any complex entity we may therefore perceive two contrasts of one and many, each legitimate if it is understood that it is inseparable from the other. A] A contrast of one supervenient individual and many subordinate individuals, as for instance its cells, these in turn being conceivable in terms of the individual entities, or the families of entities that they comprise. B] A contrast between one supervenient individual and its many subordinate general levels of order, atomic, molecular, living, animal, rationally conscious. A third contrast merely rehearses the inseparability of the other two: that is C] the contrast between the individual and its many organs and other structures, which do not have the same status as possible individual entities in their own right that cells and molecules may have. These organs and structures have frequently many of the characteristics of individuals: a distinct developmental and functional pattern; the possibility of transfer to other environments, as in the case of transplants; and so on; yet they do not exist with the degree of independence (at best a relative matter) that we find in individual organisms, but merely share imperfectly the unity of the parent organism, being in this sense quasi-entities. We see their true character when we notice that certain complexes of organs, although they here contribute what I call causal or conditioning power to just *this* entity, constitute *levels* in the sense that they *could* constitute the dominant order of some lower entity. We can, in short, single out organic structural patterns that we share with many levels of lower animals, so that the manyness of organic structures can also appear either as a level or as many levels of general order. It is, of course, a commonplace that these phylogenetic features have important parallels in ontogeny.

The result is a view of causal or conditioning power that embraces something of two approaches to the problem of causation: 1] naturalism's insistence that "higher" entities are in fact complex units resulting from the combination of "lower" or simpler entities; 2] Aristotle's view of material causality as the contribution of a lower formal (and thus in part general) order to a higher formal order. But I would insist here on what the modern reader may easily miss, namely, the genuinely causal character of both features. I am *not* saying that causal or conditioning power is only the contribution of complexes of individual entities, and that we then *know* or *apprehend* this efficacy in terms of general levels. I am making the much more unusual claim that causal or conditioning power is *qua* power in part general: that the categories "individual entity" and "general mode or level of being" interpenetrate. Any subordinate level discerned within an individual is recognized as a level that could be exemplified in an individual; and the highest supervenient order manifested in an individual can itself be exemplified in other individuals. From this point of view there is no conflict between essence (taken as expressing the conception of a mode or level of being) and existence (taken as expressing the quality of an individual entity). In our fundamental contrast of the One and the Many, the manyness appears both in *many common levels* and *many individuals*, and the grounding of an individual in the common formative power is also the grounding of a level. No further explanation is thought necessary in that the very character of any individual presence that we recognize in our prolongation of radically originative reflection is present as a participation in, and therefore a level of, the common formative power.

The aim of this enlargement of the topic of causal power was simply to reinforce the point that a complex entity is present in terms of levels of *supervenient* order, present that is in terms of successive levels of ontic power, each supervening upon lower levels. Any level *qua* lower contributes causally to a higher; *qua* level it is supervenient upon such levels as contribute to it. The echo of Aristotelian analysis of the "soul" is intentional, although with a different emphasis, which reshapes the category of form.

If we now, in the *second stage* of this argument, approach the question of what it is that orders or juxtaposes causal powers to "produce" higher entities, we find that this "force" is simply coincidental with the presiding ontic power of what I have been calling the common formative power: the telic "cause" is absorbed in the category of being, since it now becomes identical with Being itself. In the presence of any complex entity two things strike us chiefly: A] what one may express either as the presence of an order making use of the presence of other and lower orders, or as the presence of a power making use of the presence of other and lower powers; B] the common roots of these levels. The levels are recognized as genuinely *supervening*, that is, as levels of being and not mere extensive complexes, and they are besides recognized as richer and richer expressions of, or participations in, what they have in common. We may say that we are dealing with the same Being, hierarchically disposed: there is simply more of it at higher levels, and lower levels, in participating in what is thus common, prepare the way for and foreshadow the higher levels; this is why we can say that the higher levels really *supervene* upon these, that is, include, make use of, absorb, and complete them, in the very act of being what the lower levels foreshadow. The lower levels contribute to the higher by being what they are, seeing that, taken as ontic powers, they are "for their own sake"; while the higher powers make use of the lower by being what *they* are—that is, by supervening as ontic powers over the extensive range of their subordinates.

But just this combination of *degree* and *common* gives us the sense in which the common formative power presides over its participant entities, not just *after the fact* that a new and higher entity has supervened, but *in the very ordering of lower powers* that is inseparable from that supervening. The ordering of the lower powers is indeed nothing more than the other face of what I have been calling a supervenient power, and, while we were troubled by the thought of the self-causation in which a not-yet-completed entity should bring about the conditions of its own presence, we need not be troubled if we think of that supervening and its concomitant ordering of subordinates as a participation in a presiding formative power that is participated in by all entities whatsoever. We do well to speak of presiding rather than supervening in the case of the common formative power because it is not associated with any particular extensive range but with the whole of extensiveness: in the case of individual entities their individuality is salient, although their roots are in what is common; in the case of Being—for it is the presiding character of Being that we are talking about—what is common is salient, and its individual character appears to us only in its role as principle of individuation.

Because the common formative power presides, there *are*

ranked levels of being, and we need look no further than what is present in the *existence* of ranked levels to account for their *origin*. Thus the ontic power that is Being manifests itself in several ways: as that in which the ontic power deployed at any level shares; as that which makes the very constitution of any level amenable to arrangements that afford opportunities for the supervening of higher levels; in the coming to pass of such arrangements; and—what is the same as the former—the supervening of the higher level. The emergence of any new level of being is coincidental with the ordering of causal powers (conditions) that we have been regarding as problematic, but the new level can now be regarded as bringing about the ordering of its *own* conditions in that *its* ontic power is a sharing in an ontic power that presided no less *in* those conditions and in the *ordering* of them.

We have so far neglected the role played by parent organisms in so ordering causal powers as to permit the supervening of successive levels of order duplicating levels present in the parents. At first glance this issue raises difficulties for the present approach to causation, but a further consideration only re-emphasizes the importance of regarding the ontic power of any individual as a sharing in that of a presiding formative power; so that it appears, finally, that our approach affords a framework within which what are crucial problems for naturalistic and neo-Darwinian views of life find an intelligible resolution.

It is not unusual to regard parental organisms as forming an environment or field within which causal powers, while breaking no naturalistic laws, undergo an ordering whose predictability is not given by those laws if the parental field is neglected. It is a field whose function varies with the levels of evolution we consider: the cell establishes the environment within which its own division takes place; a more complex parent organism furnishes the field within which the germ cells develop, within which the early stages of the embryo are laid down, or within which it is fully matured. The disposition to regard such matters as calling for a non-naturalistic analysis, though a fresh and promising one in contemporary biology, is as old as Aristotle, for whom the formal and final causes, taken now as but two aspects of essence, could be regarded as functions of the adult, which carries the essence and passes it on. It is, however, just this image, suggestive of an essence or nature inherited rather than shaped in action, that so troubled Bergson in dealing with metaphysical finalisms, that troubles many existentialists, and that might seem a difficulty for our own view. When we think of the efficacy of the parent organism as contributing to the ordering of the conditions or causes that enter into the constitution of the new entity, we seem to suppose that an achieved phylogenetic level dominates the ontogeny of the new entity, whose own ontic power thus appears to be cancelled.

The idea of a *common* formative power, capable of being participated in in various degrees, shared by parent and offspring, shared indeed by all entities, diminishes the force of this image. The parental organism, indeed the whole species in its development, participates in a common unity, so that we cannot single out any parental organism and say that *it* in its uniqueness has formed the field within which the conditions of some given entity were brought to pass. Yet this observation by no means simply reinforces the view that a common phylogenetic level is determinative of the constitution of a new entity, since all that the ordering of causal powers by the parental organism accomplishes is the preservation of a set of conditions that itself made use of. It is a preservation *by* an ontic power that is at once individual and a sharing in a common level; and it is a preservation *for* the supervention of a new ontic power that is already present *as* an individual the moment sets of possible conditions can be called the real conditions of a new entity. What troubles us is, at it were, the faithfulness of Being, as when, in any deliberate experiment in genetics, we bring it about that sets of conditions at least approximating our desire "yield" a new entity, "yield," it may even turn out, an entity exemplifying a higher level. On the present view, possibilities established by sets of genetic conditions—possibilities that can be delineated with great exactness —are possibilities themselves carried along or preserved by ontic powers, just as they are exploited by an ontic power, that of reason. And if Being responds faithfully (in this limited sense) to our importunities, it is also true that the whole situation hardly receives a sufficient explanation by thinking of it in terms of the efficacy of *our* phylogenetic level in the production of new entities. From a point of view in which we attend to long-term development, the very same situation appears as the production of a phylogenetic advance through the medium of ontogeny, for it is in individuals that a new species or a new stage in an old one appears.

The topic of freedom may now be introduced with some hope of clarity. Freedom is a precious commodity in the senses relevant to our human occasions, and in our wish to protect it we often go too far, positing something irrational and disordered as its metaphysical ground, where we should have been concerned merely with the authenticity of our attempts to produce order. The case is analogous to our attempts to protect the knowable order of things: there, a wish for precision often leads to an artificial epistemological position in which we find we have emptied our universe of precisely what it was important and interesting to grasp. On the present view there is this minimal freedom that is the birthright of any entity: the freedom that is inseparable from any ontic power. The root of freedom is the exercise of the character of entity, but it is not a freedom compatible with an ultimate unqualified pluralism, since the exercise of the character of entity is itself something shared in; nor is it a freedom that is incompatible with the display of an order, degree, or level of being that may be participated in. It is, at last, only the freedom of being an entity, and of exercising a causal power derivative from that status— derivative, that is, from its ontic power. This is not sufficient to authenticate what defenders of free will wish to defend, but it is a necessary condition for such an authentication.

Is there a freedom that carries with it that sense of open alternatives that we value in what we hope is free and rational choice? The individual "freedom" of ontic power is presumably something compatible with the fact that hydrogen will always combine with oxygen to produce water, and we presumably are interested in more than this when we talk of human freedom. We may find it perhaps in the fact that supervening levels of being differ in their character, and that what supervenes at certain high levels has within it an openness or freedom that is proper to it. To exist at an animal level is to exercise an ontic power not merely free in the sense proper to any ontic power, but free in the sense that will, mobility, and dawning intelligence afford; to exist at the level of reason is to exercise an ontic power in which those "rational potencies" that Aristotle distinguished from the rest of nature come into their own. It is not a freedom compatible with an absolute pluralism, marked as it is with what any ontic power *shares* in; in addition to which it is characterized by the reflective concern for the common and the reflectively apprehended atmosphere of the common that we spoke of earlier. It is a degree of being that is not only a level of being or order, but one whose ontic power exercises itself in the recognition of order, and in creation and action in accordance with this recognition; a level of being, moreover, concerned with the reflective recognition of its own order. This *mode* of freedom is this *mode* of ontic power, and all our long adventure with the idea of a creative autonomy not tied to this responsibility must end here at last. What was in the case of lower levels a *telos* only in the sense of being an ontic power, is here a *telos* indeed, for the order of consciousness is purposefully directed upon order and its achievement. In this mode of being purpose has supervened, allowing us to say at least this much of our common formative power, that purposeful entities participate in it. Returning briefly to the theme of Chapter 3, which will be expanded in the last chapter, we can say that rational consciousness here dwells in conditions it would enlist to its purposes. But these are tenacious in asserting their independence: they sometimes fall into place, so that the level of reason—reason in action no less than reason in contemplation—supervenes; and sometimes they do not. Even the recognition of its own order—that self-recognition we take to be equivalent to philosophy—is a supervening upon conditions that might not have yielded to its persuasions. But one hope we may have in the recognition of reason is that it may make the supervention of this mode of reality more constant and more sure.

IX. *The power exercised by an entity is a sharing or participating in the common formative power. At any moment of its history an entity exhibits a potentiality that is an aspect of its non-extensiveness. But its potentiality is not then merely "its" unexercised power, but a share in the potentiality of the common formative power. This gives the presence of an entity a depth that is in contrast with its own finitude.*

As the unity of any individual entity is in fact a common unity in which it shares or participates, so is its power, which we have seen to be an aspect of that unity, a power in which it shares. Our recognition of an entity, although it has a non-extensive aspect that radically originative reflection permits us to appreciate, has also its extensive side, whose most prominent feature, in common-sense terms, is that acts of consciousness take time. On the present view time has at least some of the characteristics of Bergsonian duration, for it is never merely extensive. That does not save us from the normal consequences of a temporal existence: we recognize entities in time-spans that are rarely coincidental with the whole life of the entity. This means that any entity exhibits potentiality by presiding over an extensive span that is incomplete and that yet appears as subject to completion. But since the power by means of which it is to complete itself is a shared power, there is also something common in that potentiality.

What from this point of view appears as a potentiality in which an individual participates, appears from another point of view as the potentiality of the extensive world itself. The common formative power is present as a partially unexercised power, upon which the very continuation of extensiveness— the very persistence of the world, that is—depends. This is the other side of our inability to survey the whole of possible experience, an inability represented in Chapter 5 as the problem of macroscopic extensiveness. The common formative power is present as something unexhausted by the totality of its manifestations; therefore its presence is always, for all the non-extensive features of it, qualified by potentiality.

We speak of potentiality here by contrast with the actuality of the extensive world as we know it. But in another sense, made familiar by the terminology of Aristotle, we speak of the presence of the common formative power as actual over against the potentiality that extensiveness embodies. The multiplicity of entities that make up the "actual" world come into being and pass away: extensiveness, we may say, is always potentially the entities that will supplant the present ones; and the actuality that any entity possesses in its day rests upon another actuality—that of the common formative power. What terminology we adopt depends largely upon whether we give "actuality" the auspicious sense of an abiding, or the inauspicious sense of a transient, reality. The intent, however, is to characterize the common formative power as possessing its power non-extensively, to the extent that its presiding over an extensive range is a non-extensive presiding. A *fortiori*, an individual entity, presiding over an extensive range in virtue of its non-extensiveness, would be said to exhibit power *qua* non-extensive. An indispensable feature of ontic power is non-extensiveness.

In each individual entity there is, then, an intimation of the resources of the common formative power, which it shares or participates in merely to exercise its birthright as an entity: its resources are not just those now realized or about to be realized in the course of its history. They are, to be sure, limited in the sense that it is just *this* entity, with just *this* extensive span, we are concerned with, but they are never limited in the sense of being utterly private. They are participations in or expressions of a common power and carry anticipations, foreshadowings, tentative sketches of possible beings that exceed whatever degree is here realized. The other face of this is that any individual entity in its presence is present *as* a degree of something common, this being part of what we ought to mean by the expression essence. An essence expresses a limitation, but a limitation of a common possession whose superior degrees are present as we realize that we are concerned with a limitation. In this sense the resources of any individual entity, however slight, flood into it as from a superabundant source, giving it a character that we miss if we attend only to the notion of *limit*. A limit is also an achieved order, or as the ancients would have said, a form, and carries with it its kinship to all the order of which it may be rightly said to remind us. At any moment in its history, then, an individual entity is what it is by virtue of unexpressed resources that are only in part "its own," no less than by what we can recount precisely of its extensive details. It is this that causes an access of wonder—that same wonder of which the first stages of our reflective act were already an intimation—at the chrysanthemums or asters on the desk, at the chestnut—that great rooted blossomer—in the corner of the garden, at the child swinging on the old apple tree. It is moreover what makes the general powers of extensiveness exceed whatever abstract analysis we can make of them: what I likened to matter becomes a two-faced god, the energy needed to create or destroy; and time itself takes on some of its ancient attributes of fate or providence.

X.   A reformulation of the Platonic insight: the individual entity is taken to be a sharing or participating in
a common formative power; and the status of formality (and therefore of order and law) is derived from
this participation. The common formative power is
indeed common, but it is also a principle of individuation; the individual is unique, but not merely unique.
No conflict between individuality and formality is
entertained since any level of order is established by
way of the ontic power of individuals.

Throughout the earlier sections of this chapter, sometimes directly, and sometimes by way of the conception of a level or
degree of being, we have been dealing with the idea of order.
The idea was indeed implicit in that of a common *formative*
power, but we must now consider the association between
form and order more directly, trying to do justice to the real
aspect of things that we name by these words—an aspect that
seemed so important to Plato, Aristotle, Leibniz, and Whitehead, to name only a few—without attenuating the ontic
power that characterizes the real presence of beings and Being.

A correspondent who once taxed Whitehead (so the
story goes) with some difficulty in the doctrine of Eternal
Objects was infuriated to receive the tranquil reply that Whitehead "accepted the difficulties of the Platonic position." Without wishing to accept Whitehead's, or indeed any, Platonism
that would make Forms more substantial than the entities
participating in them, one may still see the force of the observation. I remarked earlier that philosophy must always come
to terms with the Platonic insight, and I may now point out
that in adopting the present view one does to a degree accept
the difficulties of the Platonic position; not, however, with
regard to Forms or Eternal Objects, but with regard to the
presence of *any* entity. We are already accustomed to the claim
that individuality is not to be identified with the merely
unique: that to be an individual is precisely to share in a

common power. We must not hesitate to pursue this to its deepest consequences, for if it gives us a new difficulty to accept, it also takes us behind some of the traditional perplexities about individuation. We go beyond the attribution of the formality or definiteness of an entity to its participation in the common formative power, for we claim that it is to just this participation that it owes its character *as* an individual as well. There is, on the one hand, no definiteness in the individual that is not in principle open to further exemplification, except its character as just *this* individual; yet on the other, the privacy of even this latter character is qualified by being a share in the principle that establishes such privacy.

The importance of thus rooting individuation in what is common is that we need no longer think of the formality of the individual as standing in radical opposition to its incommunicable uniqueness. This felt opposition has led to two great views of individuation, each of which misses something important in the individual. The first is the traditional Aristotelian view, in which we embody our respect for the definiteness of an entity in the idea of a (specific) form, which is exemplified in the entity; with the result that the individuality itself comes to appear as the most contingent thing in the world: the work of a matter that individuates the form even as it is shaped and ordered by the form. The second, arising in opposition to this, ascribes individuation to a form (the *haecceitas*) that is exclusively the form of the individual in question; with the result that the definiteness of the individual is protected at the expense of what I am here calling its ontic power. On my own view, on the other hand, the formality of the individual, in the sense of its repeatable definiteness, and in the sense as well of its incommunicably private definiteness, appears as a function of its participation in the common formative power, to which neither the common definiteness nor the unique definiteness is alien. There is *nothing* in the form or order that we apprehend in an individual that is not a participation in the common unity; and nothing, therefore, that we do not regard as capable of multiple exemplification—

except what distinguishes it as *this* individual. And this last, though it is incommunicable, we do not regard as an intrusion, because it is the very vehicle by means of which all communicable definiteness is established, and, as such, itself a participation in the common formative power.[12]

It is the individual that carries the very stability with which any existing level of order manifests itself, just as it is the individual in which newer and higher levels, capable in their turn of multiple exemplification, emerge. Any level of form or order presents itself as a potential multiplicity of individuals, which do not escape formality by their individuality since they are the vehicles for it. It is part of the tragedy of individuation that it rests upon, and must wait upon, the causal power of individuals of lower rank; it is part of the tragedy of any level of form, order, law, or being, that it rests upon and must wait upon lower levels; but this cannot turn us aside from the central point, namely, that the uniqueness of an individual, though incommunicable, is not at war for that reason with its formality: in its uniqueness the individual shares in the common formative power, and the individual, if not *merely* unique, is *also* unique. The corollary of all this in the sphere of causation is the earlier principle that ontic power is more fundamental than causal power.

All this has consequences for our conception of formality. If we sum up our new version of the Platonic difficulty in the formula "everything that is communicable in the individual, and everything that is incommunicable as well, depends upon its participation in a common formative power," our root sense of form must be one that is appropriate to the individual. Form is indeed exactly what distinguishes any entity we attend to and constitutes it *as* an individual. When an entity unifies, presides over, dominates, supervenes upon an extensive span, it has given form to it since there is then present throughout the span a structural definiteness that is precisely that unity, dwelling in the parts, yet also that *in which* we find the parts and recognize them as such. This is a dark enough saying, which tells us no more than that that form is an *aspect* of an individual being. One might just as well have said "order" as "form," for we are merely concerned here with the definiteness of an entity as giving us a root sense of form and order. It is not, of course, a merely structural definiteness that concerns us here, for this emerges from an orderly development and is sustained in an orderly process. What has just been said of the interdependence of form, order, and being forbids us to suppose that we can erect senses of form and order that are totally independent of these origins. Thus, although we might well express characteristics of orderly processes in terms of "purely formal" mathematical laws, we do well to remember that we are then dealing with a more abstract sense of form, detached for some special purpose from a matrix in which the alliance between "form," "order," and "being" is permanent. It is in fact an apprehension of form or order at a more concrete level that first *interests* us, and leads us to wish to apprehend it in ways more suited to our interest in the extensive side of things. Here we merely reformulate in terms of form and order the general distinction made in Chapter 5 between our concerns in the speculative-empirical cycle, and our philosophic concern with the background in which that cycle is properly pursued. In terms of the present chapter, the attempt to establish senses of form and order "purified" of a dependence upon our recognition of an entity as a unity presiding throughout an extensive span is a threat to our understanding of the significance of form or order.

It is the participation in the common formative power that makes a participating entity just *this* entity, of just *this* kind, of just this *genus*. All the successive formal differences of the entity, working downwards to *infima species* and to individuality, are given by this participation. And since to participate in the common formative power is to participate in what others must participate in too, formality is also finitude and limitation—precisely what *many* can share in, limited by and limiting one another. It is not, however, limitation alone that is the issue, for if formality is a finite limitation *of* something, what is thus limited shines through it—"*Am farbigen*

Abglanz haben wir das Leben." Formality then—and this was at issue earlier when I described it as in no sense in conflict with individuality—is definiteness in the sense both of limitation and of what is positively given *in* the limitation. Formality is thus sustained *within* the common formative power: it has no "separate" existence. In one sense, it is Being, thought of as capable of being limited. In another sense, it is Being taken as the principle of limitation. There "are" forms in this sense. And doubtless this is the reason why our cognitive awareness flowers in the articulation of discourse, and why that articulation is not ever a pure and contentless formality.

7

THE TRANSFORMATION OF SUBJECTIVITY

CONCLUSION: *We are now in a position to display reason, and indeed the self-recognition of reason, as the supervention—in several senses—of a higher level of order, form, or being upon a lower. The "relation" of reason to its supporting subjective dynamism is now seen as a special case of this supervention. We accordingly transform both our knowledge of this dynamism and the dynamism itself as reason exercises its autonomy. Our difficulties about the role of subjective dynamism in our philosophic enterprise, as well as analogous difficulties about the "relation" of body and mind, become less intractable. We are also able to throw a new light upon the conflict between creativity and tradition in morality and in the arts.*

But this was not intended to be a book in systematic metaphysics, and even though the preceding chapter deals at least glancingly with some of the more traditional problems, it was meant merely to establish the metaphysical direction in which our new beginning takes us. We must return now to the motive in which these investigations originated, and ask how it now appears to us—ask, that is, whether or not we did well to take it seriously.

I hoped at the beginning to make an advance in reason's self-knowledge, and supposed the need for that advance to manifest itself in various ways, the chief of which, from the point of view of the general cultural situation, was the philosopher's uncertainty about his own task. The urgent desire each of us feels to recognize reason in order to live under its order was taken to be the private form of what in the world of science, learning, and art is an uncertainty, not only about a central principle of organization, but besides about our very right to raise the question whether such a principle is possible. We saw, however, that the self that wished to make the advance had something so problematical about it that it menaced at the outset the authenticity of any supposed advance. It menaced authenticity, moreover, in a very profound way, by calling in question any method of authentication that we might propose. That was the problem of subjectivity, whose transformation was represented as something we might at least hope for. Even before its prolongation in the kind of metaphysical task that concerned us in the last chapter, radically originative reflection purported to give us that transformation, representing itself as an ontological expansion, in which reason, presiding over, or supervening upon, a web of conditions, made them what they might not otherwise have been, conditions furthering the best exercise of its powers. Our concern now is to complete that transformation.

Our thesis in this chapter is a relatively simple one: that the difficulties we normally feel about the involvement of subjective dynamisms in our philosophic outlooks stem from our contemplating that dynamism either in terms of the speculative-empirical cycle, or in terms of an alternative philosophic approach whose authenticity is questionable. These difficulties disappear when seen from the point of view that our reflective act has permitted us to reach. I shall state the basis of this claim in summary fashion and then apply it directly to the matter of subjective dynamism. It is a claim that incidentally affords a completion of our account of recognition, and indeed of radically originative reflection itself.

From the point of view reached at the end of the preceding chapter, the release of the creative and responsible autonomy of reason in radically originative reflection is an example of the supervening of a higher level of being, form, or order on a lower level. It is a grade of ontic power levying causal or conditioning power to its own uses. It is, however, an example of unique importance, for the level that now fully supervenes is that of a creative and responsible autonomy reflexively employed to confirm all its rights, including its rights to that reflexive employment. Our way of understanding reflexivity itself is recast, so that we see it in its pellucidity and finality. Without it we have no right to any other examples. With it, we may bring forward two ways in which the supervening or presiding of a higher level is exhibited in the immediate sphere of reason and its everyday activities.   a] Speaking of reason taken in its own right, and without any reference (for the moment) to its dependence upon a bodily apparatus, we may say that the act of recognition presides over the extensive span of what we recognize, taking as a unity what could from another point of view be described as a diversity of sense impressions, or as a sensuous manifold. This presiding is also the attainment of the common non-extensive power in which what we recognize is rooted, and it is this that makes our recognition the value-laden acceptance of a *level* of being.   b] Speaking of reason as one among the higher functions of a living being, we may say that the reasonable consciousness supervenes upon or presides over a group of levels of order—neural, general physiological, cellular, physico-chemical, and so on. Recognition, as the chief function of reason, *makes use of* its extensive involvement in subordinate levels in dealing with any level of being that comes under its attention.

The role of the mind in [a] or [b] remains "mysterious" —but only if one supposes that the only alternative to naturalistic explanation is mystery. The preceding chapter purports to offer an alternative to naturalistic explanation. Perhaps sufficient attention has already been given to the role of the mind as considered under [A]; as touching [B] it may help to point out that the mind-body problem is now dealt with as an instance of a more general doctrine: we are not to look for a principle that "relates" mind and body, establishing the possibility of their interaction, because we are not to look for a principle relating *any* level to a higher one. The point is rather that the supervening of any higher level is coincidental with alterations in the lower. More generally, both levels in such a "relationship" are what they are in virtue, in part, of the other. It is as useless to look for a "connection" between mind and body as it is to attempt to reduce any of these levels to the other. Our mode of explanation consists in noticing that there *are* two levels, and that they have a common, that is to say, a non-extensive root: we explain the "relation" by attaining the presence of both levels and of their common root.

Beyond this immediate sphere of reason and (as it would seem) its purely theoretic activities, but connected with it because ours is the reason of a complex affective nature, there is another sense in which reason is a supervening upon lower levels. c] Reason supervenes not only upon levels constituting the body, and upon the extensive particularity of the body, but besides upon an affective complex itself merely rooted in the body, being no more a mere product of it than is reason itself; and the supervening both adjusts this complex and is dependent upon it. It is just here that radically originative reflection permits us to look for the transformation of that affective complex, which is of course the subjective dynamism discussed earlier.

Consider our needs, appetites, desires: we share them with the animals, but our ability to discriminate them by focusing self-conscious attention upon them, examining them, and evaluating them, is presumably our own. I may conveniently single this feature out by speaking of our needs, appetites, and desires as *interests*. A need that is articulated, attended to, perhaps evaluated, is an interest. I do not mean to suggest that we are always accurate in this self-conscious function; only that it is peculiar to ourselves that subjective dynamism also takes on an articulate self-conscious form, and that we have no reason to suppose articulation to be inevitably a disguise.

To make this point is not to suppose an atomism operative in our affective sides. There may be interests that summate, generalize, or indeed, in our present language, supervene upon, a number of others; thus, an interest in all our needs gives rise to a self-conscious interest in the control of our environment, and this doubtless contributes to our interest in extensiveness as such. It is indeed impossible to establish the limits of our interests, saying, just *this* is the pattern of our interests; although sometimes, from the point of view of the speculative-empirical cycle, we may be tempted to think so. Still less can we claim to know exactly what our pattern of interests *ought* to be.

The whole idea of an interest, as here defined, presupposes rationality, and the realm of our interests grows as rationality itself expands. Thus, an interest in extensiveness becomes, in the presence of rationality, not merely a *generalized* interest in the satisfaction of *all* our interests, but itself a transformed component of a complex interest in science. Yet it is also true to say that rationality itself expands as the pattern of our interests grow: the growth of rationality is at once the gradual articulation of an interest—this is the correlate of the ideal of a completed reason that played a role in Chapter 3— and the outcome of that tending or dynamic side of interest that I stressed when I spoke of needs, wants, and desires. Under rationality we are *interested* in the *pattern* of our interests, and it is never wholly any existing pattern of interests that ought to command us: it is a cry *from* the heart that is a cry *for* the heart—a cry for an ordering we wish the heart to have. I have already marked a parallel with Kant: noticing that the pattern of our interests, understood in utilitarian fashion, must often seem in conflict with the demands of the categorical imperative, to whose reign no such interest moves us, he spoke of our "taking an interest" in it. It is the leading of one level to another that is at issue; the adumbration, by virtue of their common root, of a higher order by a lower.

To some of this even a hostile critic will agree. We need not even abandon the footing of a speculative-empirical cycle grounded in the common-sense world in order to acknowledge that our interests undergo reorientation. It is a commonplace of most approaches to cultural evolution that drives originating in biological needs are often altered subtly while still continuing their old function. Thus, even setting aside what in Freudian psychology might seem an over-emphasis on sexuality, one can hardly doubt the presence of an erotic element in art, religion, and indeed in many personal relationships that overtly have nothing to do with sexuality; in that form the theme of the erotic announced itself at the very beginning of philosophy. The real question is only about the significance of the "higher" interests that present themselves as novelties emergent from the background of our animal wants. Are they what they seem to be, higher interests, suffused with the movement, warmth, and fervor of the lower ones? And are the lower interests, which obviously in some sense continue in their wonted courses, in any sense transformed, or are they merely disguised? A Platonist, or indeed anyone working in the classical metaphysical tradition, will give one answer; a naturalist another. As for the interest that moves us to the kind of philosophy of which this book is an example, most observers will grant it to be in some sort continuous with a pattern of interests that can be found in any pre-philosophical phase of human or individual history. The question is whether it is really nothing but an unworthy interest in cosmic security, itself in effect a generalization of other and pre-existing interests that would perpetuate themselves; or whether these latter merely establish conditions for a new interest, which then partially transforms them as it begins to grasp its object.

To make our point hold, we have to return to the sanction given by our reflective exercise. Our commanding interest in philosophy represents itself as an interest in an advance, and it emerges to be identified and named only as a concomitant of what in turn represents itself as the expansion of a creative and responsible autonomy—an autonomy concerned with authenticating interests to just the extent that it is concerned with authenticating our grasp of what the interests are directed upon. The authentication permits us to think of reason as supervening upon and partially transforming an affective complex; I say "partially" because old wants do not now go unsatisfied, but their satisfaction is colored by their association with new goals as well as with the old; while these new goals are now sought with all the dynamism of a full and concrete affective complex. The arena in which we are to contend about interests and their status is suddenly quite other than that in which a naturalist supposes himself to be contending. Knowledge of our subjective dynamism, as distinct from its entry into any cognitive effort, may be either by way of the philosophic mode of knowing that radically originative reflection liberates, or by way of the speculative-empirical cycle; and we here call the advocate of naturalism to the former, acknowledging, however, that the speculative-empirical cycle may itself take on a new status if it is pursued against the background of a philosophic mode of knowing. Nor can he refuse to contend in this new arena without, it would seem, invoking that same creative and responsible autonomy that establishes the new arena. By what right should he otherwise marshal just the peculiar complex of rational and empirical criteria that we call the naturalistic outlook against the present one?

Study of our affective lives by way of a speculative-empirical cycle carried on, as it may be, while a philosophic mode of knowing is denied, will usually offer us an image of a *complex* of interests that adjust to one another as the whole complex adjusts to its environment. Any hierarchical ordering of interests will depend upon some standard of ideal adjustment. We may, for instance, value highly the pursuit of those interests that permit us to maximize other interests, and we may, therefore, ultimately value social interests and social virtues because we recognize that any lasting standard of maximization must be social. The same interests that we thus prefer, we may nevertheless suppose to be disguises assumed by our real interests, which lie much deeper, and which assure *themselves* of maximization in this way. But from the point of view of philosophical knowledge we find it impossible to treat any pattern of subjective dynamism as wholly autonomous, and as quite free therefore to establish some working relationship with the environment. We think of any pattern as incomplete and as working from within towards its own supersession, as we seek to determine not just how conveniently an existing pattern may satisfy itself, but how it might best recast itself. It is a pattern that awaits adjustment at the hands of something that cannot come into being without its energy, and that therefore cannot adjust it without making use of it.

There are various anti-Kantian themes in this book, which is, for all that, more indebted to Kant than it is to any of the contemporary efforts to circumvent the difficulties he poses for philosophic knowledge. One such theme is that of the interdependence of action and knowing (things separated by him), an interdependence implied in the view of causation developed in the last chapter. Philosophic knowledge is now taken to be action in the broadest and most radical sense: action in which a new level of being supervenes to transform the springs of action. This ancient theme has emerged again in the many fresh and promising forms voluntarism has taken in the last hundred or so years. James's emphasis on what he called the passional side of a larger rationality is a particularly clear-cut instance, but one could advance any number of similar, if less immediately clear, instances from the various forms of existentialism. The present point is nothing less than that our personalities—and therefore reason in the species— grow in a *generalized* mode of action in which our subjective dynamism issues in theoretic insight, which then partially transforms that dynamism. There is a concomitant effect on our choice of *particular* actions, for even if we should continue in much our same courses in spite of philosophy, our choices will still inevitably be qualified by a clearer conception of what it is that we choose and of how we choose it. Our subjective dynamism will have been in the first place qualified by our particular choices, so that the cycle is complete. This last point is as old as Greek ethics, and all that is offered here is a fresh setting for the interplay of action and knowing.

The story of the relations between action, production, and knowing that are brought about by radical reflection, are of course more complex than this suggests. The most deep-seated effect of our reflective exercise lies in its being a release of creative and responsible autonomy. This release gives us the confident exercise of a freedom that, though we have always in some sort possessed it, has often been crippled by its own self-denial.

As to action, we are in a position to make intelligible the exercise of free choice, which now appears, like the rationality that informs it, and the reflective act that permits us to recognize it, to be the supervening of ontic power over the causal or conditioning powers represented by our particular circumstances and the alternatives for action existing within them; by the particularities of our bodies and of the affective complexes supervening upon them; and by the particular value frameworks we inherit. Free choice will often involve a judgment of alternative courses of action in matters of some importance; just as often it will involve nothing more momentous than that envisaged by James in his well-known example of a choice between Oxford Street and Divinity Avenue for his walk home from the lecture.

As to value frameworks, whether inherited or otherwise adopted, our relation to them may be similarly understood. Our acceptance of a particular value framework may be merely inveterate, as indeed may be our performance of certain actions, but we may also acquiesce even in an inherited one through an informing rationality that supervenes as an ontic power over the conditions represented by our breeding. Such an acquiescence must then, however, have been made in full reflective awareness of the creative and responsible autonomy that we can exercise in either acknowledging or reshaping any value system. In such a creative acceptance we do not acquiesce in something imposed or taken for granted, but in something we understand to have been won to by other selves from the reality to which we everywhere win our way. To acquiesce in an inherited value system in this spirit is in fact to claim that we are autonomous before all explicit value systems, having the right to re-shape them, not indeed as we will, but as we ought. The full exercise of creative and responsible autonomy in the elaboration of a matrix for all "rational" and "empirical" standards, gives us also, when our attention is directed upon action, a matrix from which we may detach analogous ethical standards. We may expect a correspondence between the "rational" side and the theme of law or universality in ethics, and between the "empirical" side and the theme of affective satisfaction (happiness, pleasure, love, etc.) in ethics. This is a way of saying that action partakes of knowing not just in the obvious sense in which, say, a utilitarian ethics depends upon knowledge in the mode of the speculative-empirical cycle, but in the sense of a direct involvement of knowing in the evaluation of acts and codes.

If we turn to the arts, we can say of production or making much what has just been said of action. The situation is rather more complicated, for in art the elements of knowledge, of production (creation), and action (expression) are inextricably interwoven, so much so as to make philosophy of art, with its abundance of one-sided theories, probably the most chaotic of all branches of philosophy. This is not the place to attempt to deal with that issue, but surely the release of the creative autonomy of reason can help us conceive of a work of art as something in its own right, while still making intelligible its relation both to the particular circumstances of life out of which it grows and to the styles, rules, and standards that, as the case may be, it invokes or violates. The production of a work of art—let "production" stand here for an activity admittedly more complex—can be thought of as the supervening of a new level of being upon the particular affective, physiological, social, and historical situation—upon in short the full particularity of the situation out of which the work arises, not forgetting even the subject matter, physical ingredients, and other raw material of the work. The same point holds also for the finished work of art, whose presence presides over an extensive span which may involve elements of sight, sound, their imagined counterparts, feeling, and conception: we enjoy it *as* a work of art and we judge it *as* a work of art by the exercise of a creative and responsible autonomy. It holds finally for the autonomy of the artist in his acquiescence in a style, with its rules, standards, tradition, and technique, and for the creative responsibility with which he might, shaping a new work, reshape a style as well.

The importance of the point lies not merely in the understanding that it might yield an esthetician, no more than the importance of the points made above about ethics lies merely in the understanding that an ethical theorist might get from it. The important point is the liberating effect upon the arts and upon action of the entry of reason into the enjoyment of its own autonomy and responsibility. There is no wish here to have philosophy usurp the functions of art, morals, religion, or science. But what is at issue in the present case is how the artist understands his task—a matter inseparable from how he carries it out, and not a matter that artists have ever settled quite independently of speculation. Here it is deemed important that the consequences of radically originative reflection should help release for the artist his own mode of creative and responsible autonomy.

Our concern throughout has been for the Self in its uniqueness and in its common character; our wish, that in all its courses it should exercise in full confidence its creative and responsible autonomy. This has been envisaged as a life under reason in a sense not at all detrimental to the life of feeling, for our effort to recognize reason has issued from the first as a cry from the heart that is also a cry for the heart. Because this was the theme of the partial transformation of the import of lower levels as they subserve higher, the life of reason has been envisaged as self-integration—the production, no less than the understanding, of a hierarchical organization. Riding a current of blood, living along the lines of the nerves, we both make of these levels more than they are, and understand in cooperation with them more than they are in themselves. Throughout the book the theme of Reality has been celebrated in what is openly intended as a restoration and renewal of metaphysics. The reiterated theme of creative autonomy reflects our passionate and confident apprehension and use of a level of reality that returns upon itself; our equal reiteration of the theme of responsibility reflects our concern to make of all creativity an acquiescence in the presence of the Real in its many dimensions. We may well say,

> The noble hart, that harbours vertuous thought,
> And is with childe of glorious great intent
> Can never rest, untill it forth have brought
> Th' eternall brood of glorie excellent:

provided that we acknowledge that we then do no more than enjoy and celebrate in our art and action what lies all around us.

NOTES

INDEX

NOTES

1. [*page 6*]

I am well aware that my summary account of this movement may perplex some readers and annoy others. I have discussed it at some length in an article, "To Live at Ease Ever After," *The Sewanee Review*, LXVI, no. 2 (Spring 1958), pp. 229–51.

2. [*page 20*]

This agreement is expressed in a number of very different and very familiar complaints that come at us from every point of the philosophical compass: we fail to understand the bounds of the meaningful and therefore frequently utter nonsense (logical positivism); we commit the fallacy of misplaced concreteness, and are unable to judge the abstract for what it really is (Whitehead); we try to say what cannot be said (Wittgenstein); we will not let things themselves speak for themselves (early phenomenology); our sense of experience is too abstract, insufficiently radical, and fails to cope with what is truly primordial in our life-world (Husserl's later phenomenology); our intelligence is bewitched by certain features of language, so that we fail to understand the very ample and flexible logic of our everyday language (Wittgenstein and the ordinary language movement); we must find our way back into the ground of metaphysics (later Heidegger); we deceive ourselves into thinking that common-sense certainties are not really certainties (G. E.

Moore's common-sense approach, which contributed to the ordinary language movement); the pragmatically oriented intellect prevents us from exercising our intuition to gain absolute knowledge (Bergson).

3. *[page 33]*

The Myth of Sisyphus (New York: Knopf, 1958), p. 27.

4. *[page 44]*

It was of course the intention of this whole development to expel these entities from consideration in their own terms, and technically this whole revolution could be expressed by saying that it is an effort to deal with the problem of causation without relying on the category of substance. The history of the last term is the history of many confusions, but I have in mind at this point only the sense of "substance" that is the legitimate descendant of the Aristotelian conception of the individual being or entity (*ousia*)—a sense that would have been expressed more aptly by the word "entity," as translators are just beginning to realize. We must of course exempt Kant from this stricture: for him the category of substance and the category of cause were, as they should be in any concrete usage, interdependent; but since he viewed both of these synthetic *a priori* categories as merely subjective, some of the force of the stricture stands.

5. *[page 62]*

Something very like this double paradox is familiar enough to us from other circumstances. There are many higher capacities we do not at first enjoy, or indeed clearly understand the possibility of, but whose first quickenings we surely feel obscurely, and as a necessary preliminary to their full realization and exercise. There is a kind of prescience that presides over the gradual realization of any mental faculty whose development depends upon its use, a prescience inseparable from our enjoyment of the discharge of energy by means of which we bring it about. The history of the race and of the individual afford many examples. From one side this is merely the confidence in which life advances, and we should have no reason to be especially suspicious of it in an issue like the present one, if it were not that in some presumably related spheres the exercise of this same confident spontaneity may lead instead to a stage of merely subjective confidence in which not the exercise of a faculty, but its stupefaction, is brought about. I am thinking, of course, of all the voluntaristic exaltation of belief from Pascal (and long before) to such recent developments as the existentialist leap of faith and James's will to believe. I would clearly distinguish from all this the impulse that I think moves us now to set free the pent-up resources of reason, for the latter resembles faith only in that it grows out of dynamisms for which the old term "will" is at least an approximation; but what is at issue is not so much a will to believe as a will to understand. To ignore all this is to court the danger of a practical impulse which presumes to create its own theoretic truth, a way of thinking into which James fell when, noticing correctly that the establishment of many relationships, including any possible relationship to a deity, will require some preparatory advances from *both* sides, he went on to suppose that the impulse that creates the relationship creates also the truth that the relationship was a possible one. A correct appraisal of the dynamism we associate with faith would seem to lie in another direction: it creates not its own object, but a state of readiness that prepares us rationally to embrace the object should it exist; putting it so, we are less tempted to set too high a value upon the obscurities of faith, for we now regard its dynamism as directed ideally towards the abolishment of that obscurity. It is, of course, our lot that some obscurity must always remain in any rational enterprise, but we need not go out of our way to court it, especially as we are so constantly reminded that our obscure dynamisms carry us into error as often as they bring us to truth.

I do not mean to suggest by all this that there is no place for faith except as a preliminary to conceptual understanding. There is indeed a kind of "obscurity" that is shared by art and the side of religious faith that expresses itself in terms of concrete personages and events, although we miscall it so. What we then have in mind is merely the proper characteristic of legitimate modes of apprehension which, whatever may be the dynamism they issue from, are themselves goals in their own right, and not just the dark forebodings of conceptual clarity. This "obscurity" arises from what gives these modes their excellence and intensity, namely, the concreteness—in the restricted sense arising from the roles played by particularity, the feelings, the senses—that is their vehicle. One meets two common mistakes here, utterly opposed in their intent:

we can speak pejoratively of the "obscurity," and contrast it with the clarity of conceptual thought; or we can speak of "obscurity" in some deeper honorific sense, in which we should intend to impugn the clarity of conceptual thought as factitious because out of touch with some deeper ground of meaning. But the conceptual mode of understanding and other modes of apprehension are complements rather than alternatives: art and religion are neither obscure dynamisms tending towards an ideal mode of conceptual understanding, nor are they inevitably more concrete and "deeper" than understanding. It is simply that we do not understand these modes of apprehension unless reason "places" them, and that reason does not understand itself unless it understands just how it is involved in them.

6. [*page 95*]

By the "inferential relationship" I mean whatever it is that permits us to assert some proposition on the sole ground of some other asserted proposition or propositions. This relationship displays itself in the various laws of logic, some one of which we might invoke to justify an inference in a particular case. We can, of course, construct formal logistic systems in which, without using any explicit formulation of this relationship, we are able to derive some portion of the laws of logic, and thus, as we might suppose, the inferential relationship that underlies them. But we should then have had recourse to this same inferential relationship in at least two ways: (1) in the informal reasoning we use to establish the formal logistic system (the "metalanguage" in which we construct the "language" that is our formal logistic system); (2) as the *end* we aim at in establishing that system: we wish, that is, to develop some portion of the laws of logic in which that inferential relationship displays itself, and we know in advance the kind of law we are interested in. In the second case these known goals determine the significance we give our symbols, as well as what we shall regard as a "well-formed formula" within the system. Since Gödel's famous paper on undecidable sentences in arithmetic a demonstrative support for the above interpretation has existed with regard to systems of a certain degree of richness. (See Kurt Gödel, "Über formal unentscheidbare Sätze der *Principia Mathematica* und verwandter Systeme I," *Monatshefte für Mathematik und Physik*, vol. 38 [1931], pp. 173–98. For a simplified version of this paper and a clear discussion of its significance see Ernest Nagel and James R. Newman, *Gödel's Proof* [New York: New York University Press. 1958].) The foregoing considerations are, however, independent of this: they apply also to relatively simple systems that are demonstrably complete (systems in which all propositions expressible in terms of the language of the system are decidable—i.e., can be demonstrated to be true or false). Professor Michael Polanyi makes claims similar to my own in his discussion of the "tacit" component in the development of logical systems. (See *Personal Knowledge* [Chicago: University of Chicago Press, 1958], pp. 117 ff., 190 ff., 255 ff.) I made the acquaintance of this book only when the present one was receiving its last revision. Professor Polanyi's starting point is in reflection upon the sciences, while my own was in reflection upon the role of philosophy today; he makes much of faith and commitment as being fundamental to knowledge, while I am wary of such existential categories and stress reason's autonomy in its self-justification as a *reasonable* grasp; yet there are important parallels, and this would have been a better book had I met his earlier.

7. *[page 148]*

And so this movement, in its general bent at least, only makes common cause with that "rationalism" that is the workaday rationalism of the scientist—a rationalism founded on our success in returning from our speculation to the common-sense world to deal with it and control it by means of the theoretical constructs we have produced. "Do not be troubled by the setting of the speculative-empirical cycle," the linguistic philosophers tell us in effect, "accept the world articulated in common language as the empirical pole of that cycle—*really* accept it—and all will be well. You will not be troubled by the cycle itself." But the working scientist, in his everyday "rationalism," will not have been troubled—he will have accepted the common world as his final experiential standard long before.

8. *[page 166]*

Certain aspects of these theories are especially encouraging to this effect. Thus Freud, speaking of the analyst's efforts to get at the unconscious: "What is preconscious becomes conscious, as we have seen, without any activity on our part, what is unconscious can, as a result of our efforts, be made conscious, though in the process we may have an impression that we are overcoming what are often very strong resistances. When we make an attempt of this kind upon someone else, we ought not to forget that the conscious filling up of the breaks in his perceptions—the *construction which we are offering him*—does not so far mean that we have made conscious in him the unconscious material in question. All that is so far true is that the material is present in his mind in two versions, first in the conscious reconstruction that he has just received and secondly in its original unconscious condition. By persistent efforts we usually succeed in bringing it about that this unconscious material too becomes conscious to him, *as a result of which* the two versions come to coincide" (italics supplied). *An Outline of Psycho-Analysis*, tr. Strachey, J. (London: Hogarth Press, 1949), p. 20. It is hardly surprising that the two versions should come to coincide.

9. [*page 170*]

If the "empirical" side of the cycle were a reality recognized under the guidance of radically originative reflection, we might well devise speculative constructions by means of which we might fit the pattern of life and its evolution into the pattern of physical explanation so far as that may be done, without at the same time supposing that such a new pattern relieved us of the obligation of trying to understand the order of life in a way appropriate to the ideal adumbrated by our so-persistent interest in purpose. There is much in any prospective further development of physical law that promises the inclusion within it, in some sense, of the pattern of life. But that qualification is important. The pattern of life will not set aside the orderly patterns we find in non-organic nature, but we have no warrant for saying that the latter necessitate the former. If we are to make any such further claim, we must rest it on one of two assumptions: A] all existence is pervaded by a universal determinism, in which any event is in principle predictable from the beginning, in accordance with the laws of nature; B] whatever events are compatible with the laws of nature will at length come to pass through chance rearrangements. From the beginning "chance" and "fate" have displayed a curious family resemblance, so that there may be little to choose between these assumptions; certainly, though, we have no good grounds for maintaining either. One curious fact is worth noting in passing: what we call the laws of nature are inseparable from the facts as we have them; and when we suppose that these same laws have brought about the facts, it is to be suspected that we do not quite know what we are saying. One may say of an isolated system that it is what it is because it belongs to a wider system in which these laws *prevail*, but one can hardly say of the widest system imaginable that it is what it is "because of" these same laws. The laws are, on the present point of view, abstract versions of an existent order, and not in any sense producers of order.

10. [*page 199*]

I am thinking of accounts congruent with Laplace's ideal of causal description. In these accounts the "formal" element expressible in "laws" is taken to be descriptive, rather than, as in the case of the formal cause of Aristotle, prescriptive.

11. [*page 200*]

The Laws of Nature (London: Allen & Unwin, 1955), p. 171.

12. [*page 225*]

In the preceding sections of this chapter we regarded the complex individual now as a hierarchy of levels of order, form, or being; and now as a hierarchy of individuals, in which the relationship of subordination was elucidated in terms of the contrast between causal or conditioning power and ontic power. The latter way of regarding the individual leads us ultimately to what appears to be a principle of extreme contingency, for as we move downward in a hierarchy, considering any given entity as levying just *these* conditioning powers to its own supervention as an ontic power, we must come at last to founding individuality on just *those* entities that form the lowest level in the hierarchy. If, following Whitehead's terminology, we call the members of the lowest level *primates*, we should be founding individuality upon some *particular* selection of primates. Presumably we should then be finding the source of individuality in something approaching a mere numerical distinctness, founded upon a bare extensiveness. This, of course, does not mean that we should be regarding two complex individuals of the same species as differing only in their extensive "locations"; only that what differences we should find—including important differences that appear to be "formal"—would be explicable finally in merely extensive terms. Yet we should not because of this have reduced individuality to a mere numerical distinctness, for even at some supposed primate level we are dealing with individual entities that owe their individuality to a sharing in the unity of the common formative power. The really telling point is that *any* level of order manifesting itself in individuals is a level of order *carried* by individuals, with all the consequences that this entails. In the case of primates distinguished merely numerically from one another (if this should indeed be the case), what is at issue is that *that* level of form, order, or being is congruent with (though by no means exhausted by) its being carried by individuals having a merely numerical distinctness. The principle here is that the level of order is *carried* by individuals, with no detriment to its being a *level*, and with no detriment to the individuals that make it up. And this applies no less to higher levels of individuality: any level must have its own mode of "contingency," "chance," or "freedom," associated with just the fact of individuation within that level; but this means only that we do not account for the full individuality of any entity either by referring it to the level of order, form, or law that it carries, or by thinking of it as something that flaws what would otherwise be a purer mode of order.

INDEX